Radio Controlled

MODEL AIRCRAFT

Radio Controlled

MODEL AIRCRAFT

BY ADRIAN VALE

First published by Gresham Books 1979
Revised 1982
Revised 1984
Revised 1986
Revised and enlarged 1986
Revised and enlarged 1987
Revised 1989
Revised 1991
Published, revised and enlarged by Traplet Publications Limited 1995

Traplet Publications Limited
Traplet House
Severn Drive
Upton upon Severn
Worcestershire WR8 0JL
England

ISBN 0 9510589 2 4

A Traplet Publication

Cover Photograph by Neil Blowers
Cartoons by Raf and Simon Bates

Printed and bound by Stephens & George Limited
Merthyr Industrial Estate, Dowlais, Merthyr Tydfil, Mid Glamorgan CF48 2TD

Contents

Chapter 1

Introduction

The beginner to any sophisticated hobby is faced with two main problems – understanding the technical jargon that drops so effortlessly from the experts' lips, and deciding what sort of equipment he or she should buy. What budding photographer has not been confused by shutter speeds, "F" numbers, light values, film speeds etc? What budding angler, looking at all the beautifully made equipment in a sports shop, has not listened with a mixture of awe, admiration and growing perplexity as the proprietor and a customer discuss the finer points of various expensive rods or reels? Beginners to the hobby of radio controlled flying have these problems in full measure. The technical terms seem to be endless and the magazines contain advertisements for such an incredible range of model kits, engines and radio control equipment that there seems to be little hope of making a rational choice. The writer was fortunate in that he started radio controlled flying long before these problems really existed – the technical jargon was minimal, there were few, if any, "experts", and a sample of every single item of commercial equipment (kits, engines and radios) available to radio control flyers in the UK could have been put on top of the average model shop's counter. Today they would probably fill the entire shop and stockroom three times over.

In the early days commercial radio control equipment was technically very simple, yet often unreliable, and gave nothing more than a three-position control of the model's rudder. It could be set left, straight ahead or right, but nowhere in between. It was called "single-channel" and the people who bought it were invariably aeromodellers of some experience who wanted to be able to steer their models in the sky so that they would land somewhere near the point of launch or take-off. The writer was a fairly typical example. He had built his first flying model when about ten years old. Others had followed in endless variety – gliders, rubber driven models, models powered by miniature engines, "Jetex" motors and cordite rockets; models "controlled" by pendulums and controlled by lines. Some were successful, others weren't, but they all reflected a passionate interest in anything that flies, and they kept him out of mischief during his adolescent years. He shared with his contemporaries the dream that one day radio control would enable him to make his models take off, fly under complete control, do loops and rolls like the real thing, come in to a perfect landing and taxi back to the side of the runway. Marriage, and the need to study for a professional qualification, put a temporary halt to these activities, but in the course of time children provided the excuse to start again.

Two or three firms in the UK were then selling single-channel radios and thus it was that, some twenty-five years after cutting his first bits of balsa wood, the writer designed and built a glider with a radio controlled rudder. Engine powered models followed, using more sophisticated radio equipment, but the real breakthrough, not just for the writer but for the whole hobby, was the introduction of "proportional" radio control. For the first time *complete* control of a model was possible, in that every control surface could be moved in either direction *by as little or as much as was required,* and all controls could be operated simultaneously.

Early commercial proportional equipment was very expensive and the writer, in common with many other enthusiasts at that time, built his own. But increasing competition and a steadily widening market soon brought lower prices and improved reliability, and by 1970 prices had "bottomed out" in the UK and most of the better outfits then on sale could be bought "off the shelf" with a reasonable degree of certainty that they would work accurately and go on working. The hobby expanded rapidly and displays of radio controlled flying, coupled with a certain amount of television publicity, acted as a further stimulant. But this rapid expansion caused, and yet at the same time was due to, a fundamental change that was taking place in the hobby. It was now attracting "outsiders" to aeromodelling. People who had never built any sort of flying model were seeking out their local model shop and buying proportional radio control (R/C) outfits in steadily increasing numbers. They had seen a display of R/C flying at some local fete and gala, or had seen it on television, and the attraction of flying one's own model "just like the real thing" had proved irresistible.

Now there is a world of difference between flying a stable free-flight model fitted with single-channel rudder control to "steer it in the sky" and flying an advanced aerobatic model fitted with full proportional control. The former will fly quite happily without any control whatsoever, whereas the latter, like its full-size counterpart, *must* be controlled virtually at all times otherwise it will crash.

The modelling magazines were urging beginners to start with a stable, slow-flying "trainer" and published plans of suitable models, but these "outsiders", by definition, did not read the modelling magazines, and most had neither the inclination nor the ability to build a model from a plan. They wanted to "get in the air" as soon as possible, and many bought ready-made models or highly prefabricated kits that were totally unsuitable, in that they were designed for people who already *knew* how to fly a fully controlled model. Many soon found out the hard way that proportional R/C will not, in itself, prevent a fully "controlled" model hitting the ground – even the best radio control equipment is only as good as the person operating it. At that time there weren't as many radio control clubs as there are now, so that help and advice were at a premium, and only those outsiders lucky enough to find a model shop where the proprietor knew something about proportional R/C flying, and wise enough to heed his advice, stood any real chance of success.

By 1972 the writer had designed, built and flown four or five models for this new form of control. He was past the learning stage as regards the actual flying and the long held idea of turning his hobby into a business seemed very attractive. So he took the plunge, abandoned his career as a Chartered Quantity Surveyor, and opened a model shop specialising in R/C. He soon learnt that there is more to running a model shop than being madly keen on R/C flying, but that is another story. He was able to start many beginners on the right lines and most Sundays found him at the flying field of the then small but very active Swansea & District Radio Control Club, test flying customers' models and, in company with the other club tutors, teaching their proud owners how to fly.

The business prospered and it was soon realised that one cannot spend a whole hour on a busy Saturday explaining the "do's and don'ts" of R/C flying to a potential customer while there are half-a-dozen other customers impatiently waiting to be served. At the same time the shop's reputation for giving sound advice to beginners was spreading, and requests for advice and information were coming in from all over the UK and even from overseas.

This lead to the publication of the shop's own "beginners guide" to R/C flying in booklet form, which was advertised in the modelling magazines and revised and enlarged through the years as the hobby advanced. Later editions naturally reflected the writer's experiences in flying an endless variety of beginners' models and teaching "learners" of all ages and widely differing abilities. The booklet became well known in modelling circles and was favourably reviewed by Aeromodeller magazine, who kindly stated that it "should be compulsory reading for the non-modeller wishing to take up R/C flying".

In 1978 Unwins suggested that a revised and illustrated edition, in "proper" book form, could be sold through bookshops and thus reach a much wider public. Gresham Books published the first edition in 1979 and the six further editions that followed. In 1994 Traplet took over, "repackaged" the book with major revisions, new illustrations and new covers and generally made it brighter and more attractive. Like its predecessors it aims to whet beginners' appetites, to unravel the technical jargon in everyday terms, and to tell beginners enough about the hobby to enable them to spend their money wisely and to ensure the maximum possible chance of success.

Many soon find out the hard way . . .

Chapter 2

About the Hobby

Radio control flying is one of the most challenging and rewarding of all hobbies, and each year it attracts a large number of devotees of ages between about twelve and sixty, and from all walks of life. Nearly all R/C flyers build their own models, so that this is an indoor as well as an outdoor hobby, to be enjoyed whatever the weather, and right through the year. The desk-bound professional man or office worker appreciates the chance to use his manual skills in building, and the factory worker can exercise his mind designing his own models or practising the more intricate manoeuvres demanded by competition flying. Whatever one's work is, R/C modelling can probably provide more outlets for one's creative talents and energies than any other hobby, and whether one is building or flying the worries and troubles of everyday life are completely forgotten.

Radio controlled model aircraft come in an endless variety of types and sizes. Powered models, that is models fitted with engines, range from simple "trainers" to advanced models fitted with retracting undercarriages and flaps and capable of every known aerobatic manoeuvre. There are biplanes, triplanes, canards (tail-first aeroplanes). models with circular or triangular wings and no tails, pylon racers (models built solely for racing against other models designed to the same specification), jet fighters, flying boats, seaplanes, autogyros, even a Zeppelin! Almost every category includes "scale" models -replicas of a particular full-size example, sometimes built with extraordinary accuracy and detail. The

This is an indoor as well as an outdoor hobby . . .

The writer with his little 33in (825) wingspan Tipsy Nipper, which was dogged by engine problems.

smallest radio controlled model was claimed to be a biplane of 6¾ inch (170) wingspan with a minute R/C system operating the rudder only. At the other extreme the writer's last club boasted a half-size Auster of 14 foot (4200) wingspan powered by a lawnmower engine! Gliders range from large, lightweight models designed for thermal soaring (using "thermals" or upcurrents in the air to stay aloft) to smaller and heavier "slope soarers" designed to fly in the upcurrent created when wind blows against the face of a slope. Slope soarers, too, can be fully aerobatic. The design of many gliders is compromised so that the model can perform reasonably well in a wide range of wind and site conditions.

So far no mention has been made of helicopters, which are becoming increasingly popular among R/C flyers, although they are looked down upon by some purists, perhaps because of their mechanical complexity and perhaps because of their incessant noise. Some wag once remarked that a thermal soarer rides on the air, a sleek aerobatic plane cuts cleanly through it, but a helicopter thrashes the air into submission! Not strictly true, of course, but it emphasises the fact that model helicopters are fundamentally different from conventional model aircraft. To start with, they are much more difficult to fly. A fixed wing model will always go the way it's pointing or, if you like, point the way it's going. Not so a model "chopper", which is only too willing to spin round on is axis or come at you sideways when you least expect it! Choppers are also more expensive, require far greater accuracy in final assembly and balancing, cannot stay up without the engine running (hence the potential noise problem), are more easily damaged and much more expensive to repair. On the other hand, they can out-manoeuvre anything with fixed wings (loops, rolls, the lot!) and can be made to hover motionless, or fly backwards, or even loop the loop backwards! Experienced model flyers may argue over the attractions of fixed or rotating wings but virtually all are agreed that they required completely different flying skills. This book has been written for the fixed wing flyer and if you are taking up model helicopters you will find it of little use. Nor will learning to fly a fixed wing model help you to fly your chopper.

"What about autogyros?" a few readers may be wondering. These are usually mechanically very simple or mechanically rather complicated. The former have rotors that are driven round solely by the model's forward movement through the air, and the blades of the rotor(s) are not controlled in any way during flight. The complicated ones usually have rotors that are speeded up mechanically before take-off and the angle of the blades can be altered in the air. The simple ones are controlled in the same ways as a fixed wing model but the complicated ones are very similar to helicopters and this book will not help you build or fly them.

Whatever type of fixed wing model is your ultimate aim, you'll have to start with a trainer (a simple, stable model capable of flying reasonably slowly to make learning easier) and you'll need an experienced model pilot to give you tuition. You may need help in building your model and you'll almost certainly need help in learning to start its engine. What this boils down to is that you'll save a lot of time and money, and avoid an awful lot of frustration and disappointment, by joining a radio control flying club.

Chapter 3

About the Clubs

These clubs range from the large and formal, with over a hundred members, interested in all aspects of R/C modelling and flying, to small informal groups with perhaps five or six members who are interested only in slope soaring gliders. The benefits of club membership are many – the chance to fly in the company of others, to see how their models, engines and R/C equipment perform, to exchange ideas and to benefit from each other's experiences generally. Most larger clubs offer third-party insurance and have their own private flying site(s).

As mentioned previously, R/C flyers come from all walks of life, but club members are united by their common interest and life-long friendships are formed that would never otherwise occur.

But most important of all for the beginner is the fact that any club worthy of the name has a number of safe and experienced flyers who give quite a large proportion of their time to test-flying beginners' models and teaching their owners to fly. The advantages of proper tuition *cannot* be overstated.

Most clubs are affiliated to the BMFA (previously the SMAE) who arrange insurance and provide invaluable legal help in obtaining and safeguarding model flying sites.

BRITISH MODEL
FLYING ASSOCIATION

Finalists in a club scale competition – a motor mechanic, an electricity board engineer, a model shop proprietor, an electronics engineer and a furniture salesman.

Chapter 4

Learning to Fly

You may have been flying free-flight or control-line models for many years, you may be a fully qualified airline pilot, you may have built your model beautifully and have read lots of books and magazines on the subject, but the sad fact remains that if you try to fly an unsuitable model without proper tuition there is at least a 90 per cent chance that within ten seconds, repeat *ten* seconds, of the model leaving the ground it will hit it again – hard. The model will probably be damaged badly and you may damage the engine and radio as well.

Even more perturbing, when you come to ask yourself "what did I do wrong?" you just *won't know*, so if you repair the model and try again in a few weeks time, the same sorry story will probably be repeated. By then, however, you will have realised that you have to *learn* to fly a radio controlled model just as you have to *learn* to fly a full-size aircraft. Similarly, you *must* start with a trainer. You would not expect to learn to fly "full-size" by climbing into an executive jet straight off the production line (and therefore untested by the maker's test pilot) and taking off without an instructor in the seat beside you. You cannot therefore expect to succeed with an unsuitable model, which has never even been test-flown, and with no instructor at all! Beginners with full-size flying experience will accept the need for a trainer, but may think we are over-stressing the difference between flying full-size and flying a model. The examples below will illustrate some of these differences:

A superb model – but not a good subject for a student pilot!

- (a) There is no "feel" to a model's controls; the full-size pilot feels his plane's reaction to the controls "by the seat of his pants". With a model the information comes back visually, and is, in a way, second hand.

- (b) The full-size pilot will know the vital importance of airspeed during take-off and landing. With a model this has to be judged visually – no easy task when the model is flying away from, or heading straight towards, the pilot.

- (c) A full-size aircraft will always turn (or, at least, yaw) to the left when left rudder is applied. So will a model, but when it is flying *towards* the pilot it will turn or yaw to the pilot's *right*.

Yes, model flying really is *different*! So, whatever your experience in other fields, don't set out to learn on your own unless you have to. With the right model and a suitable engine you may succeed, but there is no doubt at all that it will take you longer, and cost you more, than if you have proper tuition from model flyers at a R/C club.

Your local model shop should be able to put you in touch with your local club. If it cannot it probably doesn't merit your custom. Try the local newspaper or council office. If they cannot help either, send a stamped addressed envelope to the British Model Flying Association (previously the S.M.A.E.) at 31 St Andrew's Rd., Leicester LE2 8RE to see if they can. If the nearest formal club is a long way away that club may be able to put you in touch with a smaller group in your area. If not, then accept the fact that a thirty mile journey to the club's flying field, if it results in good tuition, will certainly be cheaper in time and money than repairing a badly damaged model after each solo "flight".

If you are reasonably young, and if you learnt to drive a car without any great difficulty, and are fortunate enough to have a good tutor, you could be good enough to fly on your own after about ten flights of fifteen to twenty minutes. Other, possibly older, newcomers to the hobby may need up to thirty such flights or even more. Either way you will still need a lot of practice in all weather conditions before becoming really proficient.

A good instructor will help you succeed in the minimum time – and at minimum cost!

Chapter 5

Power Model or Soarer?

Many R/C modellers enjoy power model flying and soaring, and often let the weather dictate which sort of model they will take with them when they go out flying. Obviously it would be both expensive and unwise to start on both these branches of R/C flying at the same time, and the beginner must make up his mind as to which he will tackle first. This decision is, of course, strongly influenced by one's own ambitions. If you have a lifelong dream of flying a scale Lancaster with retracting undercarriage and flaps you'd better get onto power modelling right away, because you'll need a lot of experience and a lot of models before you are ready to start flying the "Lanc". If, as many do, you regard anything with an engine as slightly improper and consider soaring the only true form of flight you wouldn't enjoy power flying anyway. So even if there is a power model site on your doorstep and the nearest soaring site is twenty miles away, you might as well stick to your principles and start with a soaring trainer.

For those with no prejudices the choice is often dictated by the availability of a flying site, or the fact that there is already a prospective tutor lined up experienced in one or other branch of R/C flying. For those with a choice of sites and no tutor we will list out the main advantages of each.

Soarers are cheaper and much quicker to build, much cheaper to fly, require less routine maintenance, can be flown from National Trust property, don't cause noise, rarely upset householders or officialdom and don't usually upset farmers (though only a fool flies from farmland without seeking permission first). Many soaring sites are suitable for picnics so it can be a family affair, and a soarer in the car boot won't dribble fuel onto the lunch basket or mess up your clothes. Soarers, however, can only be flown if the weather is right, particularly so in the case of slope soarers. That apparently attractive slope quite near your home can be unflyable through weeks of fine weather if there is no wind or if the wind is from the wrong direction.

... it can be a family affair ...

Power models can be flown in nearly all weathers and, providing a suitable flying field is available, the model can be taxied out from the "pit" area and taken off, and after the flight can be landed, taxied back close to the pilot and the engine stopped. All very blase! A lot of modellers enjoy the speed and power of a fully aerobatic model without being in any way interested in entering aerobatic competitions – flying a high speed low-level run across the field (*away* from the spectators) followed by a rolling vertical climb gets the adrenalin flowing in much the same way as driving a thoroughbred sports car all out around a deserted race track. It is also very much less expensive!

Scale models offer opportunities for soaring enthusiasts as well as power flyers. Power scale soarers (PSS) have grown increasingly popular and on many slopes you will see scale fighters, bombers and airliners flying with the more conventional gliders. They won't usually be very highly detailed and they won't have undercarriages (they land on their bellies) but nevertheless they will look very much like the real thing in the air. Those intent on progressing to highly detailed true scale models will find the power side of model flying offers more scope. Nearly all full size gliders are designed with broadly the same purpose in mind – to stay up in the air as long as possible should nature not oblige with the necessary lift – and to the untutored eye most full size gliders look pretty similar. But powered aircraft have been designed over the years for literally dozens of different purposes, from small single-seat "fun" planes to heavy transports, from fighters like the Sopwith Camel to bombers like the Lancaster, from army-cooperation aircraft like the Lysander to dive bombers like the Stuka, and from spy planes like the Lockheed U2 to tank-busters like the Fairchild A10. The differing design requirements and the technology available at the time have produced an almost unlimited variety of shapes and types to be modelled. But most power models are rather noisy and all are rather messy, in that they soon become covered with fuel residue which gets onto your hands and clothes. Also the average power club's flying field is hardly the ideal spot for a picnic, so that while you are still in the learning stage your family life must suffer rather more. When you no longer need tuition a friendly farmer may let you use a suitable field and this disadvantage will disappear.

Scale Sopwith Camel by Ray Stuart of Llandyssul, South Wales.

Cost is another consideration. We have already mentioned that soarers are cheaper to build. You don't have to buy an engine nor its quite expensive accessories and since you won't need a throttle control, the radio will have one less function to perform. It will therefore cost a little bit less. In the mid 1990s a typical first power model, with engine and accessories and throttle control, cost about £100 more that a typical first soarer.

That more or less sums up the pros and cons of these two branches of R/C flying. The choice is yours, but remember that for every R/C flyer there are probably a hundred people who regard us and our "toy aeroplanes" as a menace to them and their property. Only a fool starts looking for trouble – the prudent modeller takes positive steps to avoid it, and enjoys his hobby far more as a consequence. So don't let your choice be influenced by a site that is not really suitable and don't join a group of people continually at war with their neighbours. Above all, don't fly with an engine that is not effectively silenced.

Bell Aircobra and Chance – Vought Corsair, two power scale soarers from the R/C Model World range of plans.

Chapter 6

Getting Started

You made the best possible start by buying or borrowing this book! We'll assume you have found what you hope will be a suitable R/C club and you have gone along to their flying site to see them in action.

In some clubs and on some occasions visitors are largely ignored, in others one or two members make visitors welcome and answer their questions, and in others the unfortunate beginner is seized upon by more than a few people who are better at talking than flying, and is positively bombarded with advice as to what model to build and what engine and radio to buy. Such advice can be far from good and it is particularly unfortunate when this happens to a really young beginner. At this impressionable age he will naturally assume that anyone capable of flying a model by radio control is an expert. His father could point out, possibly from bitter experience, that many people capable of driving a motor car are very far indeed from being expert, and any advice they give should be ignored. The situation is even worse when, as quite frequently happens, the advice offered is conflicting. We *have* to be a little big headed here and say that the advice offered in this book is based on the writer having personally taught dozens (yes dozens) of complete beginners right through to their first solo and beyond, and, as a shopkeeper, having guided hundreds (yes hundreds) of beginners successfully into the hobby. "Alright" you may be thinking, "I'll build the sort of plane you advise but how do I find a competent tutor?" Well, as hinted above, you avoid those members who spend most of their time talking and very little time flying. Avoid also the show-off who flies his model low over other people's heads. He may be a very competent (if foolish) flyer but he would probably make a bad teacher. Talk to and listen to the more senior members of the club *and* to those still in, or just past, the learning stage. You have to find someone who is first and foremost a safe and competent flyer. Next he has to be a reasonably good teacher (one does not automatically follow from the other), next he has to be a regular visitor to the flying site on the days and times that you can be there, and lastly, he has to be willing to take you on as a pupil! Clearly such a person may be difficult to find and you may need to visit the site two or three times before you succeed. You'll probably find on your second or third visit that the competent flyers are then more willing to talk – they will now regard you as an interested beginner rather than a casual spectator. You'll also find them more willing to talk when they are relaxing after a flight – no one can give you his undivided attention when he is starting his engine or flying his model.

Whether or not you can persuade someone to teach you to fly may well depend on your being able to convince him that you will heed his advice and you won't waste his time. Many an experienced flyer has wasted the best part of a whole flying day trying to sort out a badly built and unbalanced model that has its controls moving the wrong way and an engine that has never even been started, let alone run-in. In trying to get this mess into a flyable condition he has received little help and no thanks at all and has resolved there and then never again to offer his services as a tutor. So you'll do no harm at all by taking this book along with you and assuring those who will listen that when you turn up for your first flight your model will be properly built and balanced, the radio will have been installed correctly, the controls will move the right way, and the engine will have been properly run in. How to do all this is, of course, fully described in later chapters.

You may also find it helpful to refer to the future when asking a potential tutor if he will take you on as a pupil. If he already has one or two pupils "in tow" he won't have much time for flying his own models and any request to take you on as well is likely to be refused. But if you book your place in the queue as it were by asking him if he will teach you *after* he has finished teaching his current pupil(s) a favourable reply is much more likely. If this is received you'll be wise to turn up at the flying field on some of the weekends during the interval, both to "keep your place in the queue" and perhaps to help your intended tutor to clean his model down after each flight and make yourself generally useful.

During these visits try to get a look inside as many models as you can. You'll see how the batteries and radio receivers are packed in low-bounce foam plastic to help protect them in a mishap, how the servos (the little black boxes which actually move the controls) are fixed in the model and connected to the controls, and how the wiring is all packed away safely to resist vibration. You'll later realise that modellers who take care in matters such as these are the ones who fly the same models year in and year out. The ones who are more casual and leave wires flapping about are the ones who always seem to have bad luck.

Before buying your radio control outfit you'll need to find out whether your tutor has the engine throttle operated by the left or right hand stick of his transmitter, because your transmitter will have to be on the same "mode" as his. Next you'll need to decide, of course, on what make of radio control you should buy. Your instructor's transmitter may have provision for what is called a "buddy box lead", a cable which can connect instructors' and pupils' transmitters together to give a form of dual control (more of this anon). If it does then you'll be well advised to buy the same make of R/C as his, and pay extra if need be for the lead and for an out-

Avoid the show-off . . .

fit with a transmitter into which the lead can be plugged. If not you'll probably be best advised to buy the make most popular in the club. The features you should look for when selecting the particular model from that maker's range of outfits are dealt with at some length in the chapter "ABOUT RADIO CONTROL".

If you decide, as most beginners do, to build your own model you will need a flat board to build it on, preferably about 3 feet (900) long and at least 1 foot 6 inches (450) wide. It must be free of warps and ¾ inch or 1 inch (18 or 24) blockboard is satisfactory in this respect, but try to find a board with a reasonably soft surface so that modelling pins (used to pin down parts of the model during construction) can be pushed in rather than hammered in. A way out of this problem is to cover the board with thin cork tiles as sold by DIY shops. Chipboard, similarly covered, is equally satisfactory.

To start with you'll need very few tools and most trainers require only a modelling knife with thin, very sharp blades for cutting balsa wood (the Swann-Morton Craft Tool is excellent and inexpensive; single-sided razor blades are a good substitute), some modelling pins and sandpaper. A modelling knife and/or pins are included in some trainer kits. Some even include a sheet of polythene to put over the plan to prevent glue sticking to it. If yours doesn't, rub the plan all over with soap or a candle before you start building.

The structure can usually be finished and covered before you need to buy your engine or radio, but don't fit the engine mounting until you have bought the engine because sometimes it has to be fitted slightly off-centre so that the silencer clears the side of the fuselage.

We have already stressed that the easiest way to learn R/C flying is with a proper trainer, and there is no shortage of excellent trainer kits on the UK market, both for power flying and for soaring. Unhappily there are, and probably always will be, models advertised as trainers that are by no means ideal for that purpose, and the beginner will need to be able to identify these.

Now a trainer is, essentially, easy to fly, difficult to damage and easy to repair. The latter two qualities are discussed in detail later, but one cannot understand fully why one model is easier to fly than another without understanding just what it is that makes an aircraft fly in the first place, and how it is controlled and why it responds to these controls. We have tried, in the next chapter, to unravel the mysteries of flight as simply and as briefly as possible in a way that everyone can understand. We have assumed that the reader knows *nothing* about aircraft or flying, and no mathematics or formulae are used.

Please therefore do *not* "skip" the next chapter – you cannot expect to get very far in a hobby such as ours without a basic knowledge of the "whys and wherefores".

Besides, you might even find it quite interesting!

Chapter 7

Very Simple Aerodynamics

A conventional aeroplane has a wing, a body (called the fuselage) and a tail. The wheels and bits of metal holding them to the fuselage are collectively called the undercarriage. The noisy thing at the front is called the engine or motor; this drives the propeller (sometimes called the airscrew) which whirls round and drags the whole contraption through the air. Well, we said we'd keep it simple, didn't we! Although a bird has two wings, an aeroplane of the monoplane type is thought of as having only one. Perhaps this is because a bird can move each wing independently, whereas the two halves of a monoplane's wing are rigidly connected together for flight. We now have to define various parts of an aeroplane because we need to mention them in explaining how it flies. If these terms are new to you, turn down the top corner of this page so that you can find it easily when required.

The front of the wing is called the leading edge and the rear of the wing is called the trailing edge. The outer ends of the wing are called the tips. The distance from the leading edge to the trailing edge is called the chord and the distance between the tips is called the span. In most aircraft the wing slopes upwards slightly from the centre to the tips, and this upward slope is called dihedral. The wing is fitted in such a way that the leading edge is a little higher than the trailing edge when the aircraft is flying level; this slight upward angling of the wing is called incidence. Dihedral and incidence affect the way an aircraft behaves to a very large degree, and it is important that they are not confused. So remember, dihedral is the angle of the wing you can see if you look at the aircraft from the front; incidence is the slight upwards slope of the wing that you would see if you looked at the aircraft from the side while in level flight.

The tail comprises a fixed horizontal surface called the tailplane and a fixed vertical surface called the fin (think of the fin on a shark). Each of these has a moveable surface hinged to its rear edge which controls the aircraft in flight. The one behind the tailplane is called the elevator and the one behind the fin is called the rudder. Sometimes similar moveable control surfaces are hinged to the back of the wing; these are called ailerons. Although you cannot see it, every aeroplane also has what is called its centre of gravity or CG. This is the point at which the whole weight of the plane can be considered as concentrated. If it could be somehow picked up at this point it would balance exactly, whether it were held upright, or upside down, or on its side. We shall see later that the position of the CG in relation to the wing is important. The aeroplane is

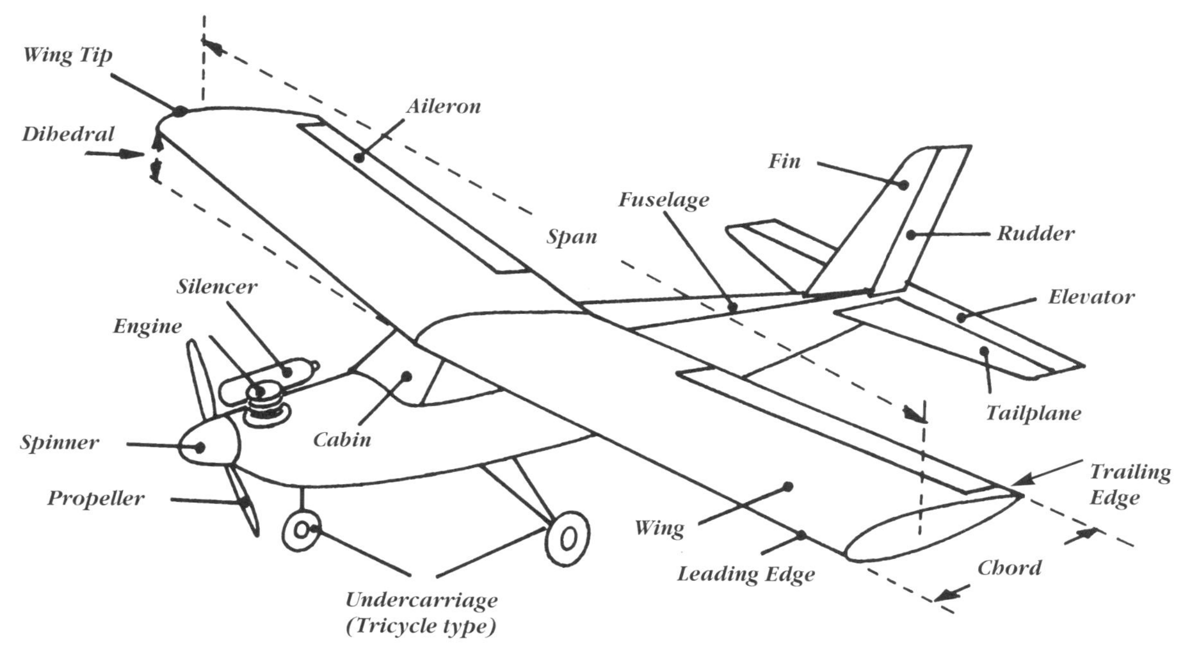

designed so that the CG occures under the wing, usually about 30% of the way back from the leading to the trailing edge.

Having defined the parts of an aeroplane we can now discuss what it is that makes it fly. Very simply it is two things, the wing and the wind. In case you are already wondering why planes fly quite happily on a calm day, when there is no wind at all, we must hastily explain that the aeroplane generates its own wind by moving forward through the air that surrounds it. If you put your head out of the window of a car travelling at, say, forty miles per hour you'll experience the car generating a wind in this way. It is the action of the wind on the wing that provides the upward force or lift that keeps an aeroplane up in the air. If the wing were to break away from the fuselage the aeroplane would fall out of the sky; if the wind gets too slow the same thing will happen, and the plane will not be capable of flying again until it is falling fast enough to make enough wind for the wing to work again. Sufficient speed is every bit as vital as having the wing firmly fixed to the fuselage.

"But how" you will be thinking "does the wing actually work?" You'll remember that the wing has incidence – the leading edge is a little bit higher than the trailing edge. So the wind rushing past the underside of the wing is pushed downwards. Now the action of the wing in pushing the air downwards causes what is called a reaction – the air pushes upwards on the wing with equal force. In scientific terms action and reaction are always equal and opposite. Readers puzzled by this scientific "law" should think of two skaters, a man and a girl, standing close together and facing each other on the ice. The girl puts her hands on the man's chest (keep your mind on the subject) and pushes him away. Assuming he doesn't fall over he will slide backwards away from the girl. But the girl also will slide backwards, for when she pushed against the man's chest she caused a completely unavoidable reaction – the man's chest pushed against her. If it hadn't, her hands would have broken his ribs.

So the bottom of the wing, providing it has a little incidence, can give us lift. The top of the wing can give us much more. Now wings can be flat in section, like a wide board, but don't work very well if they are. Early aviators soon realised that if the top of the wing is curved to a sort of banana shape, rounded off at the leading edge and sloping down to a sharp trailing edge, a lot more lift can be produced. The wind, or airflow as it is called, will follow this curve down to, and past, the trailing edge. This airflow has a more downward direction than that from under the wing, and when the two merge behind the trailing edge the resultant downward deflection of the airflow is much greater than if the top of the wing were flat. So more lift is produced.

Readers with a more scientific turn of mind will realise that the wing, in pushing the air downwards, produces an increase in air pressure under it and a decrease in air pressure above it. This decrease in pressure is enhanced if the wing has a curved upper surface, for the airflow over it has to travel further and therefore faster, and the faster the air flows the lower its pressure will be. Lift can be considered as a force resulting from the difference in air pressure above and below the wing. But most beginners will find it easier to think of the wing as simply deflecting the airflow downwards and producing lift by the air's inevitable reaction.

We can, of course, increase the strength of the downward airflow and therefore produce more lift by making the aeroplane go faster, though it will need a more powerful engine to do this. Every part of the aeroplane creates what is called drag – it needs power to pull it through the air. In approximate terms to make the plane fly twice as fast an engine with four times the power will be needed.

We can increase the lift from the wing in another and apparently more attractive way, that is by increasing its incidence. But only to a limited degree. Rarely in real life and *never* in science does one get something for nothing. As the incidence is increased so also is the

If the wing were to break away from the fuselage . . .

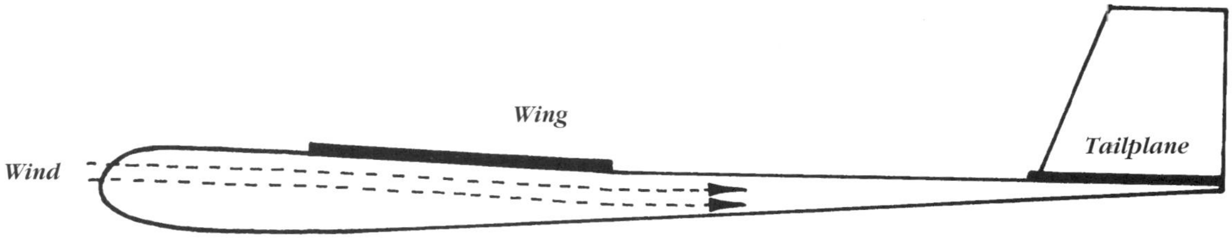

The wing of a simple sheet balsa glider is tilted so that it slopes upwards slightly towards its front, i.e. it has a few degrees of incidence. This enables it to provide lift by pushing the wind or airflow' downwards. The air reacts by pushing upwards on the wing with equal force.

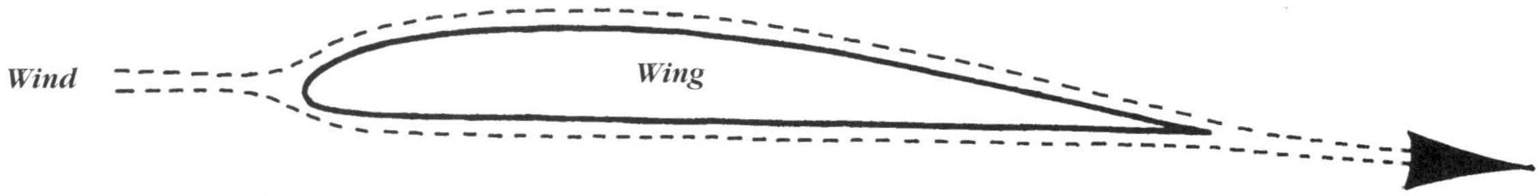

If the top of the wing is curved to a sort of "banana" shape the airflow over the top will be deflected downwards more than if it were flat. The deflected airflow behind the trailing edge will provide more lift.

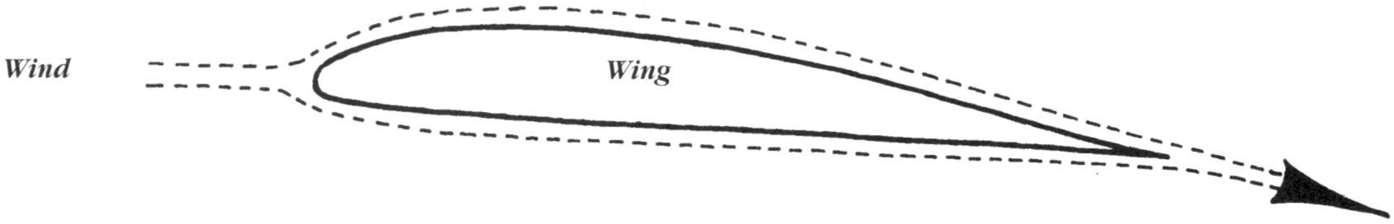

Even more lift can be obtained by increasing the wing's incidence.

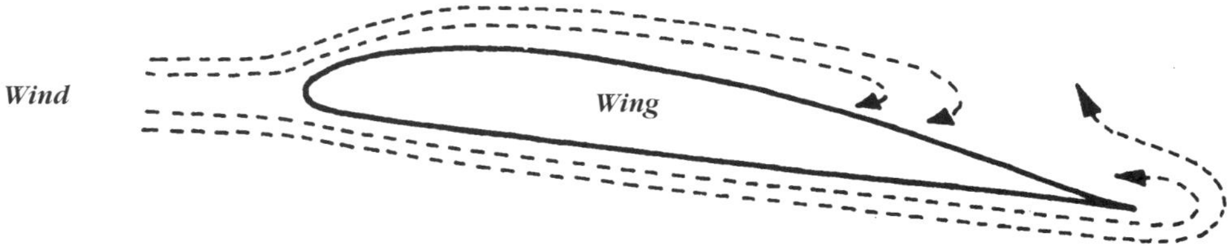

But if the incidence is increased too far the airflow over the top of the wing will break down and the wing will "stall".

drag, meaning that a more powerful engine will be needed to keep the aeroplane moving at the same speed. Increasing the incidence produces another and very important effect – the lift acts further forward towards the leading edge of the wing. At normal incidence all the lift can be considered as concentrated at about 30% back from the leading edge, and it was for this reason that the plane was made to balance at that point. But as the incidence is increased the centre of lift, as we shall call it, moves forwards in front of the centre of gravity, and unless something is done to prevent it, the nose of the plane will begin to rise. We prevent this happening unintentionally by fitting the aircraft with a tailplane, and we shall see later how the tailplane does its job.

But let us assume for a moment that the aircraft doesn't have a tailplane. If the nose is allowed to rise the plane will start to climb, but will only *continue* to climb if the engine produces more power. Without this, the plane will carry on about level but with a more nose up attitude than before, i.e. with more incidence. In this attitude the centre of lift will be further forward than normal, pulling the nose up even more, which will tend to make matters worse. If this weren't bad enough something else is happening – all the time the wing's incidence is increasing so also is its drag. So without extra power the aeroplane won't even maintain its existing airspeed, it will slow down. It is trapped in a very vicious circle, a deadly combination of rapidly increasing incidence and steadily reducing speed. If the incidence is allowed to increase too far, or the speed is allowed to get too low, the wing will stall. What happens when the wing stalls is described later, for the moment we will merely state that a stalled wing doesn't produce any lift.

It is to overcome this inherent instability of a wing that we fit the aircraft with a tailplane. But it is important to realise that neither the tailplane nor anything else can stop a wing stalling if the pilot allows the speed of the aircraft to get too low. Every aircraft has its minimum airspeed in level flight, usually called the stalling speed, and even if it is well above this speed a stall can still be induced by trying to make the wing operate at too great an incidence. The tailplane prevents the aircraft building up to a stall unless the pilot does something silly. *It cannot prevent a stall occurring if he does.*

The word "stall" is now an everyday expression (people talk of their cars stalling on a cold morning) but it is really an aeronautical term to define the breakdown of the airflow across the top of a wing. With too much incidence, or too little speed, or both, the airflow will no longer obligingly follow that banana curve down to and past the trailing edge, giving a nicely deflected airflow and producing lift. Instead, it will break away from the wing surface into a series of little eddies, rather like inverted whirlpools, rising upwards from the top of the wing. These don't produce any lift at all – the wing has stalled, the nose will drop and the plane will start to dive towards the ground.

Now a stall can be gentle or vicious or anything in between. If we let the airspeed gradually get too low in level flight the stall will be gentle and the resultant dive won't be very steep. Before too long the plane will have speeded up enough for the wing to start working again, and the plane can be brought back level without too great a loss in height. There will be a much greater loss of height if the plane is allowed to stall when it is climbing, and this is a particular hazard to the pilot of a R/C model trying to clear some obstruction soon after take-off, before sufficient speed is available. This is easily done – the model will be flying directly away from the pilot, so that its angle of climb is not easily determined, and remember that the model pilot doesn't have an airspeed indicator conveniently in front of him so that he can keep a constant check.

The stall that results from this sort of situation is anything but gentle. The resultant dive will be steep, and in its early stages the pilot might as well forget the transmitter and bite his nails, for there is absolutely *nothing* useful that he can do. Only when there is sufficient airflow over the wing can he put it to the not inconsiderable task of hauling his model out of that dive and back towards level flight. If the ground happens to get in the way before this is achieved he can only blame himself for letting the stall happen in the first place, and console himself with the thought that no-one else could have got the model out of that situation either.

The other classic stall situation occurs on the landing approach. The model is coming down nicely towards the landing area in a gentle dive when it becomes apparent that it may not clear some obstruction, possibly the hedge or whatever that bounds the flying field. There is a great temptation to put the nose up to induce a climb, but by doing so the drag is immediately increased and airspeed is reduced. Unless there is plenty of airspeed available the pilot will very soon be biting his nails again! Only by increasing the power of the engine can one get out of a situation like this with safety.

We have seen how a wing works and why it sometimes doesn't, and have related this briefly to the particular problems of flying a model. We'll now go back to the wing itself and see how its design can affect the flying qualities of a trainer.

For years trainers had what is called a flat bottom wing. As the term implies the bottom was flat and only the top was curved. The flat bottom made it easy to build – it could all be pinned down onto the building board and, when completed, would be free of warps or twist. At the other extreme aerobatic models frequently have what is called a fully symmetrical wing, a much thicker wing in which the bottom is banana curved to exactly the same degree as the top. Since an aerobatic model is intended to perform in exactly the same manner whether it is flying the right way up or upside down (inverted) this is entirely logical.

Sports or intermediate models usually have a semi-symmetrical wing, in which the bottom is banana curved but not to the same degree as the top. Now the flat bottom wing can be flown relatively slowly without stalling but when the stall does come it is rather pronounced. A semi-symmetrical wing is more difficult to build accurately but has a slightly more gentle stall. It also has another important advantage – because it is thicker it will be appreciably stronger and only very slightly heavier than a flat bottom wing of exactly the same construction. In approximate terms if we make a wing spar twice as wide it will be twice as strong; but if we make it twice as *deep* from top to bottom it will be four times stronger.

Now the kits of many trainers on the market today contain ready-built wing halves which are simply a centre core of expanded polystyrene covered all round with a thin veneer of wood (usually obeche) glued on. These are factory made, and the easy-to-build advantage of the flat bottom wing has, to a large degree, disappeared. More and more trainers are now therefore designed around a semi-symmetrical rather than a flat bottom wing. The shape you would see if you sawed through a wing from leading edge to trailing edge is called its airfoil section, and strictly speaking a flat bottomed wing is a wing of flat bottomed airfoil section, and so on.

So far we have discussed the wings of powered models but not those of gliders. With a glider the choice of airfoil section is obviously more critical, particularly so in the case of a thermal soarer were the pilot may be continually fighting for lift. The wing must be far more efficient so that the glider has the lowest practicable sinking speed. Yes, it is important to remember that, without a reserve of speed, any glider must always be moving forwards *and downwards* through the air that surrounds it – there is no engine to sustain it in level flight.

Now the flat bottom wing section is a very good choice for a thermal soarer and is frequently used, but with one important difference – it is used at a higher angle of incidence. We have already seen that at high incidence a wing will produce more lift and more drag. The ideal incidence is where the ratio of lift produced to drag created is at its greatest, and this incidence is not very far below the incidence at which the wing will stall. Now thermal soarers usually have long, slim wings, not because of their graceful shape (although this is an added attraction) but because such a wing is more efficient than the more short, stubby one fitted to the average power model. In technical terms the span divided by the chord is called a wing's aspect ratio, so a thermal soarer's wing will have a high aspect ratio.

The Kamco Kavalier, once a popular 'first' low-wing model. There were no wing tips as such – merely thick end ribs – and this photo shows clearly the semi-symmetrical airfoil section used.

Such a wing poses an added problem to its pilot. When the model is turned the wing will rotate – one tip of that long, slim wing will move through the air faster and the other will slow down. With the whole wing at a high incidence anyway there is obviously a danger that the wing tip that has slowed down will stall, particularly as it has been found that those beastly little eddies that destroy our lift tend to start at the wing tips and spread inwards along the wing.

If one wing half stalls and the other doesn't the soarer may well drop into a spin. To avoid this risk, and to ensure that, if the wing does stall, the stall will at least start near the fuselage with consequently less risk of a spin, many soarers have a wing incorporating what is called washout. This somewhat peculiar term means that the incidence is deliberately reduced towards the tips. The tips are thus unlikely to stall first, and indeed the whole wing may then be operated at a slightly higher incidence. Some power models incorporate washout to enable them to be flown more slowly, particularly on the last stages of the landing approach.

The wing of a slope soarer is much more akin to that of a power model than to that of a thermal soarer. Slope soarers are normally designed on the assumption that there will be plenty of lift available, and the wing is set to operate at a lower angle of incidence than that of an out-and-out thermal soarer. The airfoil section of a typical slope soaring trainer is usually either flat bottomed or semi-symmetrical but the aspect ratio is much lower than that of a thermal soarer.

The tailplane doesn't normally produce any lift at all. It is, as the Americans call it, merely a stabiliser, and is fixed to the rear of the fuselage so that it is level when the plane is in level flight. In this condition the wing will probably have between three degrees and five degrees of incidence, meaning that a line joining the foremost point of the leading edge to the rearmost point of the trailing edge will be angled three to five degrees above a line parallel to the tailplane.

Although the wing's incidence has been frequently mentioned previously we have deliberately not mentioned any typical figures because they could have been misleading. The incidence of the wing in relation to the fuselage, or to its centre line or datum as it is sometimes called, doesn't much matter. What does matter is the incidence of the wing *in relation to the tailplane.* The tailplane's job is not to keep the aeroplane level, it is to keep the wing at its correct incidence *to the airflow past the plane at any particular time.*

Let's consider a stable trainer type model in steady, level flight, suddenly disturbed by a gust of wind putting it into a nose-up attitude while still flying level. Straightaway the wing, which now has increased incidence, will produce more lift and the model will start to climb. But when the model suddenly went into a nose-up attitude the tailplane suddenly acquired a positive incidence to the airflow and acted like a back wing. It deflected the airflow at the tail downwards and as a result was very quickly pushed upwards until it wasn't deflecting the airflow any more – i.e. until it was parallel to it. So the wing is back at its correct incidence *in relation to the airflow* and the tailplane has prevented that vicious circle of more incidence plus forward movement of the centre of lift plus increased drag leading to an immediate stall. But the model is still in a slight climb, and there has been no increase in engine power to sustain that climb. Let's see how the wing and tailplane in combination cope with the situation.

Without extra power the model will slow down and the amount of lift produced by the wing will consequently be reduced. The nose will fall and the model will for a moment be level again. But it won't be flying as fast as it was before the gust upset it. It has gained height without more power and paid for this in terms of speed. With less speed there will be less lift than before all this started so the model will ease into a gentle dive. As the speed increases so will the lift, until ultimately the model will level out slightly below its original height (it wasted a little energy going through this manoeuvre and paid for it with a few feet of altitude).

Had the model stalled and dropped into a steep dive after the gust of wind upset it, it would not have reverted to level flight straightaway. The excess speed as it pulled out of the first dive would have resulted in a climb and there would have been two or three switchbacks or oscillations of diminishing intensity before level flight was once more attained.

This ability of an aircraft to revert to level flight after a sudden change of attitude or speed is called longitudinal stability and results from it having the correct incidence on the wing and the CG correctly positioned to suit that incidence. If the wing has too much incidence, and/or the CG is too far back the aircraft will not recover, unaided, from the situation just described. It will go on climbing, diving, climbing and diving again until some correction is applied by the pilot. If the wing has insufficient incidence and/or the CG is too far forward there won't be enough excess lift to pull it out of a dive without the pilot intervening.

A plane that is longitudinally stable can, of course, be made to climb or dive simply by altering the power produced by the engine. More power means more speed means more lift resulting in a gentle climb. Less power means a gentle dive. The climb out from take-off and the descent before landing are made by using the engine in this way. During the remainder of the flight a model is normally flown with an excess of speed so that it can be made to climb simply by pointing the nose upwards a little. But it is important to remember that the resulting climb will only last while there is still excess speed available, and once this is lost the model must be levelled off again. Speed and height are thus closely inter-related. An excess of speed can quickly be turned into additional height if required, just as height can be swopped for speed simply by putting the model into a dive.

We need a tailplane to hold the wing at the correct incidence to the airflow, but we also need something to prevent the plane "yawing" or skidding sideways through the sky. This is the job of the fin, which acts in much the same manner as the tailplane, except, of course, that it is working sideways, not up-and-down. If for some reason the tail were to slew round, say, to the left, the airflow past the fin will be deflected to the left. The result will be (you've got it!) that the fin will be pushed back to the right until it isn't deflecting the airflow any more. The fin has a much easier job than the tailplane, it doesn't have to contend with a wing trying to misbehave and make a climb worse, or with gravity trying to hold the plane in a dive. Consequently the fin needs to be only about one third to one half of the area of the tailplane.

Neither the tailplane nor the fin can help if, for some reason, the aeroplane tilts over to one side so that one wing tip is lower than the other. If nothing is done the plane will begin to sideslip – to skid down sideways in a direction more or less parallel to the wing. We prevent this happening by giving the wing dihedral (by making the wing slope upwards from centre to tips). If the aeroplane is tilted over and skidding down sideways in a sideslip there will be a sideways airflow along the wing from the lower tip to the upper one. The upper half of the wing will then be acting like a tailplane with negative incidence – because of the dihedral it will be deflecting this sideways airflow upwards, and consequently it will be pushed down. It will continue to be pushed down until the sideways airflow stops, i.e. until the sideslip has been halted. If the sideslip is exactly parallel to the lower half of the wing then that part of the wing will be doing nothing to assist. But if, as is more likely, the lower wing half has a positive incidence to the sideways airflow it will be lifting and thereby helping to get the plane on an even keel again.

If the plane tilts over to one side it will tend to skid down sideways or "sideslip" as this is called. This will cause a sideways airflow over the wing. If the wing has dihedral (i.e. slopes upwards towards its tips) the lower half of the wing will be pushed upwards and the upper half will be pushed downwards, and the plane will get level again without any action from the pilot.

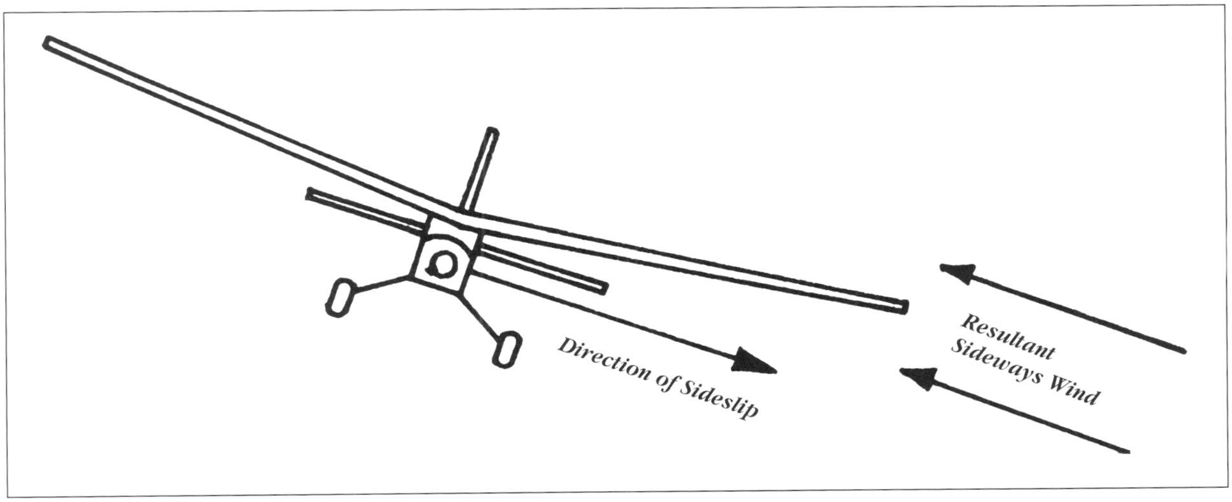

Not all aircraft have dihedral; in the full size world it is quite common for planes with a high wing (fixed to the top of the fuselage) or a parasol wing (held above the top of the fuselage) to have no dihedral at all. These rely on the pendulum effect of the rest of the aeroplane hanging under the wing to bring the plane back level should it have been tilted over sideways, with perhaps just a little assistance from the pilot.

We have now discussed all the major parts of an aeroplane except the fuselage. We left this until the end because, in terms of flying, it doesn't do very much – it merely holds the tailplane and fin in their correct positions. It does, of course have to provide fixings for the undercarriage and the engine and sufficient space for fuel tank and radio gear, but in this chapter we are concerned with how the plane flies and how it is controlled. The reader will, we hope, now have a good understanding of how it flies. Let's now see how it is controlled.

All the aeroplane's control surfaces work basically in the same way; they deflect the airflow and thereby produce a reaction that will push the control surface in the opposite direction. Taking the elevator first, if it is raised it will deflect the airflow upwards, and will consequently be pushed downwards. This will force the tail down and the plane will begin to climb.

Similarly, if the rudder is moved to the left the airflow will be deflected to the left and the tail will be forced round to the right. But note that this will not, in itself, cause an aeroplane to turn properly. In this condition it will be yawing or skidding sideways. The engine will ultimately pull the plane round the turn, but the engine might have stopped. We need something to raise the right half of the wing and lower the left half so that the plane is banked over to the left. When this has been achieved part of the wing's lift will be in a leftwards direction, and only then will the plane start to turn correctly. Happily the wing will bank over for us automatically *provided it has sufficient dihedral.* If a dihedralled wing is yawed the forward half has more incidence, and the rearward half has less incidence, than if it is flying normally.

Even experienced modellers have difficulty in understanding this relationship between incidence and dihedral but it can easily be demonstrated with a piece of stiff paper or a postcard. Fold the card or whatever in two and press it flat. Now open it out again and arrange it so that the two halves are sloping upwards from the centrefold at about twenty degrees. These now represent two wing halves with plenty of dihedral. Hold it by one edge at arm's length so that the centrefold points at your eyes, then lower the far edge of the card slightly so that the centrefold pints to about the top of your head.

You can now see the underside of both halves, and it can be considered as a wing, with plenty of incidence as well as dihedral, flying towards your eyes. Now, without moving your fingers but by using your wrist, twist the card away from you slightly to give it "yaw". You will immediately see that the nearer wing half has increased incidence, and that the further wing half has less.

Ailerons, which we hope you'll have remembered are the control surfaces hinged to the back of the wing, are used in more advanced models, which usually have little or no dihedral, to bank the model over into a turn, or to turn it onto its back so that it can be flown inverted, or to make the model roll. They are connected up in such a way that when one goes up the other goes down, and vice-versa. They work, as previously stated, by deflecting the airflow and it should be immediately apparent that if the left aileron is raised and the right one lowered, the left wing half will be pushed down and the right half will be raised. But they do not work in precisely the same way as elevator or rudder, for they are really re-deflecting an airflow that has already been at least partially deflected by the wing, i.e. they affect the amount of lift being produced by each half of the wing. A raised aileron is better thought of as destroying lift and a lowered aileron as increasing lift, and there are very good reasons for this thinking, apart from the one that this is what actually happens!

In this diagram the elevator is shown raised by about 20°. You don't need a science degree to appreciate that the wind or airflow will push the elevator and hence the tail of the aircraft downwards. In technical terms the elevator will deflect the airflow upwards and the air will react by pushing downwards on the elevator with equal force.

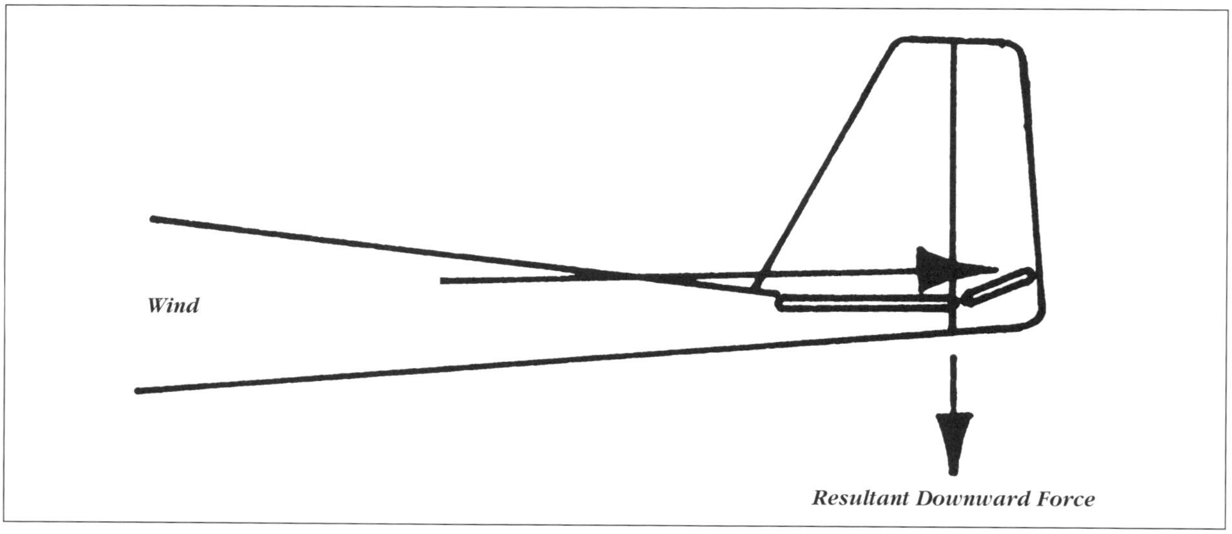

A simple experiment with a postcard will demonstrate the important relationship between a wing's dihedral and its incidence when the plane is yawed.

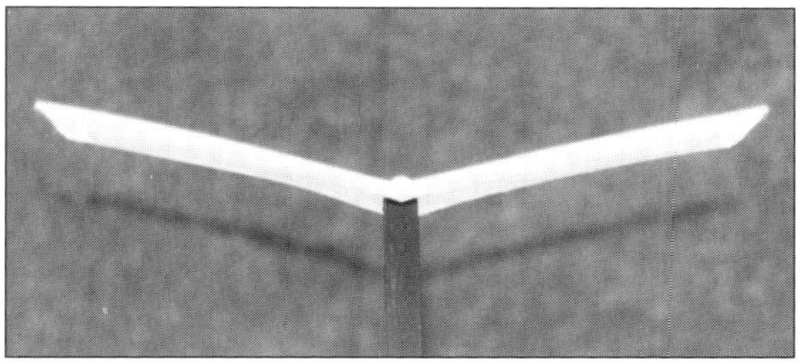

a). Underside of "wing" in normal flight

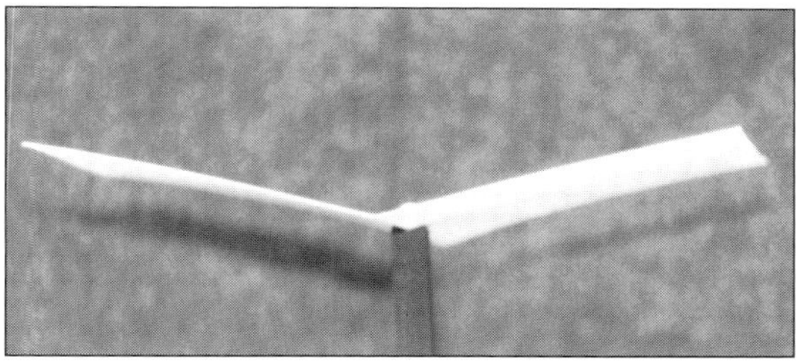

b). Underside of "wing" when plane is yawed

It is important to think of a lowered aileron as increasing lift because it can produce a stall. This is a particular risk on a thermal soarer where the wing will be operating near the stall anyway. For this reason many thermal soarers rely on rudder alone for turning. A too-sudden application of rudder can stall the wing half that is slowed down, but this is far less likely to happen than if an aileron is suddenly lowered near a wing tip.

One final point about ailerons – a raised aileron produces, perhaps surprisingly, less drag than one lowered by the same amount. This can induce a yaw which, in connection with the dihedral, will actually resist a turn we are trying to initiate. When, say, the left aileron is raised and the right one is lowered to induce a turn to the left the extra drag on the right wing slows it down and yaws the plane towards the right.

Too much dihedral would convert this yaw into a turn, or at least prevent the ailerons turning the model the intended way. This is one of the reasons why models fitted with ailerons normally have only a small amount of dihedral. The real remedy is to arrange the linkages in such a way that the ailerons move rather more up than down, so that the extra drag is balanced and no tendency to yaw occurs. A second advantage is that, with less downwards movement, the chances of an aileron inducing a stall at low speed are reduced. The usual name for this arrangement is differential ailerons.

Now what we have written about ailerons does not directly concern the beginner, who shouldn't be using a model fitted with ailerons anyway, but keep it in mind when you build and fly your first aileron model.

Before leaving the whys and wherefores of flight we must explain why engines in R/C trainers are not mounted exactly in line with the fuselage. Look at the plan inside any high wing model kit and you'll see that the engine is pointed downwards by some three to five degrees in relation to the fuselage centre line, and similarly pointed to the right (as we look down on the model from behind) by two or three degrees. An engine thus installed is said to have downthrust and sidethrust.

The former is needed because, on a high wing model, most of the drag is created by parts of the model situated above the engine (the wing being the obvious creator of drag in this respect). Now in level flight at a constant airspeed the thrust of the engine is exactly balanced by the drag of the model, and if the centre of drag, as it is called, were in line with the engine no downthrust would be needed. But with a high-wing layout the centre of drag is above the engine, and the two opposing forces (thrust pulling forwards low down on the model, and drag pulling backwards higher up the model) result in a turning moment that will pull the nose up and push the tail down. The faster the engine is going the more powerful this tendency will be.

By giving the engine downthrust we build in a compensating force to pull the nose down, and the faster the engine is going the more powerful *this* force will be.

Getting the downthrust exactly right is usually a matter of trial and error, part of the process that is called trimming out the model, and ideally if the engine is suddenly stopped in level flight the model will settle into a safe gentle glide without any action being taken by the pilot.

Sidethrust is needed because the action of the engine driving the propeller round produces the inevitable reaction; the propeller tries to drive the engine, and hence the model, round in the opposite direction (those skaters have a lot to answer for!). Viewed from behind, the engine rotates clockwise, so the reaction will be to rotate the model anti-clockwise, i.e. the left wing will tend to drop resulting in a left hand turn. So we point the engine a couple of degrees to the right to compensate for this.

Again the exact amount can only be found by trial and error, and will possibly vary very slightly if we use a different propeller, but generally speaking the two opposing forces can be made to cancel each other out more or less exactly whatever the engine speed. Ideally if the model is flown on a straight course it will not tend to turn if the engine speed is varied, and will continue to fly (or rather glide) without change of direction when the engine is stopped.

Sidethrust to the right has another effect – when the model is banked over and turning to the left, part of this sidethrust will be in an upwards direction, and will help to keep the nose up during the turn. When it is turning to the right it will tend to pull the nose down. This is probably the reason why most beginners find they prefer left-hand circuits, a preference that often continues right through their flying careers.

Armed with this knowledge we can, in the next chapter, see just how correct design can make a trainer immeasurably easier to fly than a more advanced model, and we can draw up a list of features that the reader should look for.

Chapter 8

The Ideal Trainer

Virtually everything in this chapter applies equally to power models and soarers (though comments on engines and undercarriages obviously don't apply to the latter) and to write another chapter on soaring trainers would merely involve a great deal of repetition. We have therefore dealt with power models first and have then turned to the particular desirables of the ideal soaring trainer.

The ideal trainer should be ready-built, easy to fly, crashproof and cheap!

Those who enjoy building might disagree with the ready-built bit, but if it *were* possible to buy a good ready-built trainer for no more than a kit they would be wrong. The sole purpose of a trainer is to teach you the noble art of R/C flying with the minimum expenditure of money and time. However, you have to pay about twice as much for a ready-built model as you do for an all balsa kit, so naturally most beginners start with a kit.

Kits are available with varying degrees of prefabrication. All-balsa kits aren't actually all-balsa, the term really means you build it all, though usually all the tricky pieces of wood are ready cut to shape. The typical all-balsa kit has a wing of ribs and spars, a fuselage of sheet balsa with ply reinforcement at the nose, and a sheet balsa or built-up balsa tail. For a little more money you get ready-made wing halves of expanded polystyrene with a thin obeche veneer glued on. More money again buys a ready-made fuselage, usually of glassfibre. Next up the scale are the ARTF or "almost ready to fly" kits (they aren't!) which feature ready-made wing halves and fuselage.

The ready-built models usually have wing halves which plug together, control surfaces fitted and hinged, linkages connected to the control surfaces, and wing and tail are already covered with a coloured, fuel-proof plastic film. The plastic or glassfibre fuselage is self-coloured, inherently fuel proof, and doesn't need painting. Some even have the engine and fuel tank ready fitted. But you still have to fit the radio, connect up the throttle and flying controls and make the model balances correctly.

To do this properly can take quite a long time because you cannot rush through the "installation" as it is called.

No mistaking the purpose of this model! This all-balsa kit went out of production when more and more beginners demanded kits with ready-made wing halves. Photograph: Ripmax Ltd.

The ideal trainer should be easy to fly.

The control surfaces have to move the right amounts; the movement on the engine's throttle lever must be matched to the servo (more about this later); the battery and radio receiver have to be packed in place with foam plastic; and all the wiring has to be secured against vibration. So a ready-built model is by no means ready to fly.

To put this in perspective the writer, who is a slower than average builder, can build a fuselage and join a ready-made pair of wing halves in less time than he takes over the installation. Don't despair, therefore, if finances dictate that you have to build an all-balsa kit. As long as you are reasonably patient and are reasonably good with your hands you should have no real difficulties, and you won't be human if you don't feel a growing pride as your creation takes shape, and the admiring remarks of the children may help to change your wife's attitude if she regards the whole project with a certain amount of female cynicism!

Having built the model you will have a very good idea of how to go about repairing it should this become necessary later on, whereas many beginners who start with a ready-built model are at a complete loss as to how to repair even quite minor damage. It is however very important that the wing should be free of warps or twist. If, having studied the plan and seen how the wing is built, you feel it may be beyond you, you'll do better to spend a few pounds more and get a kit with ready-made wing halves.

One other factor which may affect your choice is the time of year. If you get hooked on our hobby in the spring you'll want your model finished as soon as possible so that you can learn to fly during the summer. If you start in the late autumn there won't be this hurry and you'll very likely soon discover that model building is a far more relaxing and rewarding way of spending your winter evenings than "gawping at the box".

The ideal trainer should be easy to fly. For this the first essential is that it should be reasonably large so that you can fly it at a "safe" height in the sky and still see clearly what it' s doing. We regard a wing span of about 55 inches (1375) as a minimum. Models rarely come to any harm in the sky – you can break or "fold" a wing trying to get your model out of a steep high-speed dive by jerking on full up elevator in a panic, and your model might be hit by another model. The first danger you can avoid, the second does happen but happily very infrequently. Models are normally only at risk near the ground, and if yours is 200 feet (60 metres) up and you do get into bad trouble your instructor will have plenty of time to take over and sort it out.

The second essential is that the model should be stable, meaning that, once it has been trimmed out, it will fly quite happily on its own, and will revert to straight and level flight whatever attitude you get it into *providing* you throttle back the engine and neutralise the flying controls. If you survived the chapter on aerodynamics you'll already have a good idea of the factors that contribute to stability – a high wing to give pendulum stability, plenty of dihedral, generous tail areas and plenty of room in the front of the fuselage so that the battery and radio equipment can be used to balance the model without extra weight having to be added.

The third essential is that the model should be reasonably light for its size, or have a low wing loading, as it is called. The lower the wing loading the slower it can fly with safety, and you'll have an easier task controlling a relatively slow model than one that has to pound around at 40 or 50 mph merely to stay up in the air. Also, of course, sooner or later you're going to have to land the thing, and although the landing approach is made well above the stalling speed the slower the approach speed the easier this will be. Now the battery and radio equipment of most standard R/C outfits weigh about 10 ounces (285g), which is another reason for regarding a span of about 55 inches (1375) as a minimum – the same load in a smaller model must inevitably result in a higher wing loading. A foam wing will add to the overall weight a little, and a glassfibre fuselage rather more. A model featuring both these should therefore be kept as light as possible – don't paint the fuselage and use a lightweight covering such as Solarfilm (described later) on the wing and tail.

We have now dealt with the three essentials of an easy-to-fly trainer – its size, stability and wing loading. Another factor to be considered is the undercarriage. Some trainers have a two-wheel or "taildragger" undercarriage, others have a tricycle undercarriage. The former is more suitable for landing on uncut grass and if you will be flying over rough fields, where hand launching is essential, you should choose a trainer with a two wheel undercarriage. If the ground is very rough you will do better to leave the undercarriage off altogether, and rely on a heavy gauge wire skid to protect the front of the model during landings. If you are fortunate enough to have a flying field with a cut grass or paved take-off area then go for a tricycle undercarriage. Providing it is tracking straight (a little "toe-in" on the rear wheels helps enormously in this respect) little or no rudder correction will be needed during take off, whereas a two-wheel model can, in the hands of a beginner, need a lot of work on the rudder to keep it on course.

The ideal trainer should be crashproof . . .

Trainers with tricycle undercarriages usually have a fixed noseleg, and are steered during the take-off run with the rudder. The engine will be at full throttle and, as the rudder is directly in the blast of air blown back by the propeller, plenty of control is available. Some trainers have a steerable nosewheel, which turns when the rudder control is operated. This can be a tremendous asset, as the learner can become familiar with the rudder control by taxying the model away from him, turning it round and taxying back. He will then experience the major difference between model and full-size flying referred to earlier; when the model is coming towards the pilot and left rudder is signalled, the model will turn to the pilot's right.

If the learner will practise until he can taxi the model accurately, and correct any deviations from the intended course as soon as they begin to develop, he will be amply rewarded once the model is in the air. The only drawback to a steerable nosewheel is that in a bad landing the noseleg will be bent back. Since the noseleg is mechanically linked to the rudder servo, damage to the servo can result. If your instructor is going to land the model no problem should arise, but before you attempt your own first landings you should disconnect the nosewheel linkage from the rudder servo and fix it to a temporary anchorage inside the fuselage so that the nosewheel is set straight ahead.

The ideal trainer should be crashproof. None of them are, nor ever will be, and you'll do no good by beefing up the structure here, there and everywhere in an attempt to achieve this. You'll merely end up with a heavier model that flies faster, and the heavier they are the harder they fall. Unless you can see an obvious weakness in the design which can be remedied for a very small weight penalty, build the structure exactly as the plan.

Now the essence of a model that is to be as nearly as possible crashproof is that the wing and undercarriage should be attached in such a way that they can "give" or even come away completely in a crash. If they are fixed rigidly a lot of unnecessary damage will result.

Although the standard of trainer kits has improved a great deal over the years one must remember that kit manufacturers are in business to sell their kits, and the untutored beginner can be influenced too much by a model's appearance. Regrettably, in attempting to produce sleek, streamlined models with more sales appeal, certain features are sometimes introduced which are positively detrimental. Fortunately these are easily remedied and, if your kit has any of the design faults listed below, we strongly recommend you build-in the minor modifications we suggest, rather than have to incorporate them later when the fault has been proved to exist in practice!

Some models advertised as trainers have the wing fixed to the fuselage with bolts. Admittedly the bolts are usually nylon which can give a little, but nowhere near enough. So if you must buy a trainer with a bolt-on wing you should convert it to a "knock-off" wing by reverting to the traditional system where ¼ inch (6) dowels are built through the fuselage, about 1 inch (24) below the leading and trailing edges of the wing, and left projecting about ½ inch (12) outside the fuselage at each end. The wing is held with strong rubber bands (at least four) looped diagonally over these dowels. If you don't have any dowel handy, pencils will do. Reinforce the inside of the fuselage around the dowels with $\frac{1}{16}$ inch (1.5) ply plates about 1 inch (24) wide running the full height of the fuselage. The outside grain of the ply must be vertical. If knocked the wing can then slew round. In a bad bump it will slew round so far that the bands will come off the dowels – you may lose the bands but you'll have saved the wing and the fuselage. Try to get proper white wing-fixing bands as sold by model shops. These are more easily found and if you crash on grazing land you must find them. Cattle have been killed by swallowing rubber bands which cannot be digested.

Similarly some trainers with a tricycle undercarriage (U/C) have a rigid preformed aluminium main leg assembly which is bolted to the bottom of the fuselage. If the fuselage is fibreglass and there is plenty of reinforcement moulded in this may be all right, but a bad landing on rough ground could still damage the fuselage badly. If yours is this type cut halfway through the bolts with a fine hacksaw before fixing the U/C. Buy a spare set of bolts, cut these in the same way and keep them in your flight box as spares. The cut bolts will be plenty strong enough for normal use, but will "fail safe" if the U/C hits something hard. If the fuselage is balsa and the same arrangement is used, forget the bolts altogether and hold the aluminium on with strong rubber bands looped over ¼ inch (6) dowels just like the wing. Glue a hardwood or plywood stop under the bottom of the fuselage against which the back of the aluminium can bear. This will keep the legs straight during take-off, but in a bad landing the rubber bands will allow the whole assembly to pivot backwards.

Some trainers feature a knock-off tail where the tailplane is held on by rubber bands and dowels. Although this seems logical it doesn't work well in practice. Unless the tailplane gets fixed in exactly the same position each time the model is assembled on the flying field the elevator won't be at the same angle as previously – it will be slightly up or down as dictated by the linkage connecting the elevator to its servo. So a little re-trimming may be necessary. Also, of course, if the tailplane gets a bump and slews round either the elevator or its linkage must give – if it doesn't the servo could be damaged. Models don't crash tail first so the tail is least likely to receive really hard knocks, and in our experience it is better to have the tailplane firmly glued in place.

Some trainers have a glazed cabin, i.e. celluloid windows to make the cabin area look more realistic. If there is a good strong ply reinforced structure under the wing to hold the wing dowels this will probably be all right. If there isn't the wing dowels could break away in flight (disaster!) or the cabin area could collapse as the wing slews round in a cartwheel landing. Better to fill in the whole window area with hard ⅛ inch (3) sheet balsa. In general a model with all three of these design faults (bolt-on wing, bolt-on rigid undercarriage and glazed cabin) wasn't designed as a trainer anyway, and a model with two probably wasn't. No matter what claims are made on the box top, such models should be avoided.

The reader should now have a pretty good idea as to what makes a good trainer and what doesn't. We must now deal with a particular group of beginners to R/C flying, those who have been aeromodelling for many years and now want to buy a radio control outfit and realise a long-held dream, to build a scale model of some full-size light aircraft that they have owned, flown in or admired. They are not the least interested in progressing (if that's the word!) to a high-powered aerobatic model, what interests them is a scale Piper or Cessna or whatever that they can taxi out, take off, fly round at scale speed and land. To them the reproduction of the full-size flight of such an aircraft is the true purpose of, and the only justification for, radio control.

Now many planes such as these are high-wing monoplanes, having inherently stable flight characteristics, and kits are available for large Pipers, Aeroncas and other similar models which have a light structure, are capable of flying very slowly, and feature knock-off wings (though the rubber bands are cleverly hidden inside the fuselage). On the face of it, therefore, models such as

... those who have been aeromodelling for many years ...

these would make good R/C trainers, and the scale enthusiast is often tempted to start with such a model instead of a purpose-designed trainer.

This is the wrong approach on many counts. The first snag is that a scale model always has a more intricate structure than a trainer, so that building will take longer. Then again no true scale enthusiast will be happy with anything less realistic than a nicely glazed cabin area and a proper paint job in authentic colours complete with appropriate registration letters etc., which again will take more time. But the result will be more easily damaged and take *far* longer to repair than a trainer, and psychological barrier will have been created in that the builder will be more reluctant to attempt, say, his first landing for fear of damaging his beautiful but time-consuming creation. And if, as can happen, a bad crash occurs during the training period, he may be tempted to abandon the model altogether, knowing it will never again look quite as good as it did when first finished, whereas a simple trainer suffering quite serious damage can be repaired and flying again by the following weekend.

So, if you are a scale model aspirant, forget the aesthetics and start with a proper trainer. Build it accurately but don't waste a lot of time trying to achieve a scale standard finish. It is, after all, merely a means to an end, not an and in itself. Your eventual dream will be realised quicker, and at less expense, if you accept that all your aeromodelling skills have to be put aside temporarily while you learn the quite different art of flying by radio control.

So far we have said nothing about the controls to be fitted to a trainer, and it is every bit as important to get these right as it is to select a suitable model. Fortunately nearly all trainer kits have got it right. For power modelling the standard trainer today is fitted with a throttle control on the engine, and elevator and rudder controls for flying, and therefore requires what is called three-function proportional radio gear. (Proportional means that the controls move in proportion to the movement of the appropriate stick on the transmitter. In other words if you move the rudder control stick a little to the left the rudder will move a little to the left. If you move it fully to the right the rudder will go to the full right position, and so on).

Beginners are sometimes puzzled as to why a throttle control is regarded as essential, and are tempted to save money on a power model by using two function R/C gear operating elevator and rudder only. *This is very much a false economy.* The throttle is an invaluable safety valve if something goes wrong on the ground or in the air. The model may turn badly when released for take-off, so that it would be flying across rather than into the wind if it left the ground. Even for an experienced pilot this is a dangerous situation. Or it may leave the ground quite safely but, once airborne, prove to be badly over-elevated, so that the pilot has to hold in a lot of down elevator to stop the model climbing too fast and stalling. In either event (and in many, many other situations) it is safer to throttle back and prevent or curtail the flight for appropriate adjustments to be made.

The reader will have noticed that we recommend a trainer that doesn't have ailerons, but relies on rudder and dihedral for turns, yet there are many models advertised as trainers with little dihedral and ailerons fitted as standard. This is because the writer saw, from personal experience over many years, that those who started in this way, and "converted" to ailerons once they had mastered the basics, almost always made quicker and safer progress than those who wanted to "start as I intend to finish", i.e. with a model fitted with ailerons from the word go. Happily you don't have to build another model to convert – the best-selling power trainer kits are almost all available in what are called three or four function versions, and if you start as we advise with three functions (rudder, elevator and throttle controls) you'll find an aileron wing kit can be bought, when it is required, for a reasonale price. Just in case you are still thinking of starting with ailerons, we'll give you some examples in the following paragraphs.

Let's assume you have throttle and rudder controlled by the left-hand stick on your transmitter and elevator by the right-hand stick (probably the most popular mode). Your trainer is standing on the runway pointing directly into wind, engine idling, and you are about to do your first solo take-off. Your tutor is holding the model's tail. You push forward the throttle stick to full throttle, have a last nervous test on the other controls, and shout "OK". The model is released and speeds off down the runway. She starts to veer off a little and you hold on a little rudder to keep her into wind, building up plenty of speed before take-off. Then you ease in just a touch of up elevator and she lifts off. At that moment the undercarriage has no more effect on the model – it's now being supported by the wing, and what was the correct rudder setting on the ground won't necessarily be exactly right in the air. Also she probably won't be heading *exactly* into wind. Whatever the reason the model will almost certainly bank over into a slight turn. But no worry, you've been using rudder on the ground and your reaction will be automatic. A quick touch on the same stick gets her back into wind again. She still has no real reserve of speed and as she comes back into wind she puts her nose up a little too high for comfort. A quick touch of down elevator remedies this and she's climbing away safely into wind, steadily gaining height. "No sweat" as the Americans say. Well – not the second time you do it!

Now let's assume you have ailerons (instead of rudder) and throttle on the left-hand stick, and rudder and elevator on the right (this would be the arrangement when you convert to ailerons – ailerons become the primary turning control and replace rudder on the transmitter). Let's go through the same take-off again. She's speeding down the runway and with your right hand you're holding on a little rudder to keep her on course. Then, with the same stick, you ease in just a touch of up elevator and she lifts off. Now, at this most critical moment, when the model is just airborne with no reserve of speed, you have to centralise the rudder (without disturbing the elevator) on the right stick, and correct that turn with ailerons on the left stick. But the nose starts to get too high. It won't be surprising if you can't switch your mind back to the right stick to put in a quick touch of down elevator before that potential stall develops into a real one!

In case you're thinking that all this won't apply to you because your field is rough and your model will be hand launched anyway, bear with us while we illustrate the difference between a rudder and an aileron model as it is flown through the very first manoeuvre it will ever do, the 180° turn at the end of the climb-out after launching. With a rudder model you ease in a little rudder *and hold the stick in that position.* The model banks over until its natural stability stops it banking any more (the angle of bank will be about 20 degrees it you've got it right). Now the nose always tends to drop a little during a turn so you ease in a touch of up elevator at the same time. When the model has turned the intended 180 degrees you release rudder and elevator, and within a couple of seconds she's flying straight and level again. We're not pretending you'll get it exactly right first time, she might have gained or lost a little height, but you've done a safe turn. Note that only four signals are given – rudder and elevator to start the turn, take off rudder and elevator to come out of the turn.

Now let's do it with an aileron model, remembering it has little or no dihedral so is less stable, and that the elevator must be used to pull the model round the turn as

The throttle is an invaluable safety valve if something goes wrong

well as to maintain height, so that a steeper bank (say 30 degrees) will be required. You ease in a little aileron to bank the model over. When you've got your 30 degree bank you *take off most of the aileron* (if you don't the bank will go on getting steeper and steeper). You ease in up elevator to pull her round the turn. When the model has turned the intended 180 degrees you have to apply *opposite* aileron to get the wing level again (because the model isn't sufficiently stable to do this for itself), *and* release the elevator at the same time, *and then* put the ailerons back to neutral. One day all this will become instinctive, you'll do it without thinking, but for the average beginner – it is *not* easy!

Can we now look ahead a little till the time you think you *are* ready for ailerons? Please don't convert too early in your flying career. Time and time again we have seen beginners who have been making excellent progress throw it all away by converting too soon. They learn the new take-off technique and soon discover that a tight turn with ailerons seems remarkably easy. All you do is to bank the model well over, say to 60 or more degrees, haul in a lot of up elevator and she pulls round in no time at all. So she does, providing there is sufficient speed and power available. If there isn't the wing will stall and a stall at that attitude means real trouble.

The other danger is banking over just that little bit too far. Once the wing is past vertical, up elevator starts to pull the model downwards, and the relative beginner, seeing the model rapidly losing height, almost always reacts by giving still more "up", thereby making matters worse. The only remedy is to take off the excess bank with the ailerons. This seems obvious written here, but you won't have time to think it out in the air! So disregard the advice of the "loudmouths", who have probably forgotten (or chosen to forget) the problems they had when still learning, and resist the temptation to fit ailerons until you have done, say, fifteen to twenty *solo* flights without having given a wrong signal.

One other and equally important point before leaving power trainers. Don't be tempted to fit a too-powerful engine with a view to using it in an aerobatic model later. The faster it flies the quicker things go wrong. It's better to start with an inexpensive training engine, which you won't wear out anyway, and sell it or trade it in for a high power engine when you are ready for your first low-wing aerobatic model.

When you get your trainer kit check the contents before you do anything else. If something is missing the sooner the shop knows about it the better, particularly if there isn't another kit like yours in stock from which the part can be taken, and the manufacturer has to be chased to supply one. Next, read the instructions right through to get a general idea as to how the model is built. Then read them through again slowly and carefully because you may find the order of building suggested isn't always the easiest. Don't misunderstand us here, we are not suggesting you depart from the instructions without a good reason, and you must think out all the consequences before departing from the suggested sequence.

An example of what we have in mind is fitting and shaping the block balsa tips used on some foam wings. The instructions frequently tell you to do this after the wing halves are joined together. Now a complete wing is quite a handful and carving and sanding the tips to match the wing section is obviously much easier done while the wing is still in two halves. We freely admit you should be able to follow the instructions exactly, knowing that you'll be building your model in the easiest and quickest

When you get your trainer kit check the contents . . .

way. But most kit manufacturers are small firms serving a relatively small market and are unwilling to face the expense and delay in testing out a new kit on an experienced modeller *and* on a complete beginner before putting it into production. This is a great pity but it is perhaps symptomatic of our times, when all too often goods are judged by price alone. We know of many kits that could be considerably improved if the selling price could be raised by only a few pounds. But doing this could turn away so many customers that the manufacturer would be courting financial disaster. Nevertheless there is no excuse at all for carelessly written instructions, let's hope they will become a thing of the past.

Now for the soaring trainers. The requirements of stability, plenty of room for the radio and knock-off wings still apply and you'll again find that this last essential quality is often compromised for the sake of appearance. More than a few soarer kits feature a wing held on by rubber bands in the correct way, but which can only knock-off by smashing the canopy! This incredibly stupid arrangement can usually be overcome by re-arranging the way the canopy is fixed so that if it gets pushed from behind by the wing it will slide upwards and forwards at its front until the front fixing is disengaged, and can then fly off altogether.

The requirements for size and slow flying ability differ completely between slope soarers and thermal soarers. The former are flown closer to the pilot than power models. If you fly too far out from the slope you'll lose lift, and if you get the model behind the slope you'll be in turbulent negative lift and the model will very soon be out of sight anyway, so large size won't help you see it! Probably 50 inches (1250) is the realistic minimum span if the wing is built-up, 60 inches (1500) if it is foam. There is much less building in a slope soarer than in a power model of equivalent size, so probably less incentive to go for a foam wing, but a true wing is absolutely vital on any form of soarer, and again if you doubt your building abilities a foam wing should be your choice.

Thermal soarers *must* have a low wing loading and a wing of at least 6 foot (1800) span is the minimum; 8 foot (2400) span or more will be better. The choice as to what type of soarer to build will probably be dictated by the existence or otherwise of soaring slopes within easy reach of your home – it is pointless building a "sloper" if all the land around you is as flat as a pancake, equally pointless building a lightweight delicate "thermaler" and heaving it off a steep slope in a 30 mph wind.

If you have found a group of slope soarers near you and intend flying with them, they will be better able to recommend a suitable trainer than anyone else. They will know how much lift is usually available and may well have already found which trainers suit their site best. They also will probably suggest minor modifications (a fly-off canopy or perhaps a tail skid to keep the tailplane further off the ground) and you'll obviously be wise to incorporate these. If you cannot contact any slope soarers near you but think you have found a flyable slope, work on the assumption that it is only just flyable and build one of the large slope-or-thermal soarers mentioned earlier.

We don't want to be pessimistic but the interest in slope soaring is now so great that if you never see soarers on the slope you have "discovered" there is probably a very good reason why – insufficient lift. An apparently attractive slope can often give less lift than anticipated, either because of geographical features upwind from it, or simply because the slope just isn't long enough and a lot of the wind goes round the slope rather than over it.

Before you select a large trainer give a thought to transport – some kits have two piece wings which are plugged together with metal dowels and tubes on site, others have one piece wings and it's a bit disappointing if you find you can't get it in the car! Quite large wings can often be carried safely under the car roof on elastic supports fixed with contact cement or whatever to the roof lining and slightly stretched across the width of the car. Your wing is then safely out of the way of the children and their day out is not spoilt by father continually nagging them to sit still and mother nagging father not to nag the children!

Whereas fuselages on power trainers are almost always balsa or glass fibre a lot of soarer kits have fuselages of ABS or other plastic, sometimes with plywood reinforcement. These are lighter and less expensive to produce than glass fibre but ABS will crack in all directions if hit hard, particularly on a cold day, and is more difficult to repair. If your soaring site is nicely covered with grass or ferns ABS should be all right, but if it's hard ground with rock outcrops stick to balsa or glass fibre.

For either slope or thermal soaring almost all trainers are fitted with rudder and elevator controls and require two-function proportional gear. Again adequate dihedral is essential for the rudder to work properly, so don't be afraid to compare the picture of the trainer you have in mind with pictures of others in the magazines and catalogues and ensure yours has as much dihedral as most.

Again you'll be asking for trouble if you start with rudder and ailerons or if you try to convert too soon. We won't be so dogmatic about ailerons on true slope soarers as we were with power models; if the wind usually blows pretty hard on your slope the quicker and more positive response to aileron control could well be beneficial. But in these circumstances use ailerons *instead* of rudder so that you still only have two controls to worry about, and don't try to learn this way without an instructor constantly beside you so that he can take over instantly whenever the need arises. For thermal or slope-or-thermal soarers designed to fly off a gentle slope in moderate winds our advice is the same as for power trainers – avoid ailerons on your trainer like the plague.

Readers completely new to our hobby may be wondering how a thermal soarer is launched. A free-flight glider is launched by someone walking or running directly into wind at one end of a thin towline 2 – 300 feet (60-90 metres) long. The other end is fitted with a ring which is engaged on a towhook fitted under the fuselage. The model goes up rather like a kite and it is important that it isn't towed too fast. The free end of the towhook slopes slightly downwards and when sufficient height has been attained the tower stops walking or running, the model flies on, the line goes slack and the ring can slide off the hook. Usually a handkerchief or piece of silk is tied to the line about 2 feet (600) in front of the ring so that its drag will help the ring disengage. It also helps find the end of the line afterwards. This technique can be used with R/C (the pilot should launch the model and let his assistant do the running) but has largely been superseded by what is called "bungee launching".

The line is about 300 feet (90 metres) long overall and is made up of about one third bungee rubber tubing (a special kind of rubber which returns to its original length

. . . if you never see soarers on the slope you have "discovered" there is probably a very good reason why . . .

after being stretched with less of a "jerk" than does normal rubber) and two thirds lightweight thread or fishing line. The rubber is held by an assistant or pegged to the ground and the ring is tied to the end of the thread. The ring is pulled back until the rubber is stretched from three to five times its natural length and the model is launched in a nose up attitude. This is a much safer way of launching than the free-flight method – a sudden gust of wind causes the rubber to "give" so that the model has a more constant airspeed and consequently behaves better on the line.

In place of the handkerchief it is usual to fit a "bungee parachute" (a strongly made parachute of about 18 inch (450) diameter when open). This actually forms part of the towline so that while the rubber is in tension hauling up the model the shrouds are tight and the parachute remains closed. When the line goes slack it opens and the ring quickly disengages from the towhook. The parachute blows downwind as the line falls and (in theory at least!) the line is more or less ready for the next launch.

This brings us to another way of launching a thermal soarer – by fitting a small engine either to the nose or on a pylon mounted above the wing. Such a pylon is frequently held on by nothing more than the rubber bands holding the wing, so that conversion from pure soarer to engine power is virtually instantaneous. Similarly a nose-mounted engine can replace a weighted noseblock with equal ease.

Now engine conversion kits are available for more than a few soarers currently on the market, but powered-launch soaring has received little publicity. This is probably because its advocates are often lone handers – in practice it really needs two people for bungee launching, one to free the line from the inevitable thistles and things and the other to launch, whereas a powered glider can be operated single-handed. Whatever the reason, powered-launch soaring should not be dismissed as "neither one thing nor the other". Correspondence in one of the R/C magazines suggested that this is probably the easiest way to learn R/C flying if you have to "go it alone", and almost certainly *is* the easiest if you have experience with free-flight power models.

It is essential to realise that the engine is there for one purpose only – to gain height. No throttle is normally fitted nor should be. After initial hand launches (down that elusive grassy slope always recommended for free-flight models) with the engine fitted but not running, to obtain a straight flat glide, the engine is set running at only about half power and with only enough fuel in the tank for about 10 seconds running. A powered glide should result and the model's behaviour will show if any changes are necessary to the engine's thrust line. If it is pylon mounted it will almost certainly need some upthrust (i.e. be pointing, say, 5 degrees upwards in relation to the wing). If it is nose mounted it will probably want 2 or 3 degrees downthrust. When the effect of the engine on the glide has been corrected power and duration can be increased flight by flight. The pilot should do nothing during this proving process other than get the nose down as soon as the engine cuts and just keep the model gliding away from him into wind.

Even when the "full power full tank" stage is reached he should do no more than apply gentle corrections with the rudder to keep the model climbing steadily into wind. Only when he has mastered controlling the thing as a glider he can start *gently* controlling it as a power model, never forgetting that he cannot throttle back if things go wrong.

Because the choice of a good trainer is so often one of the major factors that determine whether a beginner succeeds or sells up we make no apology for summarising the features you should look for when buying your kit:

- (a) sufficient prefabrication to suit your building ability;
- (b) simple, rugged construction that is easy to build and easy to repair;
- (c) adequate size, high wing layout with generous dihedral, generous tail areas and no ailerons;
- (d) thick, strong wing that can knock off;
- (e) undercarriage of the type to suit your flying field;
- (f) availability of an aileron wing for economical conversion after initial learning.

Finally, for the best possible chance of success, don't forget to select an engine from the lower half of the power range claimed to be suitable. Some of the more popular power and soaring trainer kits are described in chapters 24 and 25.

Chapter 9

About Engines

Engines for R/C models are usually referred to by their size or swept volume. For the non-technical this means the area of the top of the piston multiplied by the distance it travels up and down. The answer is given in cubic inches except that in the world of models the decimal point is missed out. Thus an engine called a 20 has actually a swept volume or capacity of .20 cubic inches and a 30 a capacity of .30 cubic inches, about 3¼ and 5 cubic centimetres or CCs respectively. Most trainers need engines of 25-40 size.

Most engines for radio controlled models are of the glowplug type, meaning that the fuel is ignited by a tiny coil of wire which glows between red and white-hot (usually bright orange) and replaces the sparking plug in the conventional petrol engine. A battery is connected to the glowplug for starting, but is disconnected as soon as the engine is running at a reasonable speed, so that no external aid to ignition has to be carried in the model. Diesel or compression-ignition engines are still popular for free-flight and control-line models and are making a comeback in radio control, but the lighter weight, lower vibration and better throttling characteristics of glowplug engines have made them remain the more popular the choice for R/C models. Of particular importance to the beginner is the fact that glowplug engines are *much* easier to start than diesels, and this book therefore deals with them exclusively.

Most model engines work on the two stroke or two cycle principle which means that fuel is burnt and power produced every time the piston reaches the top of the cylinder. Such engines are delightfully simple and the workings of a basic "crossflow" type are easily understood.The carburettor on the front of the engine mixes fuel and air in the correct proportions and this mixture enters the engine via the crankshaft, which is hollowed out internally to form a tube. An inlet is machined at the front of this tube to coincide with the bottom of the carburettor, allowing the mixture to enter the engine while the piston is rising, but closing off the carburettor when the crankshaft has rotated far enough for the piston to be at the top of its stroke. On one side of the engine is the exhaust port which is essentially a slot cut in the side of the cylinder to allow the burnt fuel/air mixture to escape to the outside air when the piston nears the bottom of its stroke. On the other side of the cylinder is a transfer passage which transfers the fuel/air mixture from the crankcase underneath the piston up into the top of the cylinder above the piston. The passage is opened by a hole or holes drilled through the side or "skirt" of the piston and is closed off as the piston rises. There are none of the valves, camshafts, coils, condensers or other complications of the four stroke motor car engine. Let's now go through one complete revolution or cycle to see how a two stroke works.

When the piston rises it will leave a partial vacuum in the crankcase underneath it, and a fresh charge of fuel and air will be drawn in from the carburettor to fill this

This photo shows that balsa wood can be used to make simple demonstration models as well as model aeroplanes. The large round disc near the bottom represents the rear of the crankshaft which supports the crank pin. This is attached, via the connecting rod, to the gudgeon pin which runs through the piston. The transfer passage is on the left and the exhaust port is on the right.
In modern engines the fuel/air mixture enters via a hollow crankshaft, not through the side of the cylinder as indicated by the hole just above the top of the piston. (Photograph: Solarbo Ltd)

space. Above the piston the fuel/air mixture (we'll see how it got there in a moment) will be compressed, and as the piston reaches the top of its stroke the mixture is ignited by the glowplug. As it burns a large volume of gas is produced and this forces the piston down until the exhaust port is exposed and the gas can escape to the outside air. As the piston is forced down it compresses the charge of fuel and air in the crankcase underneath it, and at the bottom of the stroke this charge will escape into the transfer passage and discharge into the cylinder above the top of the piston thus helping to push the last of the gas out through the exhaust port. As the piston rises once more its skirt closes off the transfer passage, the mixture above the piston is compressed ready for ignition, while a fresh charge of mixture is being drawn in under the piston from the carburettor.

Piston at top, inlet and exhaust ports closed off, cut out in hollow crankshaft about to close off under carburettor.

All we need to keep the process going is a supply of fuel, a glowplug that glows and a flywheel on the crankshaft to push the piston back up again every time the exhaust gas pushes it down. The glowplug is kept red/white hot by the burning fuel/air mixture and the propeller acts as an adequate flywheel.

Carburettors on most R/C engines fall into two different types, those with one main adjusting control or "needle" and those with two. We'll describe the more simple single needle type first. Essentially there is a large round air inlet called the venturi, a much smaller fuel inlet called the spraybar, which usually projects about half-way across the venturi, and a tapered needle called the needle valve which controls the amount of fuel that can be released by the spraybar (when the needle is screwed fully in fuel is shut off altogether). The outer end of the needle valve is bent or knurled to make finger adjustment easier. There is also a rotating barrel to adjust the engine's speed and this is rotated by a lever connected mechanically to the throttle servo of the R/C equipment. The barrel has a hole drilled straight through it and at full throttle position there is no restriction to the amount of air that can enter the engine. As the barrel is rotated the air supply is progressively closed off and less air rushing past the spraybar results in less fuel being drawn in with the air. The correct proportions of

Piston halfway down, inlet and exhaust ports still closed, fuel/air mixture being compressed under piston.

Piston at bottom, fuel/air mixture entering above piston on far side, exhaust gases leaving above piston on near side, cut out in hollow crankshaft about to open under carburettor.

fuel to air are thus approximately maintained whatever the throttle setting, though invariably the mixture is more rich (more fuel to air) at low throttle openings.

On the top of the carburettor body there is a small adjusting screw called the throttle stop which determines how far the barrel can rotate when the throttle is closed, and thus determines the idling speed of the engine. At the front of the carburettor body there is often a small hole that lets in air when the throttle barrel is closed or nearly closed. This compensates for the too rich mixture at low throttle openings and the airbleed hole, as it is called, is fitted with what is normally the only other adjusting screw, so that its effective size can be altered to give the ideal fuel/air mixture at idling speed. The normal position for this adjusting screw is about half way across the airbleed hole. It is pointless adjusting this when the engine is new – you'll not get reliable idling with any new engine, some need one or two hours running before a slow reliable idle can be obtained.

Setting up a single needle carburettor is not difficult. The correct fuel/air mixture is obtained by adjusting the needle valve at full throttle, after which the throttle stop is adjusted, if necessary, to ensure a safe but slow idling speed when the throttle is closed. The airbleed is then adjusted for maximum revs at closed throttle with the model held level. (The fact that you are getting maximum revs means that the fuel/air mixture must be at its optimum). This may result in the idling speed increasing perceptibly, in which case the throttle stop, and then the airbleed, will need further adjustment.

Two needle carburettors also have a venturi, spraybar, tapered needle valve and rotating barrel. They differ from single needle types in that the barrel is made to move sideways towards the spraybar as it rotates. A second tapered needle is mounted on the axis of the barrel and moves into the end of the spraybar as the throttle is closed, reducing the amount of fuel that can be admitted. Thus, in theory at least, a constant ratio of fuel to air can be achieved from full throttle right down to tickover. For this theory to be realised in practice four conditions need to be fulfilled – the end of the second needle must be tapered to exactly the right shape, the second needle must be positioned with almost microscopic accuracy in the barrel (it is threaded into the barrel and its free end is slotted to provided fine adjustment with a screwdriver) and there must be no free sideways movement of the barrel which would, of course, completed upset the mixture. Sideways movement is usually prevented by spring-loading the barrel towards the spraybar side. The fourth condition is that the screwdriver adjustment of the second needle, which should have been set with extreme accuracy at the factory, hasn't been messed up in the meantime by some well-meaning but damnfool helper!

Two needle carburettors are clearly more difficult to set up correctly. The main needle is again adjusted to give the correct mixture at full throttle. The second needle should, in this position, be on the verge of obstructing the spraybar without actualy doing so. Its position is normally finalised at about half-throttle and the throttle lever and hence the rotating barrel has to be mechanically clamped so that it cannot rotate by even the slightest degree. At the same time the barrel *must* remain spring-loaded sideways as normal. The second needle is then turned very slowly and carefully in each direction until maximum revs, and thus optimum mixture, is obtained. If the carburettor has a separate adjustment at idling speed the second needle can be left at this setting and the airbleed or whatever adjusted for correct mixture at tickover. If there is no separate adjustment this setting of the second needle should also give optimum mixture at tickover. To test this the lever and barrel have

An O.S. "Sports" engine with simple single – needle carburettor and therefore ideal for beginners

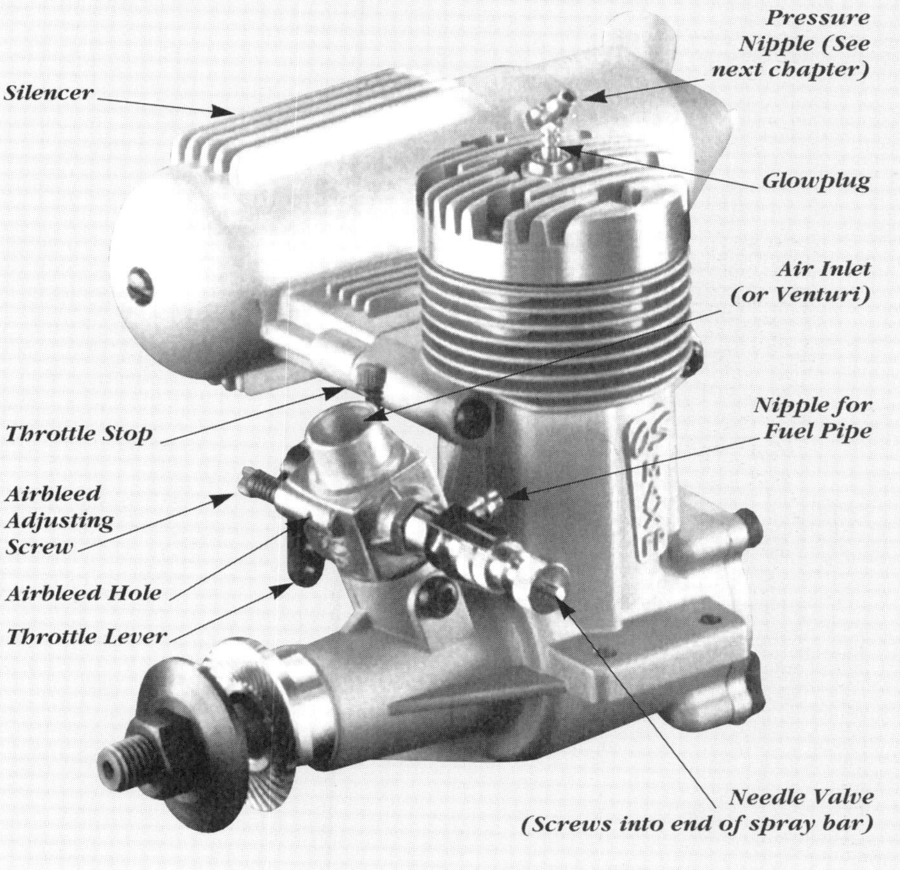

to be mechanically clamped as before to prevent rotation. The second needle is then rotated very slowly in each direction and no increase in revs should result. If it does, the carburettor is out of balance and you'll have to choose between optimum mixture at idling speed or at half throttle. It is better to opt for the former because correct mixture and hence reliable running are more important at low speeds (e.g. during the landing approach) than at half throttle.

If you suspect the writer is prejudiced against two needle carburettors you are correct. They are not only more difficult to set up correctly, they are more complicated and hence more expensive and they get out of adjustment more quickly due to wear. If very accurately made and correctly adjusted they can, of course, give a more consistent fuel/air mixture than single needle ones. But for the average club flyer's trainer and subsequent "sports" models they are simply not necessary. This is evidenced by the fact that O.S. (the oldest, largest and most prestigous model engine company in the world) retained single needle carburettors on their "sports" engines long after many of their rivals had changed to two needle ones.

Readers might be thinking that O.S. retained single needle carburettors because, like Rolls Royce, they are reluctant to pioneer new ideas, preferring not to risk their reputation on anything before it has been proved in practice over a number of years. Nothing could be further from the truth. O.S. pioneered engines with Schnuerle porting, ABC construction, were the first to put a four stroke engine into production, the first to produce a model engine with a true supercharger and are still the only one to make a Wankel. And, no, the writer does not have any shares in the Company! Schnuerle porting and the rest may well be meaningless to many readers so we'll briefly explain these terms.

Most modern engines are Schnuerle ported. This means they have three transfer passages to take the fuel/air mixture from the crankcase to the top of the cylinder. They produce considerably more power than "crossflow" engines (those with a single transfer passage) but at higher revs. High power used to be associated with difficult starting and temperamental running, but this certainly doesn't apply with Schnuerle porting. The more efficient transfer of the fuel/air mixture gives, if anything, easier starting and more consistent running.

ABC Construction. ABC stands for aluminium, brass, chrome and engines of this type have an aluminium piston in a brass cylinder liner which is chromium-plated on the inside. Brass liners have been dreamed about by engine designers for years because brass expands more than aluminium when heated, thus the clearance between piston and liner increases at higher revs. The snag was that brass is a soft metal, totally unsuited to having a relatively soft aluminium piston hurtling up and down in contact with it. The obvious answer was to plate the inside of the liner with chrome to give it a hard surface. Early attempts failed because the chrome was so smooth it wouldn't retain the oil. This was overcome by microscopically pitting the chrome, and more and more engines are using this form of construction. If you buy an ABC engine you must disregard the traditional running-in procedures and not run your engine, as one manufacturer puts it, "slobbering rich". But remember that crankshafts and bearings and connecting rods still have to be run in so build up to full revs in easy stages as recommended in the instructions. Some engines have brass liners that are nickel rather than chrome plated but are still described as "ABC".

AAC Construction. Engines of this type have an aluminium liner which also is chromium plated on the inside. AAC Construction has only found favour, in general, for racing and other very high power engines.

Four-strokes. When the OS Company put the first modern four-stroke engine for R/C model aircraft into mass production power produced per cubic inch of swept volume was way down in relation to its two-stroke equivalent, but so also was its weight. There was also a dramatic decrease in noise. Other manufacturers soon followed and newer engines are very near their two stroke rivals in terms of power/weight ratio. In doing this they have inevitably got more noisy, and they do require silencers, but the pitch of the noise emitted is much lower and far less offensive to the human ear. They also use considerably less fuel. With the complications of camshafts, pushrods, valves, etc. they are inevitably more expensive than two-strokes and are more vulnerable to damage. Thus they are not recommended for trainers, but more and more sports and scale models at club flying fields are now powered by four strokes.

Which make of engine should you buy? We can't be specific but *can* give some guidance. If you join a club you can see which makes are most used and which give most satisfaction. If not, you much choose between the big, old established makes that are stocked in depth by all the large retailers and the newer, cheaper makes from Russia, China, Taiwan, Korea, etc., etc. Those firms with the biggest share of the market are usually the safest bet for the beginner – if you were asked to advise a middle-aged aunt as to what family car she should buy you'd be pretty safe in answering "Get a Ford, Vauxhall or Toyota". So ask a few large retailers which makes they sell the most and you'll probably have a pretty safe answer.

Some readers will be wondering why we haven't, as yet, recommended electric motors instead of engines. The two main disadvantages are that the power run will last only about 5 minutes, which doesn't really give much time for tuition, and the much greater weight of the electric motor and its rechargeable battery. The weight disadvantage can be overcome, to a certain extent, by the experienced flyer, who can build an ultra-light fuselage and accept the fact that, if he has a minor prang, his fuselage will disintegrate. But minor prangs are part and parcel of learning, and if each heavy landing is to require a new fuselage the learning process won't last one summer, it is likely to last three or four!

The first disadvantage can, however, be overcome by an electrically powered soarer. Providing it is sufficiently large to keep the wing loading down then advantage can be taken of the lift from a gentle slope or of any passing thermals. The flight can thus be prolonged, perhaps for as long as the pupil's concentration will permit. Clearly the ability to switch the motor on and off will be a great advantage, and this is something that can be done relatively easily with electrics but not with piston engines! The damage that can be done by the battery in a minor prang can be greatly reduced by mounting it in a streamlined "saddle pack" *outside* the fuselage, where it can slide forward and unplug itself without damaging the structure, should the fuselage suddenly stop!

Chapter 10

About Engine Accessories

Silencers are supplied with all but a very few highly specialised engines and their use should be regarded as a must. You will not be allowed to fly with any club worthy of the name without having an efficient silencer fitted to your engine, and the selfish minority who used to fly without silencers can be blamed for the loss of many good flying fields, as well as having helped bring our hobby into disrepute with many local authorities.

Engines were traditionally primed with one or two drops of fuel on top of the piston before starting. A silencer prevents you doing this directly and some silencers are therefore fitted with a small priming tube which will direct a thin squirt of fuel onto the piston top from a squeeze bottle applied to the outside end. If your silencer doesn't have a priming tube it is probably worth fitting one. A short length of thick wall 1/16 inch (1.5) copper or brass tube can be glued with slow setting, heat resisting epoxy glue such as Araldite into a hole drilled through the side of the silencer opposite the exhaust port. Most silencers are fitted with a pressure nipple which can be used to pressurise the fuel tank. The advantages of doing this are explained later.

Glowplugs come in four basic types, 1½ volt and 2 volt, short reach and long reach. The 1½ volt types are operated off a large dry battery (usually an Ever Ready 993) and the 2 volt ones off a lead-acid rechargeable accumulator. 1½ volt batteries are quite satisfactory as long as the engine can be started easily, but cannot be left connected for perhaps ten to fifteen minutes at a time in the way that accumulators can. Although an accumulator and charger costs considerably more than a 993 you will probably find most flyers at your club use the former. Over the years the extra cost will be recouped and the much greater capacity of the accumulator means more reliable starting.

Close-up of a Hot Spot glowplug. This particular type has a soft iron core running inside but not touching the glow element, the intention being to prevent the element over-cooling when the engine is idling and to prevent it over-heating at full throttle. (Photograph: Ripmax Ltd)

Some glowplugs are advertised as "suitable for 1½ or 2 volts" but this is fallacious – if a plug will glow brightly on 1½ volts it will burn out on 2. And if it glows correctly on 2 volts it won't glow sufficiently brightly on 1½ to give easy starling. Plugs described in this way must be considered as 2 volt ones.

The "reach" of a plug is a measure of the length of the threaded part, which determines how far down into the cylinder head the glow element is positioned. Generally speaking engines over 15s (i.e. over .15 cubic inch or 2.5 cc swept volume) require long reach plugs. Most trainers therefore require plugs of this type and usually you have to buy the plug separately – you don't get one with the engine. If you do get a plug with your engine be warned – it will probably be a 1½ volt one (to suit the American market) and could well burn out if connected to a 2 volt accumulator.

Certain makes of glowplug are available in "hot" and "cool" versions as well as the standard version. These are intended for use with engines of abnormally low or high compression ratios or with non-standard fuels. The serious competition flyer may find advantages by experimenting with special plugs but beginners and sports flyers using normal commercial fuels will not need plugs other than the standard type. Some makes are also available with an "idle bar", a thin strip of metal below the platinum coil designed to protect the coil from some of the effects of combustion and to stop it becoming overcooled when the engine is idling. These are called "R/C" plugs and the small extra cost is usually justified.

Glowplugs must be regarded as consumable and no sensible flyer sets off without at least one spare. Sometimes a plug will last practically a whole flying season, yet the next plug of the same make and type will burn out after only three or four flights. There are many different makes on the market, most modellers settle in the end for the cheapest make that gives, on average, a reasonably long life.

The lead from the starting battery is connected to the glowplug by a proprietary gadget called a glowclip. This comprises two parts or arms, one of which makes contact with the stem at the top of the glowplug, the other of which makes contact between the cooling fins on the side of the cylinder. The arms have to be insulated one from another and spring loaded so that the clip cannot fall off in use. To hold firmly the "clothespeg" type pushes down on the stem of the plug and pulls up on the underside of one of the fins. The "lock-on" type pulls sideways on the stem of the plug and pushes sideways against the cylinder. There is a third type intended for boats and some helicopters called "push-on" or "tubular". These fit over the glowplug rather like a box spanner and are intended to grip around the main body of the plug. The cheap ones are forever falling off and the good ones are more expensive than the other two types without being any better.

You will see at your club flying field that many flyers have an ammeter wired into their glowplug leads so that the amount of current going through the plug can be measured. It is no coincidence that people who use an ammeter in this way have less starting troubles than those who don't. If an engine in good mechanical condition won't start it must be for one of the following reasons:

- (a) Battery or accumulator is not capable of giving sufficient current to obtain a bright orange glow.
- (b) Glowclip is not making proper contact on glowplug head or on outside of cylinder.
- (c) Glowplug has burnt out or is shorting out inside.
- (d) Engine is flooded and glowplug is not glowing because it is surrounded by fuel.
- (e) Engine does not have sufficient fuel to fire.
- (f) Glowplug is leaking, either because the insulator is loose or because the plug has not been tightened sufficiently, both resulting in lack of compression.

An ammeter will immediately indicate if symptoms (a) – (d) apply, and these are by far the most common causes of difficult starting. As regards (d), a 2 volt glowplug working off an accumulator normally takes 2-3 amps, but if the element is surrounded by fuel it will be kept cool and consequently take a larger current until the excess fuel has been burnt away. If the engine is flicked over while the crankcase is flooded the ammeter needle will be seen to kick as a fresh charge of cold fuel reaches the plug and the current momentarily increases. An ammeter costs only a few pounds and the writer regards this as money very well spent.

You'll see electric starters advertised in the magazines and these are popular with owners of four strokes, which can be quite tricky to start by hand. Good starters are not only fairly expensive, they are also heavy. So too is the 12 volt battery needed to power them. Add a half gallon of fuel and a few tools and you have a formidable load to be carried as well as the model! If you are using a two stroke engine therefore, we suggest you start it by hand. With a little practice and experience you'll soon have it running within a minute or so every time.

For hand starting you need a rubber finger stall. This protects your "flicking" finger if the engine kicks, and even the most docile engine can kick really hard if it happens to be in that sort of mood! The resultant cut can be very painful, particularly if the methanol in the fuel gets into it, and you should wash out the cut with warm water and antiseptic as soon as you can if this ever happens.

Another useful accessory is a priming bottle – a small plastic squeeze bottle with a valve and tapered nozzle

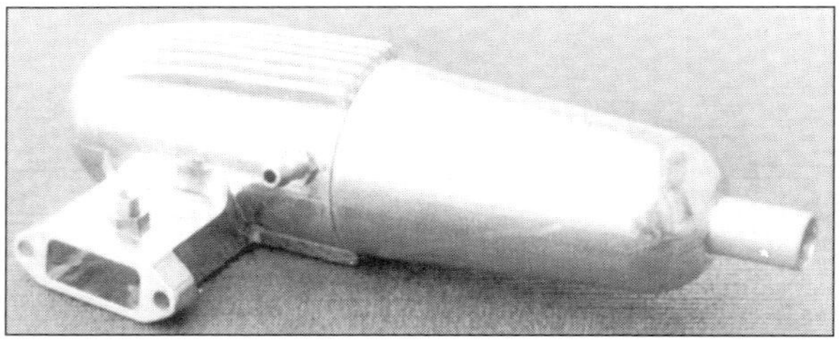

This photograph of a silencer shows the pressure nipple projecting towards the engine and the priming tube on top of the connecting manifold. The bottom of this tube is blanked off and the side of the tube facing the engine is drilled to direct a small squirt of fuel onto the top of the piston for starting. (photograph: Ripmax Ltd.)

filled to the end of the outlet pipe. Priming bottles are intended for priming the carburettor intake and priming on top of the piston before the engine is started, though many modellers fit a larger bottle to the nozzle and use it for filling the tank as well.

Another inexpensive but virtually essential accessory is a fuel filter. Model engines are made to very close tolerances and dirt in the fuel can cause difficult startling or other carburettor troubles as well as premature wear in the engine itself. A filter in the fuel line between tank and carburettor virtually eliminates this possibility.

All R/C trainers are filled with a type of fuel tank called a clunk tank. The essential feature is a hollow weight which falls to the bottom of the tank whatever the model's attitude in the air, and which is connected by flexible tubing to the rigid outlet pipe at the front of the tank. So long as there is sufficient fuel in the tank to cover the clunk weight, fuel, rather than air, will be drawn into the engine.

As well as the outlet or feed pipe there are normally two other pipes emerging from the tank, both of which terminate inside the tank near the top. One is for filling the tank, the other lets the air escape as fuel goes in and acts as an overflow when the tank is full. These are usually extended by flexible tubing so that the one used for filling projects above the top of the fuselage and the overflow discharges at the side or bottom of the fuselage. As long as they both terminate inside the top of the tank it doesn't matter which pipe is used for which purpose.

The filler pipe must be closed off with some form of stopper when the tank is full, otherwise the backdraft from the propeller will draw fuel up the pipe with consequent mess and wastage. A short length of wire or a nail or piece of knitting needle of the appropriate diameter will do the job – don't use a matchstick as wood fibres will eventually find their way into the tank. A few proprietary tanks have only one pipe in addition to the engine feed. In this case the tank is filled by disconnecting the flexible fuel tube from the carburettor or filter and pumping fuel back up the tube into the tank. A single vent pipe must not be stoppered – fuel can only be drawn from the tank if air can get in to replace it.

If you are flying practically every weekend there is no need to drain the tank after each session. But if you won't be flying for some months you can do this by squeezing most of the air from an empty priming bottle and sticking the nozzle into the end of the fuel tube disconnected from the carburettor or filter.

The body of the tank is usually plastic and can contain plastic turnings. If it does is should be washed out thor-

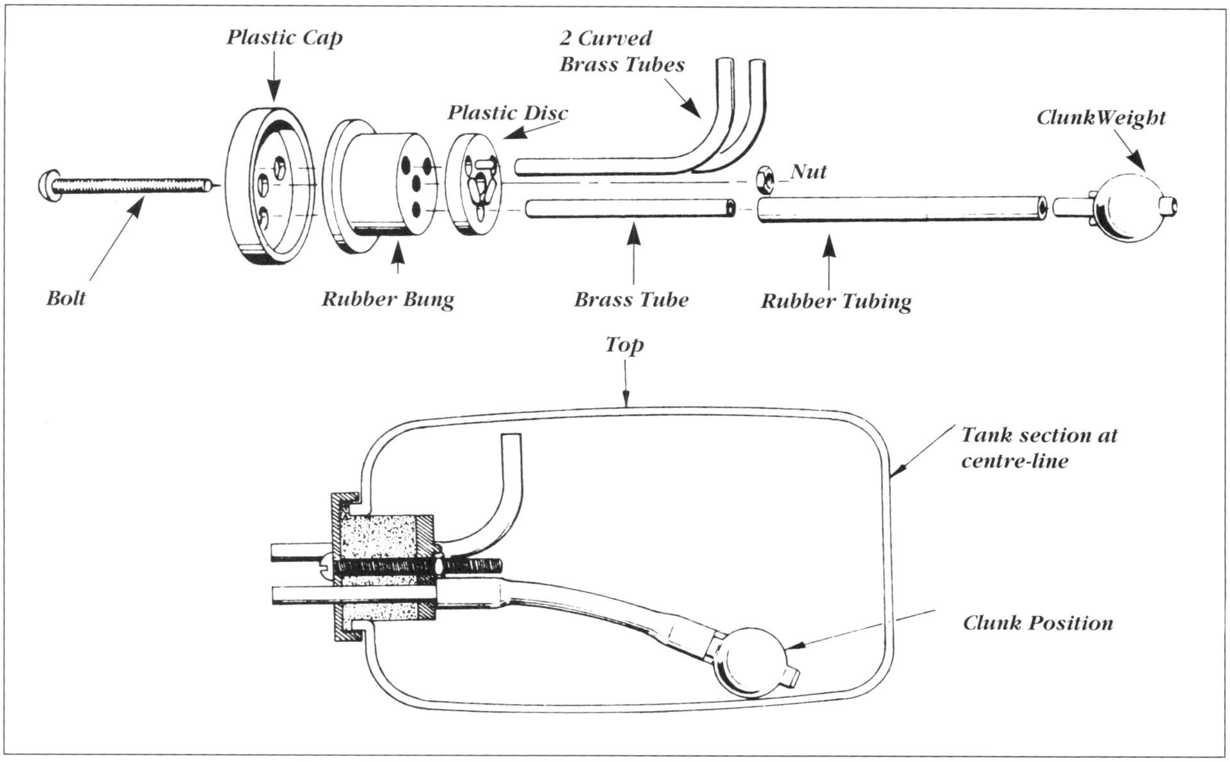

A cause of bewilderment to many beginners, the internals of a clunk tank. (Micro-Mold drawing).

oughly and allowed to dry before the tank is assembled. The flexible tubing between the clunk weight and the outlet pipe is usually rubber and this stretches with age, so make sure the weight can swing about ¼ inch (6) clear of the rear of the tank. The rubber will perish with time and should be renewed about once a year or replaced with silicone rubber which is virtually everlasting. Make sure the filler and vent pipes go up close to the top of the tank otherwise in a bad landing the clunk weight can get caught up with the ends and you'll be drawing air not fuel next time you try to start the engine.

Plastic tanks cannot be glued and are usually firmly wedged into position in the tank compartment with pieces of foam plastic. The front of the tank should be as close behind the engine as practicable, but make sure you have some packing to stop the tank skidding forward in a bad landing because this can cause the feed pipe to kink and starve the engine of fuel. Ideally, when the model is resting on its undercarriage, the top of the tank should be about ⅛ inch (3) above the needle valve on the engine carburettor. If you have it higher it will tend to flood the engine when completely full. If the tank is too low the engine will have to draw the fuel up an unnecessary height, starting will be more difficult, and the fuel/air mixture will become excessively lean (i.e. insufficient fuel for adequate lubrication and cooling) as the fuel level falls towards the end of the flight.

With aerobatic models it is usual to pressurise the tank and most silencers have a pressure nipple which is connected by translucent silicone rubber tubing to one of the filler/vent pipes emerging from the front of the tank. Providing the other filler/vent pipe is stoppered pressure inside the silencer is thus transferred to the fuel tank and fuel is pumped to the engine. The faster the engine is running the more the pressure, and this apparently crude system works surprisingly well. It helps the engine to draw up fuel from the tank when it is in a steep climb, particularly when the tank is nearly empty.

You should not be doing "hairy" aerobatics with your trainer but you'll get a more consistent engine run if your tank is pressurised. The only slight drawback is that when the tank overflows fuel doesn't pour out onto the ground, it goes up the silicone tubing to the silencer. So you need to disconnect the tubing from the silencer or to watch the tubing pretty carefully and stop filling as soon as fuel appears in it, otherwise you'll fill up the silencer as well! Some silencers don't have a pressure nipple, in which case one will have to be threaded or epoxied through the side. Don't position the nipple near the outlet as you may get a venturi effect from the exhaust gas rushing past which will unpressurise the tank rather than the reverse.

The same silicone rubber tubing is used between the tank and the carburettor. Being translucent you can see when bubbles of air are present in the fuel – a sure sign that the clunk weight has got caught up at the top of the tank, or that the flexible tubing connecting it to the tank outlet is leaking and letting in air. Or (it happens!) that you forgot to refill the tank.

Many trainer kits include a spinner, usually of plastic, which fits over the front of the engine's crankshaft and shrouds the central part of the propeller. Spinners give a neater and more realistic appearance to the nose of the model, but they can perform another and more important function as well. Should you be unfortunate enough to crash your model at an angle into a concrete or tarmac runway the spinner will often skid over the surface and convert what was partly a downward travel into a sideways one. Without a spinner the end of the crankshaft might dig in and the model stop instantly, with much more severe damage resulting.

Chapter 11

Engine Starting and Running In

Your engine must be run in before it can fly your model. This can be quite a lengthy process and is best done where the inevitable noise will not cause a nuisance. If done on the flying field you should be well away from the flyers and as far as possible from any houses etc. But you will save time if you learn to start your engine at home, and give it a few brief familiarising runs in the garage first.

The reasons why running in is necessary, and the method in which it is done, are fully described later in this chapter. We will deal first with starting your brand new engine, but must emphasise that the running in process starts here in the garage, and whatever you do you mustn't let your engine run away at full speed, and you mustn't let it get too hot. And, if it's ABC or AAC construction, you mustn't let it get too cool either. Life gets complicated, doesn't it!

The engine should preferably be mounted firmly on temporary timber bearers screwed down to a bench. Don't put it in the vice; doing this will almost certainly

The fuselage must be firmly restrained . . .

distort the crankcase. It *can* be fitted in the model but if so the fuselage must be firmly restrained so that both hands are free, and if the wing isn't fitted the top of the fuselage must be protected with polythene film or something similar to prevent exhaust fuel and oil entering the fuselage.

Fit the recommended size of propeller (see next chapter for the correct way to do this) and connect a length of garden wire or whatever to the throttle arm so that it is fixed about half open. This will prevent the engine running too fast unintentionally. Organise a fuel tank with its top level with the needle valve, shake your fuel to ensure the oil is evenly mixed, and fill up the tank. Set the needle valve at the number of turns open, as indicated in the engine's instructions, for starting from cold. Put one finger over the venturi air intake and turn the engine over once or twice to draw fuel from the tank up to the carburettor. If you use translucent silicone fuel tube you can see the fuel shoot along the pipe.

Now a new engine (or one that has not been used for a long time) is always a bit stiff as the fuel will have evaporated leaving the rather gummy oil behind. So you should next put five or six drops of fuel into the air intake and flick the engine over vigorously to disperse it round the moving parts. (For subsequent starting one or two drops will probably be sufficient.)

There is a slight knack in flicking a propeller. Turn the engine so that it is just coming onto compression i.e. the piston is moving upwards and its top is level with the top of the exhaust port. The prop should be horizontal in this position. If you are right-handed put one finger under the root of the right hand blade close in against the crankshaft and flick it up and over as quickly as possible. Make sure you follow through well clear of the prop otherwise the other blade could hit your finger when the engine fires (it can't fire at the moment because the glowclip isn't connected). If you are left-handed your finger goes on top of the left hand blade and you flick down and under. As you continue flicking you will feel the engine loosen up and it is now ready for starting but first a word of warning.

Sooner or later, in the early days of model engines, every aeromodeller used to put his fingers or his hand into a spinning propeller. This wasn't a very great danger as most modellers started with a 1 or 1½ cc slow-revving diesel engine and the result, though painful, wasn't dangerous. You will be using a much more powerful and faster-revving engine and later on you may well progress to a high-powered 40 or 61. If you put your hand into the prop of one of these at high revs it could *easily* be lacerated so badly that you'll lose the use of your fingers. So right from the outset get into the habit of making all your movements *slowly* and *deliberately* when your engine is running. Never rush to do anything, and always make sure that battery leads, scarves, ties and anorak strings can't get caught up in the prop.

Mention was made earlier of electrically powered soaring trainers and we must digress slightly here and consider the safety aspects of electric motors as well. Obviously the warnings about lacerated fingers and scarves, ties, etc. getting caught in the prop apply equally, but there is more to it than that. We can do no better than quote from the excellent instructions for the Precedent Electra Fly, described later: "The blades may look flimsy but are quite capable of severing a finger (or two). A combustion engine requires a physical effort to start it, and when running there is a loud noise that reminds you that something fairly sharp is going around. The problem with electric motors is that they start rather suddenly and with no warning...." The instructions tell you to never fit the fuse (accessible from outside the fuselage) until ready for launch, and to remove it and thus "disarm" the motor immediately you pick up the model after each flight. Sound advice indeed.

Back now to starting our piston engine. Put on your fingerstall or a gardening glove. Connect up the glowclip and flick the engine over again. There will be a surplus of fuel so it probably won't fire first time. Keep flicking, pausing a second or so after each flick, and it will probably fire after three or four flicks when some of the surplus fuel has been expelled and the mixture becomes more nearly correct. If it fires and runs very slowly, so that there seems a danger of it stopping, the mixture is too rich and you should screw in the needle valve a little (say a quarter turn) at a time to speed it up. If it fires and runs very fast you must screw out the needle valve as quickly as you can with safety to slow it down.

If the engine fires when you flick it but refuses to run you have the classic symptom of a too-rich mixture and/or a partially flooded crankcase. Continue flicking, as each flick expels a certain amount of fuel and the engine won't be drawing more fuel from the tank until it starts to run. (Of course, if your tank is too high fuel could be draining into the engine under gravity – the remedy is obvious.) If the engine continues to fire but refuses to run remove the glowplug and it's washer and flick the engine over vigorously. Without compression it will spin over very fast, and droplets of fuel will shoot out through the glowplug boss. Keep going until no more fuel comes out, shake the fuel out of the glowplug, test it and replace it, not forgetting the washer. Then try again, without any priming initially.

If the engine fires, gives a brief burst of power and then dies out you have the classic symptom of fuel starvation. It has burnt up the fuel used for priming but hasn't drawn enough from the tank to replace this. The remedy is obvious – screw out the needle valve a little (say a quarter turn) and re- prime the engine. If you can't get the engine to fire at all the battery or glowclip or glowplug are suspect. So have the plug out and check you are getting a bright orange glow.

Once the engine is going at a reasonable speed you can reach carefully over the behind the propeller and disconnect the glowclip. Lay it carefully aside where it won't short out against some metal object. The revs will probably drop slightly when disconnection takes place. To ensure that the revs are being held down by a rich mixture and not by the throttle you should now slowly open the throttle fully, at the same time richening up the mixture if necessary to hold the revs down. How you proceed from here will depend on whether your engine has a cast iron or a plated liner, as explained later in this chapter. If it has an iron liner the instructions may recommend the engine is soon stopped to let it cool down. Closing the throttle fully should do the trick, but if the engine refuses to stop you can always squeeze the fuel tube with a pair of pliers to starve it of fuel. Another way to stop the engine is to put one finger (carefully!) over the air intake to starve it of air. But this draws excess fuel into the engine with a slight risk of flooding.

If it has a plated liner, ie is of ABC or AAC construction you must quickly speed it up to prevent it cooling, but more about this later.

After the last of these garage runs it is always good policy to check the tightness of the screws on the cylinder head and the crankcase. This is done while the engine is still hot. The cylinder head screws can best be tightened if the engine is put between the jaws of a vice with the mounting lugs resting on top of the jaws. Again, no attempt should be made to grip the crankcase with the vice.

We can now discuss the much misunderstood process called running in. Engines have to be run in because even after the most precise machining, the moving parts will still have minute ridges and valleys in their surfaces which are completely invisible to the naked eye but easily discerned under a microscope. If too much stress or pressure is applied in the early stages these minute ridges could "pick up" metal from the surfaces against which they are mated, i.e. they could wear excessively quickly. Also a rapid rise in local temperature could result. So these minute irregularities have to be worn away slowly before the friction between the moving parts in contact, and the heat generated by this friction, can be reduced to the ultimate minimum.

Until the mid 1980s even the best made engines had to be run in very carefully. Pistons were aluminium and cylinder liners were cast iron. If a new engine was allowed to get too hot the piston expanded until it became a tight fit in the liner. This increased the friction between the two, generated more heat and made the problem worse. If nothing was done very quickly the vicious circle continued until the piston seized up solid inside the liner. Nasty and expensive! Happily engines are now made to much closer tolerances and plated brass liners which, as previously mentioned, expand more than aluminium pistons, are commonly fitted. The cylinder bore is now often tapered at the top so that the piston is only really closely fitted to the liner when at the top of its stroke.

All this has removed the need for the very careful and patient running in that used to apply, and many manufacturers now recommend a mere 5-10 minutes of running in on the ground followed by two or three flights during which the demands on the engine, and the speed at which it is run, are progressivly increased. The running in process is thus largely carried out in the air.

This may be good advice for the experienced modeller, but not for the novice. Any beginner's very first flight is traumatic enough without having to worry about the engine overheating if full power is needed. We suggest, therefore, you run in your engine *fully* on the ground. Before explaining how this is done we must first consider what happens inside an engine, one that has already been fully run in, as the mixture is leaned out slowly from being excessively rich (too much fuel to air) until it becomes excessivly lean (insufficient fuel to air).

At the former setting, even if the throttle is fully open, the engine will only run very slowly. There will be insufficient air for all the fuel going into the engine to be burned and most of it will be ejected with the exhaust. The engine will also be very cool, for two reasons. Very little fuel is being burned so very little heat is being generated in the cylinder head, and the unburned fuel going through the engine will emerge warm and carry away some of this heat with it. In fact considerably more fuel will go through unburned than is burned because, when the mixture is too rich, two stroke engines don't actually two stroke. They behave like four strokes and combustion only occurs every other time the piston reaches the top of the cylinder. Since the oil is contained in the fuel a huge excess of oil will be going through the engine, and lubrication will be at its maximum.

If we now screw in the needle valve say ¼ turn, the engine will speed up. More fuel will be burned so more heat will be generated. Less fuel will go straight through the engine unburned so less heat will be taken away with the exhaust. And there won't be such a huge excess of oil for lubrication. Each time we screw in the needle valve a little more will get the same result – higher revs, higher temperatures, less excess lubrication. At a certain stage the sound of the engine will change and the revs will increase appreciably.

This is when the engine first starts to two stroke or fire at every cycle. At this setting of the needle valve the revs will probably not be constant, the engine will be "hunting', i.e. two stroking for part of the time and four stroking in between. If the mixture is then leaned out a little more the engine will two stroke almost continuously, just very occasionally faltering into a four stroke for a tiny fraction of a second. The setting of the needle valve at which this very occasional faltering occurs is important on the flying field, and will be referred to later.

A further small adjustment of the needle valve, typically not much more that ⅛th of a turn, will produce a considerable increase in speed and consistent two stroking. The engine will now be near its designed maximum constant speed. The full amount of fuel in the cylinder will be burned at each cycle so the heat generated will be near its maximum. And the amount of oil going into the engine will be near its designed minimum.

A further small adjustment of the needle valve will probably produce another increase in speed with possibly a slight risk of excess wear. After yet another small adjustment there will probably be insufficient fuel going into the engine to maintain combustion, and the engine will stop.

Back to running in. Modellers and DIY enthusiasts have a favourite saying – "If all else fails read the instructions". When it comes to the initial run of your brand new engine no better advice can be given. Use the size of the propeller recommended and set the needle valve to the 2½ turns open or whatever it is they recommend. If your needle valve has a knurled end for turning and the manufacturer hasn't already done so, it's a good idea to file a vee into the outer face and rim of this knurled end to make counting the turns from the fully closed position easier. If no recommendation is given fix the throttle so that the throttle lever is about half way between its idle and full throttle positions.

We stressed the importance of following the instructions because the initial requirements of engines vary widely according to their design – e.g. parallel bore or tapered bore – as well as to their construction, e.g. cast iron liner or plated brass. Engines with iron liners and/or ringed pistons are best started initially very rich, and can be run with benefit so slowly that they are in danger of stopping. ABC and AAC engines, in contrast, should be run much quicker initially so that they cannot become too cool – remember the clearance between the piston and the top of the liner *increases* as the temperature rises – and most manufacturers recommend avoiding the engine four stroking altogether.

No engine, whatever its construction, must be allowed to race away towards its maximum revs until all the moving parts – crankshaft and connecting rod as well as piston – have had a chance to "bed in" to the surfaces against which they bear. Running in achieves this by a series of engine runs during which the speed is increased slowly and progressively towards its maximum without it slowing down due to overheating. And, in the case of ABC and AAC engines, can maintain a tickover without slowing down due to overcooling. No-one can say with certainty how long this will take, the only true guide is the sound of the exhaust.

After each slight adjustment of the needle valve you must listen very carefully to the new engine note produced. Any subsequent slowing down will indicate that the engine is not yet ready to run at this new setting, and it should be run for a further few minutes at the previous setting before trying again. Although it is impossible to state how long running-in will take your engine will guide you – if you frequently have to richen up the mixture because it won't hold its speed on a new setting then you are definitely trying to hurry things along too quickly.

If, on the other hand, you never detect any signs of it slowing down then you may be giving it more running-in than it actually needs.

Your engine is now ready for the air but it may not yet have loosened up completely, so you must be particularly careful in the early stages that the model is never released with the needle valve set too lean. Also you must appreciate that the engine will speed up considerably once the model is released, and that the mixture will get progressively leaner during the flight as the level of fuel drops in the tank. The correct setting for a newly run-in engine with a full tank, resting level on the ground, is when the engine is only just two-stroking consistently, ie with the needle valve set so that if it is screwed out by only, say, ⅛th of a turn the engine will no longer hold a constant speed, but will just occasionally falter back to a four-stroke. Should you ever get the impression that the engine is getting too lean in the air throttle back immediately and land as soon as possible.

The only true guide is the sound of the exhaust . . .

Chapter 12

About Propellers

Propellers are really rotating wings, and if you look at a prop blade carefully you'll see it has a proper airfoil section with a slightly rounded leading edge and a sharp trailing edge (take another look at the sawn-off propeller on the second cut-away engine photograph in the chapter "About Engines"). They work by pushing the air backwards and the air's reaction (back to the skaters) is to push the aeroplane forwards. The term airscrew, suggesting that they screw their way through the air without displacing it, is a misnomer. You'll appreciate this the first time the engine of your trainer cuts in flight. As soon as the blast of air over the tail is lost rudder and elevator controls become much less sensitive, and one often has to be quite brutal with the rudder control of a stable trainer to initiate a turn once the engine has stopped.

Propellers are measured by their diameter and pitch, normally in inches. The pitch is the amount a prop would move through the air during one complete revolution if the air were not pushed backwards. Thus a 10 x 6 (250 x 150) prop has 10 inch (250) diameter and 6 inch (150) pitch. This is the best size for most engines between 29 and 40 size, i.e.between .29 and .40cubic inch capacity. Most 25s use a 9 x 6 (225 x 150) and most 19s and 20s use a 9 x 4 (225 x 100), but obviously you should check the engine's instruction leaflet before buying the props. Some makers recommend a smaller prop: (to put less load on the engine) for running in.

Propellers are made from plain nylon, glass-reinforced nylon or wood. The plain nylon ones are relatively flexible and are the obvious choice for beginners. The glass-reinforced ones are less flexible and more likely to break if the tips come into contact with the ground, but give more power. Wooden props are virtually inflexible and invariably break if there is more than the slightest contact with the ground, and are therefore not suitable for beginners.

Engine crankshafts are usually but not always ¼ inch (6) diameter, and most props have a centre hole that is undersize. You'll have to drill out the hole so that the prop is a nice easy push fit on to the shaft of your engine. You shouldn't have to screw it down the thread – this would result in severe stresses in the nylon possibly leading to a dangerous failure. The easy way to enlarge the hole is to put the shaft of the drill in a vice and "screw" the prop on to the drill. Put the prop on the motor so that it is level (a quarter to three) just as the engine comes onto compression. Starting will then be easier as up and over is the natural way for a right-handed person to flick a propeller. Also, if the engine cuts out in flight the prop will freewheel round until engine compression stops it in the level position, where it is least likely to be damaged in a bad landing.

If you already have a R/C engine that is badly oversize for your trainer, put the prop on back-to-front, this will reduce power by about 20 per cent. Remember, too much power kills trainers! Propellers, like glowplugs, must be regarded as consumable, and you should always have a least one spare in your flight box, and at least two when you are learning to land!

It is always unwise to stand in line with the disc of a spinning propeller, where you could be hit by a "thrown" blade. Helpers and spectators should be similarly warned – the consequences could literally be fatal. For the same reason *always destroy immediately* a nylon prop that has been bent, before it can revert to its proper shape. It may then look alright but could have been weakened to a dangerous degree.

Top to bottom: One laminated wood, one nylon and two glass – reinforced nylon propellers. On the left a nylon one has been badly distorted but still hasn't broken. Below this a thick rubber "fingerstall" to protect your "flicking" finger when starting the engine.

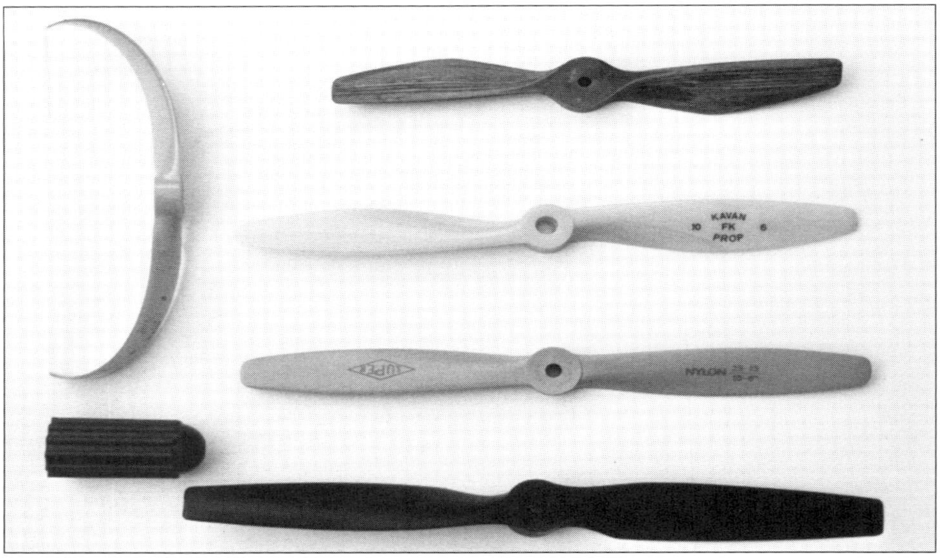

Chapter 13

About Fuels

The standard fuel for glowplug engines is 80 per cent methanol (methyl alcohol) and 20 per cent castor oil. The addition of nitro-methane usually gives easier starting and better idling in cold weather, when a small uncowled engine can often become over-cooled, and many flyers use fuel containing between 3 and 5 per cent "nitro" in the winter and straight fuel (i.e. no nitro) in the summer. Since the nitro raises the running temperature of the engine a straight or low-nitro (2% – 3%) fuel should always be used for running in. Only if the engine stops when the glowclip is disconnected, even at reasonably high revs, should you resort to more nitro, and then only after experimenting with different makes of glowplug.

Fuels with a 25 per cent castor oil content are marketed, both for running in a new engine and to extend the life of a tired engine that really needs a new piston and liner. For running in the extra oil can do nothing but good, but such fuels are more expensive and most modellers use only 1 or 2 litres of this fuel in a new engine before changing to 20 per cent oil. When you change to 20 per cent you will need to run your engine a little bit richer than before for a few flights at least. You can reduce your fuel costs very considerably by buying gallon cans rather than smaller sizes.

In the mid 1970s castor oil became very expensive, and various other oils, usually called synthetic lubricants, were tried. The R/C magazines were full of technical articles on the merits and demerits of these, and at least one engine manufacturer recommended the use of one particular synthetic. Some modellers had no trouble at all, particularly if synthetic had been used in the engine since new, others ruined engines very quickly indeed and blamed the new oil. Certainly at that time engine manufacturers and distributors were inundated with far more claims than usual for repairs under guarantee.

Within a year the price of castor had dropped appreciably, and most modellers went back to using castor oil. A few still insisted on synthetic, had absolutely no trouble at all, and regarded the extra cost of castor as a complete waste of money.

For some years one of the British distributors of a very old established and highly regarded Italian engine manufacturer, Super Tigre, had been advocating a fuel containing both castor and synthetic oil. In the early 1990s he persuaded a leading British fuel manufacturer to produce this and it became readily available in model shops. S.T. owners found it suited their engines admirably, giving more power, smoother running, better idling, cleaner pick-up. You name it, it gave it! Owners of other makes of engine found it suited theirs as well, so the overall picture got very confusing. The best advice we can give is to use the fuel recommended by your engine manufacturer – "if all else fails, etc!" If no recommendation is made then start with one of the running in fuels containing 25% castor oil.

Most synthetic oils are burned with the fuel and the model remains relatively clean. Castor oil doesn't burn, it is expelled with the exhaust, and parts of the model soon become covered with a mixture of unburned fuel and oil. It is easier if this is cleaned off with a soft cloth or paper tissue immediately after each flight, before it becomes thick and gooey. If more thorough cleaning is required you will find that methylated spirit cuts through the goo instantly and makes cleaning very easy.

The range of fuels available for model aircraft greatly exceeds that available for full-size cars and lorries – this leading manufacturer produces no less than 20 different blends in everyday use.

Chapter 14

Glues, Covering Materials and Building Hints

The instructions in many trainer kits are lamentably brief and the purpose of these notes is to amplify them and answer the sort of questions we were asked over and over again by beginners in the shop.

Balsa cement, the traditional glue for free flight models, sets too quickly to be used with many of the larger components used in R/C models – by the time the whole area has been coated with cement a skin will have formed on the cement first applied resulting in poor adhesion. It must never be used where it can come in contact with foam wing cores, since it will dissolve the foam. But it can be sandpapered down much more easily than PVA glues and is more suitable than PVA for fillets and fairings etc. where strength is not important.

White woodworking glues containing PVA (polyvinyl acetate) are the most economical choice for our sort of models. They are very strong and clean to use (surplus glue can be wiped away with a damp cloth or pushed off very easily when half dry with, say, a small steel ruler). When set PVA remains very slightly flexible and this actually increases the structure's resistance to shock loads. PVA shrinks as it dries and where maximum strength is necessary extra glue should be applied, during the drying out process, which will be drawn into the joint as shrinkage takes place. PVA glues can safely be used on expanded polystyrene and foam-cored wing halves can be jointed and subsequently wrapped with glassfibre tape using PVA. But the time saved by using epoxy and fibreglass resin as later described makes these the more popular choice for this operation.

Quick-set epoxy glues are very quick to use, very strong but rather expensive. You mix equal portions of resin and hardener thoroughly and, in a warm room, you then have about five minutes to work with the mix before it hardens too much. Five minutes later it is strong enough to withstand normal handling and the next stage of building can proceed.

Heat is generated as the two components react together and this speeds up the reaction, so the more you mix the less time you have to work. It's very important therefore that if attempting to glue a number of components together at the same time you make jolly sure these fit together perfectly before you start spreading the glue around. If something goes wrong halfway through you'll literally be racing against time to scrape off the epoxy before it's too late.

Devcon was one of the first quick-set epoxy glues to reach the UK market. You can now buy it in a double-barrelled dispenser that automatically ejects equal quantities of resin and hardener. (Photograph: Ripmax Ltd)

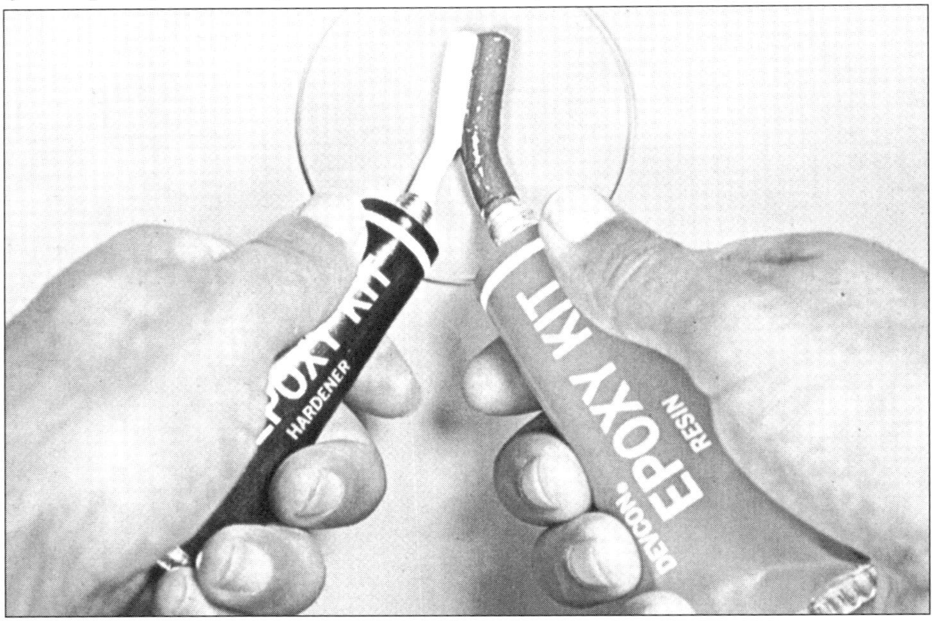

Epoxy glues have no discernable shrinkage and no subsequent filleting or other attention is normally required.

They are ideal for repairs on the flying field. On a warm day the model can be flying again fifteen minutes after repair, but in the middle of the winter the epoxy will harden much more slowly and half an hour or more may be required before sufficient strength has been achieved.

Contact adhesives, sometimes called impact adhesives,are rubbery solutions intended to be spread on both surfaces to be joined and allowed to get almost dry. The two surfaces are then brought together and pressed hard and a bond is instantly achieved. Almost all balsa fuselages have sheet balsa sides that are reinforced from the nose back to somewhere under the wing with pieces of 1/16 inch or 1/8 inch (1.5 or 3) plywood of identical shape, usually called doublers because the wood is doubled where they occur. Contact adhesives are often specified for fixing these doublers to the balsa in preference to PVA. This is not just because PVA is slower; PVA contains water which makes the balsa swell more than the ply. This causes the sides to curl up and a permanent curve can result that is difficult to eliminate afterwards. PVA is perfectly all right for ply doublers provided the sides are thoroughly weighted down and left to dry out completely (which usually means about twenty-four hours) before they are removed from the board. Whatever glue you use make sure the sides are "handed" – don't end up with two left-hand fuselage sides!

Cyanoacrylate adhesives are the instant glues advertised on TV which are particularly good at sticking one's fingers together if one gets careless! Originally they were all as thin as water but now thicker grades are available more suitable for porous materials like balsa wood and ply. They enable you to build a complicated structure like a built-up wing very quickly indeed and although they don't remain slightly flexible like PVA they penetrate deeper into the wood and are probably just as strong. They are still more expensive than PVA but to many modellers the time saved more than justifies the extra expense.

Polyester resin and catalyst (often referred to as fibreglass resin) are used in conjunction with fibreglass tape to strengthen the joint in foam cored wings, and to mend fibreglass fuselages. The resin and catalyst are also used, without the tape, for gluing wooden supports for the servos and other necessary bits of wood to the inside of fibreglass fuselages. Don't use epoxy for this, it doesn't key to the fibreglass with any real strength. Like epoxies, you mix resin and catalyst together, but only a tiny proportion of catalyst is needed. You can speed up the curing process by using more catalyst and extra catalyst is provided with this in mind. The mix makes an excellent fuel proofer and any surplus can be painted inside the tank bay of a wooden fuselage to render it fuel proof. Mixing must be thorough, and make sure you have plenty of ventilation because the smell is pretty strong. Like balsa cement, fibreglass resin dissolves expanded polystyrene, so must not be allowed to come into direct contact with foam wing cores.

Joining foam wing halves. If your wing does not have plywood dihedral braces the halves must first be glued together with quick-set epoxy. The joint is then wrapped with fibreglass tape embedded in resin. The strength comes from the tape, the resin's purpose is to bond the tape to the wing's veneer.

First you must ensure that the ends to be joined are angled to give the correct dihedral. If they aren't this can easily be remedied with coarse sandpaper pinned to a flat wooden sanding block. Sand *in one direction only* otherwise the foam will tend to pick up. Foam wing halves usually come packed in the block of foam from which the cores were cut and you'll find these ideal for holding the halves so that they don't rock about while sanding the ends.

When the ends give the correct dihedral smear a little epoxy on one end (it need only extend say 1/4 inch (6) inwards from the veneer) and bring the other wing half against it. This is best done not on the building board but by sitting in a chair with the tip of one wing half resting on the floor and the epoxied end steadied between your knees. Lower the other wing half onto it, and tilt the lower half slightly so that the upper half is vertical. Then transfer one hand to the upper wing tip and press down gently so that the surplus epoxy squeezes out of the joint. By rotating the whole thing you can see if the leading and trailing edges line up exactly. If you didn't press too hard the two halves will slide quite easily relative to each other and any misalignment can be corrected.

Don't worry if one wing half is a bit proud of the other in the middle; remember it's the leading and trailing edges that dictate the wing's incidence and you must have the same incidence on each half.

Next, the ridge of surplus epoxy has to be smoothed flat with a fingertip. Do this gently and carefully, making sure all the time that the upper wing half stays vertical. Inevitably you will disturb the joint slightly, so wipe the epoxy off your fingertip and re-align the leading and trailing edges. You might as well relax now, still resting the lower tip on the floor and keeping the upper half vertical, because you're going to have to keep it like that for five minutes or so until initial hardening has taken place. Digging the end of a screwdriver or something into the surplus epoxy mix will give you a good idea as to how hard the joint is getting. When reasonably hard you can very carefully carry the wing and lean it up against a wall or whatever, all the while ensuring that the upper half is vertical.

Cyanoacrylate adhesives, commonly called superglues, can save an enormous amount of time when building an intricate model such as this scale Auro 558 from the R/C Model World Plans Service.

Give it ten minutes or so to harden further and then carefully pare off any epoxy still projecting from the joint with a sharp curved knife. If one half is a bit proud of the other you can take out the step with a small fillet of epoxy smoothed on with the fingertip. Don't worry about the strength of the joint, the epoxy only has to hold the halves together while the glassfibre tape is being applied. All that really matters is that the leading and trailing edges match up, that the joint is filled with epoxy all round so that resin can't reach the foam core, and that no big ridges of epoxy are left standing proud that would keep the fibreglass tape away from the wing surface.

Applying the resin and tape is quite easy. First mix plenty of resin and catalyst and stir thoroughly. Using an old 1 inch or 2 inch (25 or 50) paint brush give the wing centre (top and bottom) a thin coat extending say ¼ inch (6) beyond the width of the tape each side. You can make a neat job at the edges by masking with paper tape and brushing from the centre out to the masking line. Then lay on the fibreglass, leaving ¼ inch (6) or so surplus at the trailing edge, taking it forward round the leading edge and back past the trailing edge again. Pull it reasonably tight and use spring clips to hold the two layers of tape together immediately behind the trailing edge. Then apply a second coat of mixed resin, stippling it on to ensure it penetrates the glassfibre, and finally smoothing off with the brush. Don't use too much resin – you'll only be adding weight for no useful purpose. Then peel off the masking and leave the resin to set with the wing supported flat above the building board.

When set the resin sands down easily so any little high spots are quickly removed with fine sandpaper. Don't attempt to get a smooth finish over the whole area, you're only intent on removing projecting whiskers and bubbles. If you need to sand near the edges of the tape mask the veneer again, because whatever you do you *must not* let the edge of the sandpaper cut into the veneer. It's only 1/32 or 1/40 of an inch (.8 or .6) thick, and a few ill-judged strokes can seriously weaken your wing at the point it is most likely to break – just outside the tape. Cut away the surplus tape at the trailing edge and the job is done. You can clean the paintbrush in cellulose thinners providing the resin mix hasn't hardened too much.

Many modern kits have plywood "dihedral braces" which are glued into slots machined into the foam wing halves. These give strength to the centre joint and ensure that the two halves are properly aligned. Use a slow setting epoxy such as Araldite to glue in the braces – you want plenty of time to ensure there is glue between the plywood and the foam for the full depth of, and on both sides of, each brace.

Cellulose dope. Looks and smells like nail varnish but is happily far less expensive. It is a quick-drying cellulose varnish used for strengthening the silk, tissue or nylon coverings with which all models used to be covered. It also fills in the pores and makes them airtight, which is important for wings if not for fuselages. Coloured dope has become difficult to obtain but was always very heavy anyway, and a poor substitute for using coloured silk, tissue or nylon in the first place.

Modelspan tissue. Is available in light and heavyweight thicknesses, white or coloured. On open surfaces like built-up wings it is stuck to the edges of the balsa framework with tissue paste, or paper paste. Then it is lightly sprayed with water. As it dries out it shrinks appreciably and a nice taut covering should result. It is then given two or three coats of cellulose dope, preferably thinned with about 10 per cent cellulose thinners, which fills in the pores of the tissue, shrinks it even more, and also makes it considerably stronger. Some coloured tissues don't shrink as well as white tissue, and are better put on damp rather than water- sprayed afterwards. After immersing in water the tissue is gently squeezed between the hands to get rid of surplus water, carefully opened out, laid on a towel to partially dry, and then applied with tissue paste as before.

On solid surfaces such as balsa fuselages the process can be speeded up considerably by eliminating the pasting and water-shrinking stage. The balsa is given one generous coat of unthinned dope which is allowed to dry. It is then very lightly sanded to remove the "whiskers" which the dope will have lifted from the surface. Tissue, white or coloured, is then laid on top of the balsa and a further coat of unthinned dope applied. This will penetrate the tissue, partly dissolve the dope underneath and make it sticky enough to hold the tissue in place while it dries. When completely dry surplus tissue can be cut away at the edges with a sharp blade or gently sanded off with fine sandpaper. Probably one further coat of dope will then give a reasonably good finish.

The tissue gives the balsa a hard skin as well as covering over its very deep grain, and this process is quicker and lighter than coat after coat of sanding sealer rubbed down between each coat. Unfortunately fuel for model engines dissolves cellulose dope, and when completely dry the finish must be protected with fuel proofer, about which more is written later.

Tissue can also be used for covering foam-

The Cambria Capstan. This particular example was built by the designer, John Venti, and we can be sure that a professional modeller of his standing can join a pair of foam wing halves correctly so that each has the same incidence. Yet in this photo: the nearer half appears to have far more incidence than the further one – an unintentional but perfect example of the relationship between incidence and dihedral when a model is yawing, referred to in 'Very Simple Aerodynamics'.

cored wings, but there is a risk that the initial thick coat of dope will penetrate the veneer and damage the foam. It is better therefore to use wallpaper paste to stick tissue to the veneer. The tissue is cut to size, laid on a smooth surface such as a Formica kitchen worktop, and painted all over with wallpaper paste. The tissue is then carefully peeled off the table and laid on the wing. It is usual to cover the bottom of the wing first, then the top. The top tissue is cut about 1 inch (24) oversize so that it can be turned under the edges and lapped ½ inch (12) or so over the underside covering. If the tips are rounded the excess tissue will have to be cut into short lengths which can then be turned under one at a time. When dry the tissue can be doped with safety – the paste will form a barrier and eliminate any danger of the dope reaching the foam. However if dope is used on a power model a separate fuel proofer becomes necessary, and many modellers prefer to use coloured tissue or to paint such a wing with a fuel-proof paint.

Fuel proofers are available in one-pack or two-pack forms. Clearcote is a popular one-pack proofer and is particularly suitable if the model is to be covered with Solarfilm film covering (described later) because the film sticks to it exceptionally well. It is thus ideal for fuel proofing the engine compartment before the film covering is applied to the rest of the fuselage. Extend the proofer out onto the top, sides and bottom of the fuselage by an inch or so to give a generous "lap" under the film.

Ripmax Tufcote is probably the best known two-pack proofer on the UK market and you mix the resin and catalyst together before use. The mix is very thin and it dries quickly and very hard and gives excellent protection to wings and fuselages finished with cellulose dope. If the whole of your model is doped you'll need one coat everywhere and two at the front of the fuselage.

Whichever kind of fuel proofer you use it's a good idea to apply a coat inside the fuselage where the tank goes. It is vital that fuel should not be allowed to come into contact with bare wood anywhere. If it does it will slowly soak along, increasing the weight of the model and weakening the structure. Even worse, if you have to repair the model following crash damage you'll find no glue will stick where the fuel has penetrated. You'll just have to go on cutting away the structure until dry wood is reached.

Doping or painting and subsequently fuel proofing a model are lengthy, messy and rather smelly processes and in recent years iron-on coverings have largely replaced the traditional tissue and nylon coverings for many R/C models.

Solarfilm is probably the most widely used of these iron-on covering, and comprises a very thin sheet of transparent plastic coated on one side with an adhesive which is also the colouring material (a wide variety of colours is available). The adhesive is protected by a backing sheet which has to be peeled off before the film is applied. The adhesive is not sticky at normal temperatures, only becoming so when heated.

At first sight film coverings are expensive, but in fact they are probably less expensive than the tissue plus dope plus fuel proofer routine. One occasionally reads articles and letters in the magazines claiming that tissue and dope finishes are lighter. Don't believe them. In the writer's experience Solarfilm is always lighter than tissue and any painted-on finish *as done by the average modeller*.

Solarfilm is also very much quicker – you literally cover the model, colour it and fuel proof it all in one go. On a fly-for-fun model rather than a scale model the writer always uses Solarfilm for the wing and tail, and also on the fuselage unless the nose is heavily rounded in two directions at the same time, where covering without joints is difficult if not impossible.

Let's now see how a wing is covered. The first thing to do is to borrow your wife's iron, set the control to near the low temperature end (rayon or nylon) and leave it ten minutes or so for the temperature to stabilise. The wing is normally covered in four panels, two for the underside and two for the top. The underside panels are cut the same size as the wing halves but ½ inch (12) longer at the centre, to give a 1 inch (24) lap, and ¼ inch (6) or so longer at the tip if the tip is rounded so that the covering will come up to about the centre line of the tip. (The upper panels are wider and longer so that they can be turned round the edges and lapped ½ inch (12) or so over the Solarfilm on the underside, but these are dealt with later.)

While the iron is being left to stabilise you can cut the two lower panels. Roll out the Solarfilm and weigh it down with the backing sheet uppermost. Lay one wing half on it and draw round it with a ballpoint pen. Allow ½ inch (12) extra at the centre and a bit for the rounded tip and cut out the panel with sharp scissors or a modelling knife. Test for size and repeat for the other panel, (making sure it is "handed") but leave the backing sheets in place.

Now test the temperature of the iron with a piece of scrap Solarfilm on a bit of sheet balsa. Peel off the backing. (This is easily done if the scrap film was cut from the edge of the roll, where there is a surplus of backing which can be pulled away, but if your piece is cut wholly from the centre of the roll you can spend many frustrating minutes poking at the edge with a pin or whatever trying to separate the film from the backing. The trick here is to push a sharp modelling pin or needle gently through the backing sheet about ⅛ inch (3) from one corner, then angle it so that it can be pushed up to the corner *between* the backing and the film. A little judicious wiggling and you'll have enough of the backing separated to be able to peel it off.) Now lay your scrap Solarfilm on the balsa and gently press it down with the iron, drawing the iron across the surface as you do so. If the Solarfilm melts the iron is far too hot. If it drags, appreciably, it is dangerously hot. If there is a very slight drag you've got it about right – you'll find if you leave the film a few moments to cool and then peel it off little slivers of balsa will come away with the adhesive. If the film doesn't stick to the balsa at all the iron isn't hot enough. If the adhesive sticks all over the bottom of the iron you've got the film upside down! But don't worry, cellulose thinners will remove it and placate your wife.

A purpose made iron for film covering (seen here on its stand) is lighter, more convenient and has a much more accurate thermostat than a domestic iron.

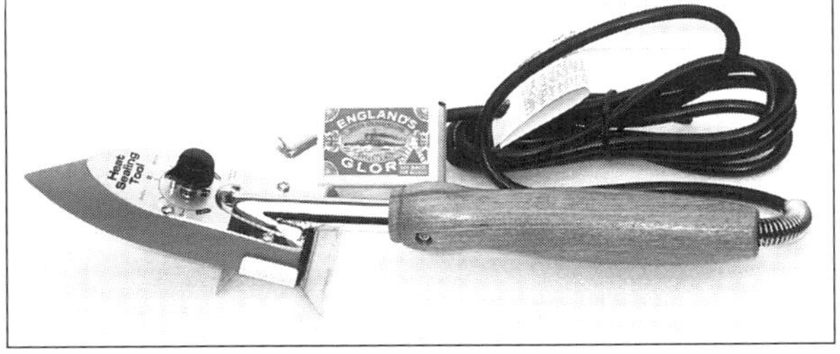

If you have to make further adjustments to the temperature setting on the iron *be patient*, you must allow time for each adjustment to take effect. Test with further scraps of Solarfilm until you have found the correct setting. When you have got the temperature right (and this is the key to success) make a note of the setting for next time. You may have to make very small adjustments as the work goes on, some irons do get slightly hotter as time goes by, presumably because the thermostat isn't as good as it might be.

Solarfilm is put on in three separate stages, tacking it in place at the edges, ironing it on all round the edges, and shrinking the remaining central area.

Peel off the backing and lay one of the panels on the underside of the wing, get it into the correct position, along the trailing edge and at the tip, and tack the film in place about halfway along the trailing edge. Just rest the tip of the iron on the film about ¾ inch (18) from the edge of the wing and draw it back over the edge. Repeat at the leading edge. Pull it reasonably tight and tack the leading and trailing edges at the tip. Repeat at the centre (it won't stick so readily to the fibreglass resin but don't worry, when the whole wing is covered and the film is shrunk its tension alone will hold it to the wing). Then tack the film, still at the leading and trailing edges, half way between the positions already tacked.

Now, still using the tip of the iron, start working along the trailing edge from one tacked position to the next, always starting with the iron about ¾ inch (18) from the edge and drawing it back to the edge, working it along a little bit with each stroke. You'll soon discover that the film stretches a little in front of the iron. When this happens pull the film tight from the next tacking so that the surplus forms a little "hump" at the edge of the wing. Leave about ⅛ inch (3) gap and start ironing at the other side of the hump. Carry on this way until you have ironed all round the panel and a continuous margin about ¾ inch (18) wide is adhered to the wood except where humps occur. Then repeat the whole process on the other half of the underside of the wing. By now the whole thing will be a mass of small wrinkles and your arm will probably be aching.

Now comes the shrinking bit. Solarfilm say do this by setting the iron at a higher temperature and very lightly ironing all over the film. The writer has found this both tiring and slow. It is easier and quicker to heat and thereby shrink the film in front of a fan heater or gas or electric fire. Start with the underside of one wing half, say 2 feet (600) from the fire. Move it from end to end and rock it from leading to trailing edge so that it heats up evenly. As it heats it will expand and go slack. Gradually move it closer to the fire, still moving and rocking it. It will slacken even more and look a terrible mess but don't despair! Keep slowly moving it closer and Bingo! Suddenly it will start to tighten up. Now concentrate more on the areas still slack but still keep the whole wing half moving so that the tight areas are not allowed to cool.

When it's all nice and tight take it away from the fire and quickly rub gently over the whole area (or all the wooden areas on a built-up wing) with a handkerchief or soft cloth to push the adhesive into the wood while it's still hot. Despair will have turned to elation, it does work after all! All those little humps have disappeared and you have a beautifully smooth and completely impervious finish that is lighter than any paint job and looks better than most. Repeat for the other wing half.

Thus encouraged, let's get on with the upper wing surfaces. The panels of film are cut about 1 inch (24) wider than the chord of the wing still uncovered, so as to give the ½ inch (12) lap at leading and trailing edges. Do some careful measuring at this stage as the curved upper surfaces will require a greater width of film than the flat or nearly flat lower surfaces. And don't forget to allow ½ inch (12) for the lap at the centre and a further ½ inch (12) for turning down under the tip. When you've got one panel the right size use it as a pattern to cut the other. But remember, they must be handed.

Peel off the backing and lay one panel on top of the wing, allowing ½ inch (12) overhang at the trailing edge and at the tip. Tack round the edges and join up the tacking to form a continuous ¾ inch (18) margin all as before. The overhanging film now has to be turned under and this is best done by rolling it around the edges with the thumb. Start at the wing centre and roll it round the trailing edge, pressing it onto the film on the underside. Solarfilm has a slight adhesion to itself before heating and it will stay there, but can be lifted with a sharp knife if required. When you have all the trailing edge turned under, iron it in place.

You'll inevitably get little ridges where the film has stretched unevenly but if you start with the tip of the iron at the trailing edge and move it carefully forward along the ridges you'll find almost all of them will disappear. You'll also get air bubbles trapped between the two layers of film. Again these can usually be pushed forward with the iron until they reach the edge of the film and disappear. If they refuse to budge just prick them with a sharp modelling pin (or needle) and iron them flat – you'll not be able to see the pinpricks afterwards.

When you have the whole length of the trailing edge lapped and ironed down, run the tip of the iron once more all along the forward edge of the film pressing just a little harder than before. This will compress the balsa or veneer very slightly and the film is so thin that the step at the edge of the film will have virtually disappeared. The writer has never had trouble with Solarfilm lifting from a wing when the edges have been fnished in this way.

After the trailing edge comes the tip, which we will

Very large wings are not easily manoeuvred in front of a fire. A heat gun blows high temperature air onto the film covering and makes the shrinking process quick and easy. (Micro-Mold drawing)

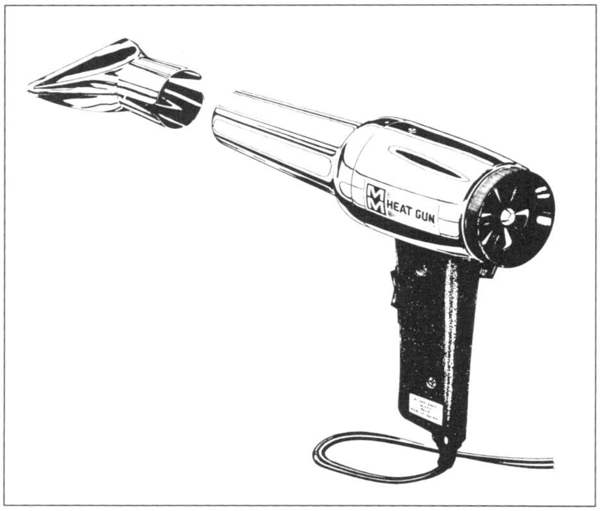

assume is rounded so that there is a compound curve to be covered. There is a limit to the overall amount that Solarfilm can be shrunk, but you can make it shrink more in one direction by stretching it in the other direction while ironing it down. So iron it down towards the tip until you can't do any more without it creasing, then hold the end of the film and stretch it round the tip, at the same time ironing it down towards your fingers. Go round the tip two or three times, all the while changing your grip and stretching and ironing a little bit at a time, and if you persevere you'll probably cover the whole upper part of the tip, down to its centre line, without any appreciable creases. You may find after all this stretching that you have more overhang than the intended ½ inch (12), in which case cut off the surplus with pointed nail scissors.

The same scissors are now used to cut a series of thin "V" notches in the overhanging film so that it can be ironed under the tip back towards the centre of the wing. If the outline of the tip is only slightly curved these notches can be 1 inch (24) or so apart, where it is sharply curved there should be one every ¼ inch (6) or so. So you now have a series of tabs of Solarfilm and these are worked round the tip with the iron one at a time, starting at the trailing edge. Then if any tabs lap over each other the lap will be rearwards and there will be no chance of the tabs lifting, either in the airflow or if you scrape a tip along the ground.

After the tip, the leading edge is simple. Roll the film round the edge with the thumb and iron it down just like the trailing edge. The other upper wing half is then covered in the same way (you'll be getting quite good at it by now!) and the central areas are then shrunk in front of a fire or whatever as previously described. But have a needle handy while doing this because quite often the covering is completely airtight and trapped air cannot escape. Just prick the film in the appropriate places to let the air out, you won't see the pinpricks afterwards. And don't forget to smooth it all down with a soft cloth while the film is still hot.

The tailplane, fin, elevator and rudder can all be covered in the same way and it's best to do this before the tailplane and fin are glued to the fuselage, and before the elevator and rudder hinges are fixed. But bear in mind that you can't glue Solarfilm, so only cover the tailplane and fin to within ¼ inch (6) of the areas to be glued. The gaps can be covered with a thin strip of film afterwards. The laps should be on the underside of the tailplane and elevator and on the port (or left) side of the fin and rudder. This is because silencers invariably discharge on the starboard side and the starboard side of the fin and rudder will accumulate more "goo" from the exhaust. Small surfaces like the elevator and rudder are usually covered completely by ironing on – it's quicker than shrinking their central areas as a separate operation in front of the fire.

If you decide to Solarfilm the fuselage as well cover the bottom first, using a piece of film the exact size required. Surplus film can be cut away easily with a brand new razor or modelling knife blade. Next, cover the sides, lapping these ½ inch (12) over the bottom. Finish with the top, lapped ½ inch (12) down over the sides. Start at the tail so that any laps in the length of the film face rearwards and the engine's exhaust will have at least chance of getting under the film.

This risk is greatest immediately behind the engine. In this area the strength of the bond where Solarfilm laps onto itself can be increased by using Solarfilm Solvent on the film to be covered. It is not expensive and one small bottle could last a lifetime. It is like very thin oil (a little goes a very long way) and best results are obtained if one drop is put on a tissue or soft cloth and sparingly rubbed onto the film to be covered. The second layer of film is then merely pressed on with the fingertip. Most air bubbles can be pushed out to the edge with the finger, the remainder will have to be pricked. Where solvent has been used it is doubtful if subsequent ironing on is necessary, but the writer always does so "just to make sure". The writer has never found it necessary to use solvent anywhere other than at the front part of the fuselage. If you've ironed the laps thoroughly the normal adhesion of Solarfilm to itself will be sufficient elsewhere.

If your fuselage has compound curves (double curvature) around the engine it is better to accept a few creases in the film, which will still be fuelproof, than to cut and lap the film. The film must always be taken round the edges of the engine compartment and ironed down a little way inside. If you can't reach inside with your wife's iron hold a putty knife or chisel against the iron long enough for it to reach the same temperature, and quickly use it instead. The edges of the film are an obvious weakness here and you'll do no harm by painting over them with another coat of Clearcote when covering is finished.

Before leaving film coverings a few more points need to be mentioned. They stick best to their intended fuel proofer or to bare untreated wood. For a really good finish you should go over the whole model with fine sandpaper but don't use sanding sealer or anything else. Brush off the dust with a dry paint brush before applying the film. Models are usually built out in the garage or workshop where the atmosphere is more moist than in the house. One of the advantages of film coverings is that they can be put on in the comfort of the lounge, and once the panels of film are cut to shape one can settle down in a chair and do most of the work with the wing or whatever balanced across one's knees. The excess moisture will come to the surface as it dries out and this can prevent the film sticking properly. So components to be covered with film should always be brought into the lounge a good twenty-four hours before you intend to start. The more lights in the room the better, the film is very glossy and one can see how it is behaving better if light is reflected from two or three different sources.

We mentioned earlier that many different colours are available. White is the colour the writer likes least. The joints soon get dirty and show up as thin black lines (joints in darker colours remain virtually invisible). But more important is the fact that white wings are difficult to see in the sky and this is particularly important to the beginner. Solarfilm light blue is, perhaps surprisingly, particularly good for the wing. When the model is banked over in a turn light from above reflects off the light blue top of the wing particularly well and the amount of bank is easily seen. A dark blue fuselage makes a pleasing contrast.

Another easily seen combination is an orange wing and a metallic green fuselage. If your distant eyesight is poor a worthwhile trick is to have a band of white film about 9 inches (225) wide all round each wing half, starting a few inches in from the tip.

The contrast here helps you see a model's attitude in poor light, and you can save money by using small offcuts of film, which might otherwise be wasted, at the wing tips.

Chapter 15

Soldering Explained

Although most trainer kits can be completed without soldering others require soldered joints in the linkages between the servos and the controls, and more advanced models invariably require the builder to be able to solder. Many people mistakenly think soldering is difficult. In fact, it is remarkably easy and the necessary equipment is not expensive. You'll need an electric soldering iron, a coil of solder and some flux. Since the iron will, in the course of time, be used for small objects such as control linkages and for large ones such as thick undercarriage wires, it will pay you to get an iron that can be fitted with different "bits" or ends. A bit of about ⅛ inch (3) diameter will be best for linkages, whereas you'll need a ¼ inch (6) diameter bit for large things like undercarriages. Make sure you buy solder intended for electrical work, i.e. the type that contains cores of resin flux. Multicore is a well-known make. The flux can be paste (e.g. Fluxite) or liquid (e.g. Bakers Fluid). Sometimes paste is more convenient, sometimes fluid. Both are corrosive to metals, and must never be used on electrical wiring for which the resin flux (which is non-corrosive) contained in the solder is perfectly adequate.

Solder such as Multicore is an alloy of tin and lead and can be used on steel, brass, tin and copper (also silver and gold) but not on aluminium or its alloys. It melts at much lower temperatures than steel, brass etc. and this feature enables metals such as these to be coated with liquid solder without damage. Providing the metals to be soldered are sufficiently hot and providing they and the solder are scrupulously clean, the solder will spread over and penetrate into the surfaces of the metals to be jointed. When allowed to cool the solder will solidify and a solid metal joint will result. Different alloys are available and solder with 60% tin and 40% lead is stronger and easier to use than 50/50 or 40/60.

Now most metals oxidise, i.e. combine with the oxygen in the air, at normal room temperatures. A copper coin fresh from the mint is salmon pink, but eventually turns brown as oxides build upon the surface. These oxides will prevent the solder penetrating or "taking" as it is commonly called. To make matters worse metals oxidise more quickly when they are heated, and heat is essential to the soldering process. It is to prevent this oxidisation that a flux is necessary. Fluxes such as Fluxite and Bakers Fluid perform two functions. Their corrosive nature enables them to eat into the surfaces to which they are applied, and assist penetration by the solder, and at the same time they prevent newly cleaned surfaces from oxidising when heat is applied. Solder also oxidises quickly when heated.

When you first use your soldering iron you will have to coat the tip of the bit with melted solder, or "tin it" as this process is called. Once it has reached a sufficiently high temperature solder should be quickly melted onto it. This will have a bright, almost chromium plated appearance, but within a few minutes a dull skin of oxide will form, and this must be wiped off or shaken off before the iron can be used. The hotter the iron gets the quicker the solder will oxidise, and one of the secrets of successful soldering is to shake or wipe off surplus solder from the iron, and to apply fresh clean solder, immediately before it is used. Don't try to load the iron with sufficient solder to make the joint, and don't use the iron to carry melted solder onto the joint. By the time it gets there it will have become contaminated with oxides. The correct technique is to load the iron with sufficient solder *to allow a rapid transfer of heat* to the metals to be jointed, and then to apply sufficient solder *direct to the metals themselves* to make the joint.

So much for the theory behind successful soldering, which can be summed up by saying that there must be sufficient heat and that everything must be scrupulously clean. Let's go through the process of soldering the end of a control cable (which is similar to a bicycle brake cable) into the threaded brass adaptor which is commonly fitted to each end. The first thing to do is to switch on your iron and ensure it is resting in such a position that it won't set fire to your workshop. It can warm up while you are cleaning and preparing the work.

Control cables comprise many strands of spring steel wire and it is obviously not practicable to clean each of these with a file. So the end of the cable is dipped into liquid flux and carefully laid aside while the flux gets on with its job. Brass adaptors are usually clean enough to require only similar treatment but if the hole into which the cable goes is dirty it must be cleaned out with a drill. The adaptor is next held vertically and a drop of flux is placed on top of the hollow end. A bit of thin wire or whatever is used to break the air lock and ensure that the liquid goes all the way down the hole. More flux is applied to the wire and the wire is jiggled about until the hole is full. It should then be left a few minutes, and in the meantime you should shake the end of the cable to remove the flux previously applied, and wash it with a couple of drops of new flux.

If the iron is hot enough it can now be tinned or coated with solder, and then the end of the cable can be similarly tinned.

Fix the cable horizontally, shake the iron to remove the oxidised solder, and melt a little fresh solder onto the iron. Bring it up against the *underside* of the cable and you will see the solder rise slightly into the strands

. . . there must be sufficient heat and everything must be scrupulously clean.

of the cable. Apply a little more solder onto the *top* of the cable, so that it melts down *through* the strands: hold the iron in position for a few seconds to let it "sweat"; remove the iron and the job is done.

Solder takes to brass more readily than to spring steel and it is not normally necessary to tin the inside of the adaptor. Just shake out the flux and fix the adaptor in the vice with the hole uppermost.

If your vice doesn't have removable fibre jaws you'll have to use bits of wood or similar non-conducting material to hold the adaptor, otherwise it will lose all its heat into the vice, and you'll never get a proper joint. Put some more flux onto the tinned end of the cable, and insert this into the adaptor. Then fix some temporary support for the cable 6 inches (150) or so above the adaptor – you won't get a strong joint if the cable is waving about in the air at the critical moment when the solder solidifies. When all is ready shake the iron again, apply a little fresh solder and hold the bit against one side of cable, immediately above the adaptor. Much hissing will result as the flux boils away. Apply the end of your coil of solder to the opposite side of the cable. For a few moments it may not melt because boiling away the flux will have taken away a lot of heat. Presently the solder will melt and run down the cable into the adaptor. Apply more solder until the adaptor is full and a bright ring of molten solder is visible all around the cable. Hold the iron in position for a couple of seconds to sweat the joint, take it away and ensure nothing is disturbed until the solder has solidified – it takes on a more dull appearance when solidification occurs. The work should then be washed under a tap to cool it and to ensure that any remaining flux is removed.

Later in your modelling career you may have to solder heavy wire undercarriage legs together. It is no easy task to hold bits of wire in contact without movement and the trick here is to clean the wires in the usual way and bind them together with fuse wire. Fuse wire is copper coated with tin, and solder takes to the tin very readily indeed. The binding acts as a reservoir and holds molten solder, which would otherwise run away, between the wires. Copper is not very strong and you can increase the strength of the joint by using strips of tinplate cut from a "tin", ie a tin plated steel can.

Small soldering irons with interchangeable bits usually have an electrical "loading" of 15-25 watts. It is easier to solder large components with a much bigger iron, say of 100 watts size. But these can be quite expensive. You can often use a smaller iron by suspending the undercarriage or whatever a few inches above the hotplate of an electric cooker so that the work is "preheated", and will not take all the heat away from the bit as soon as contact is made.

Chapter 16

About Radio Control

All proportional R/C outfits comprise a transmitter (Tx), a receiver (Rx), the appropriate number of servos and necessary batteries. The transmitter is, of course, held by the pilot and sends out the control signals, the character of which are varied by moving the control sticks on the front of the case. The transmitter is powered by its own battery housed within the case. The receiver has a thin aerial wire attached which is normally fed out of the fuselage behind the wing and attached to the top of the tail fin with a thin rubber band. This aerial picks up the signals and feeds them into the receiver, which amplifies them (i.e. makes them stronger) and decodes them so that the correct signals, and only the correct signals, are sent to each servo. The servos turn these electrical signals into mechanical forces which actually move the controls. As mentioned previously, one servo is needed for each control fitted to the model. The receiver and all servos are powered by a battery carried in the model and fitted with a switch. With three servos the total airborne weight of a modern proportional outfit is about 10 ounces (285g) and it should give one and a half hours safe operation before the batteries have to be changed or recharged.

Each stick on the Tx has a "trim" lever below it and another one alongside it. These enable "permanent" adjustments to be made to the model's controls so that if, for example, the model tends to turn to the left this can be overcome by moving the appropriate trim lever to the right rather than having to hold the stick slightly right of neutral to fly in a straight line.

The stick intended to operate the engine throttle is fitted with a ratchet or friction device so that it stays where you put it. The others are spring-loaded and return to neutral when released. You'll need to decide which side of the transmitter the throttle stick should be on (see next chapter) before buying your radio. Your R/C outfit will be the most expensive single purchase towards R/C flying, and the choice therefore requires most careful consideration.

As mentioned earlier, if you are joining a club you will be wise to rely on the advice of those members who fly regularly and well and obviously take their hobby seriously. Disregard completely the advice of the "talkers" and the accident prone, for many, many "radio failures" have been the result of a plug coming loose in its socket, a servo coming loose in its mounting, or a mechanical failure in the linkage between a servo and the control it operated.

Disregard completely the advice of the "talkers" and the accident prone,

If there is no R/C club within reach of your home you alone will have to decide which of the bewildering variety of R/C outfits best suits your needs and your pocket. If you were shopping for a brand new car you would have at least a mental picture of the type of car you would be looking for – you might need a large boot or a hatchback for family shopping at a hypermarket, or small overall size to make city-centre parking easier, etc., etc. You would not spend an extra £2000 on a

Standard size and "mini" servos compared. The output discs seem to be fitted purely for the sake of tradition – the arms and crosses also supplied are much more useful.

"GT" version with a top speed of 140 mph if you rarely exceed 60. Nor would you buy a sporty two-seater if there were a likelihood of you having to carry three or four people on occasions – you would settle for a more conventional saloon so that the extra space would be there when needed.

Having decided, perhaps subconsciously, on the type of car you needed you would then consider suitable models from various manufacturers, and probably make the final choice on a balance between manufacturer's reputation and price. You may be wondering what this digression has to do with your choice of a radio control outfit, but the analogy is very close. Before you spend your hard-earned money you must decide what features you want now, what features you are likely to require in the foreseeable future, and *then* decide between manufacturers and the different models they offer. And if your choice is wrong you will find it unpleasantly expensive to trade in your purchase for something different. We will therefore list out the various features that you should consider, with a simplified technical explanation where necessary, and try to help you decide whether or not you will need them.

1. The number of functions that the Tx and Rx can handle, i.e. the number of controls that can be operated in the model. We have already explained that you need three functions to learn power flying and two to learn soaring. Once initial learning is completed you will need a fourth function for ailerons on a power model, and a third function for ailerons on a soarer. After that additional functions become "optional extras" rather than essentials – two more functions would be needed for flaps and a retracting undercarriage on a scale World War II fighter, and an extra function for lift spoilers can be very useful on a soarer. Full size soarers all have lift spoilers – blades which can be made to project from the wing to destroy lift and thereby increase the sinking speed (but not the flying speed) on the landing approach. Many also have a retracting undercarriage (a single wheel which tucks away into the fuselage to reduce drag). So if you aspire eventually to a scale soarer you'll need five functions in all. These "optional extra" functions do not have to be fully proportional like the basic flying controls, and retracting undercarriages are usually controlled by a switch so that they are either down or retracted. Similarly, lift spoilers (in a model at least) are usually either out or retracted, though there are, of course, perfectionists who like to be able to control the rate of sink as they come in to land by using fully controllable spoilers just like their full size counterparts. The same applies to flaps – most models have flaps that can merely be switched up or down, but the true scale enthusiast will want fully controlled flaps which require a proportional slide control on the Tx rather than a two position switch.

All this must be a bit academic to the average beginner who doesn't yet know what sort of models he will eventually be flying, so we'll generalise by saying that the beginner in power flying should regard as a minimum an outfit with four functions which either has, or can be fitted with, at least one extra "switched" function for undercarriage or flaps. The beginner in soaring would only need three functions but there are now very few three-function outfits available where all functions are controlled by the conventional sticks on the face of the Tx. Most are "upgraded" two-function ones originally designed for boats or cars, and the third control is a two-position or rotating switch on the top of the Tx - fine for controlling the motor of an electrically power-assisted soarer but no good at all for ailerons. So in practice a four function outfit will probably be the best buy. Happily you don't have to buy all the servos you might eventually need at the beginning. Most five, six and seven function outfits come with only four servos as standard, and your dealer will usually be quite happy to take out one or two of these with an appropriate price reduction.

2. The frequency of the transmitted signal. Before 1981 almost all R/C equipment in Great Britain operated on six "spot" frequencies around 27 Mhz, usually called the 27 megacycle band, the actual frequency in use being determined (as it still is) by a crystal plugged into the Tx and a matching crystal plugged into the Rx. Thus up to six models could (providing they used different frequencies) be flown from the same flying field at the same time. Models using 27 Mhz were always at risk from illegal "walkie talkie" outfits and later from C.B. radios which used the same frequency, and a new frequency band, 35 Mhz, was allocated to the control of model aircraft (but not boats or cars) from January 1st 1981.

This new frequency soon became "the norm". The

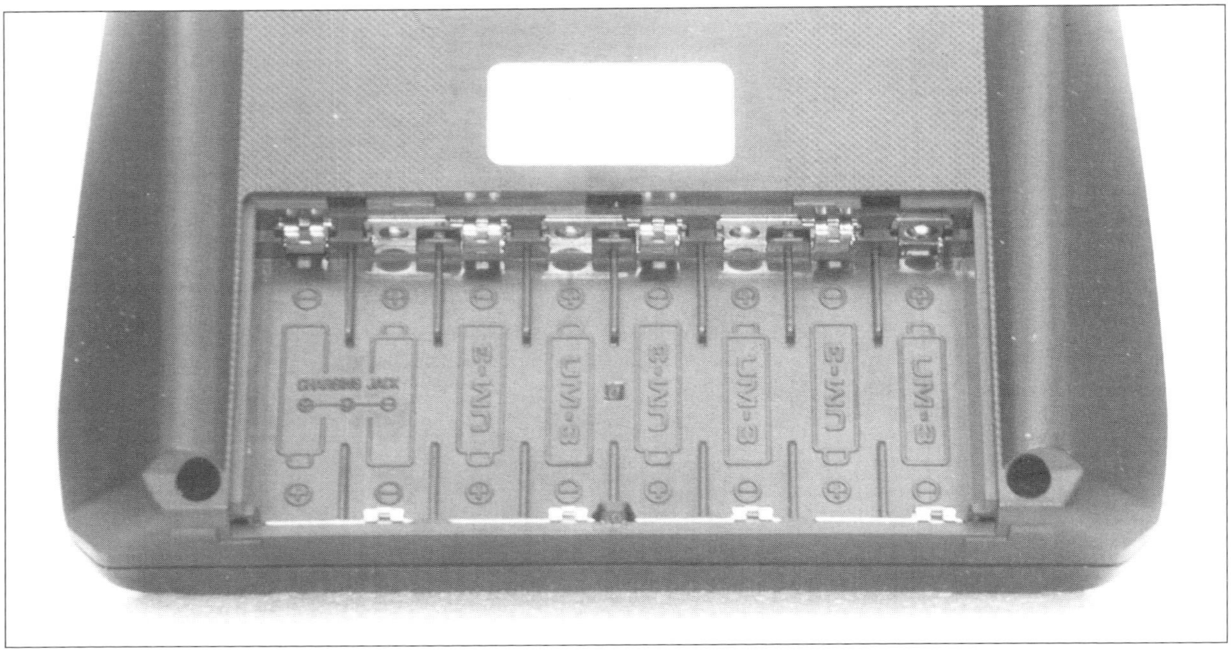

A Tx battery compartment fitted with bent metal and connectors – not recommended for anything that flies.

current legislation provides for the use of Home Office approved R/C equipment on no less than 26 different frequencies or channels (numbered 60-85) in the 35 Mhz band, which is not menaced by "walkie-talkie" outfits or CB radios. The separation between each channel is only 10 kilocycles as opposed to the 50 kilocycles between each channel on the 27 Mhz band, and manufacturers and importers must submit sample transmitters to the Electrical Research Association for type testing before Home Office approval is given. Despite this precaution there is a risk that a model flown low over another transmitter on an adjacent channel (i.e. the next number above or below the channel being used by its pilot) could suffer interference; for this reason many clubs use only "odd" channel numbers, while other clubs use only "evens". This, of course, increases the separation between channels to 20 kilocycles and renders adjacent channel interference very unlikely indeed. It also gets rid of another problem – 35 Mhz was first introduced with only 20 frequencies but when the "band" was extended to 26 a few years later it was found that a transmitter could cause interference with a receiver operating 23 channels higher, e.g. a Tx on channel 60 could interfere with a Rx on channel 83, and so on. Manufacturers quickly introduced receivers with dual conversion intermediate frequencies to combat this. Don't worry if you can't understand the term, "dual conversion" receivers as they are commonly called are simply more selective than the earlier single conversion ones, so there is even less chance of outside radio interference upsetting your model. You must appreciate, however, that the crystals used in dual conversion receivers are *not* the same as, and *cannot* be interchanged with, crystals used in single conversion receivers operating on the same channel. When the 6 extra frequencies were introduced for aircraft 30 new frequencies were introduced in the 40 Mhz band for model boats and cars. 27 Mhz is still in common use for these models and is still legal, though little used, for model aircraft.

Most manufacturers only make 35 Mhz equipment with four or more functions, and beginners starting with, say, a thermal soarer or power-assisted glider may be tempted to buy one of the very economically priced 27 Mhz two-function outfits designed for model cars or boats. The risk of interference from CB radios is less than it was in 1979/80–as soon as CB's were made legal the attraction to certain members of the community seemed to disappear! But bear in mind that these outfits may lack the range of 35 Mhz ones designed for model aircraft, and the risk of a CB enthusiast seeing your model in the sky, and calling up a friend to come and watch it, is always there. If you live in a mainly rural area you may avoid serious trouble, but we must regard a 27 Mhz outfit as an inexpensive way of "trying out" the hobby rather than a long-term buy.

3. Pulse Code Modulation. For a few years after 35 Mhz was introduced almost all R/C outfits conveyed the signal by frequency modulation (FM). This term means that minute variations of the frequency are the means by which the Tx "talks" to the Rx. This type of signal is highly resistant to, but not immune from, outside interference. Advances in the world of electronics never cease and leading manufacturers now offer outfits which (in theory at least) give complete immunity from interference, from virtually any source, by using an entirely different method of transmitting the signal, called Pulse Code Modulation (PCM). Each signal starts with a code which is unique to one particular transmitter and its receiver, so the receiver cannot respond to a signal from someone else's transmitter. Having recognised the code the receiver then accepts a series of pulses which dictate the position into which each servo shall move, and each servo is capable of 500 or so different positions - resolution of the very highest order. Should the receiver be unable to detect the

The spiral spring connectors shown here are far more reliable.

transmitter's signal, perhaps because of failing batteries, extreme range or massively powerful interference, it will go into "fail-safe". In this state the flying controls are usually centralised and the throttle is closed, though some outfits give you the option of having the flying controls set to produce (again in theory) a gentle turn. Frankly we can't see any outfit failing very safely if the model happens to be in a vertical dive (or in a vertical climb for that matter) at the moment of failure – the only really worthwhile feature of fail-safe is that the throttle is closed. Fail-safe is mandatory for models weighing more than 7 Kg and the real purpose of this regulation is not so much to stop the model crashing in the event of radio failure, it is to stop it flying around out of control and perhaps climbing into the path of a jumbo jet. PCM sets use more current than conventional ones and makers recommend receiver batteries of 1000 mah capacity or more – approximately twice as large and twice as heavy a standard ones. PCM outfits are more expensive then conventional ones and their theoretical advantages have yet to be fully proved in practice. Nevertheless, the concept of each receiver being coded to its own transmitter must be ideal, and it may be that in years to come PCM will replace FM completely.

4. Dry or rechargeable batteries. Early proportional equipment took much more electrical current from the batteries than equipment made today, and all R/C outfits had rechargeable batteries (often called "nicads" because they are of nickel-cadmium construction) and a charger as standard. Manufacturers are constantly seeking ways of reducing the initial cost of their products to increase sales, and now even five and six-function outfits can be bought that are designed to be operated on dry (or "throw-away") batteries rather than nicads. Dry batteries are normally AA size cylindrical cells, usually called pencells, and have a nominal voltage of 1½ volts per cell. Usually 8 of these fit into the battery compartment of the Tx and are arranged "in series", i.e. the positive end of one cell presses against, or is connected to, the negative end of the next cell. The resultant voltage available is theretore 1½ multiplied by the number of cells employed, so a Tx with 8 cells will be working with a nominal voltage of 12 volts. The receiver and servos almost always work off 4 cells fitted into a battery box, giving a nominal 6 volts.

These "dry battery" outfits are often significantly less expensive than those that come with nicads and charger as standard, and almost all of them can be converted to rechargeable operation when finances permit. On the face of it, therefore, they are the obvious choice for the beginner. But there can be important disadvantages which are not, of course, mentioned in the advertisements and these need to be fully understood before the

Salesman: The signal is frequency modulated and the dual-output servos incorporate remote potentiometers and cassette type gears.

final choice is made. We will go through these in the order of operating costs, convenience and reliability, first assuming that dry batteries are used and afterwards assuming that these have been replaced by rechargeable ones and the appropriate charger has been purchased.

Operating Costs. We have already stated that most outfits will give one and a half hours safe operation before the batteries need to be changed. In practice this means a maximum of four (to be safe) or five (you're stretching your luck) flights, because the radio will be switched on for about 20 minutes from the beginning of the pre-flight checks until the model is recovered at the end of each training flight. So, in practice, you'll need to buy a fresh set of batteries after every four or five flights. The batteries in the Tx will probably outlast those powering the Rx and the servos, and you may be able to economise by only changing them after every six or seven flights. To do this with safety you'll need to keep a "log" recording the length of time your outfit is switched on for each flight and the times at which batteries are replaced. You probably won't save money using the more expensive alkaline type batteries (e.g. Duracell). These should last nearly twice as long as premium quality zinc carbon ones (e.g. Ever Ready Silver Seal) but frequently cost at least twice as much. So we'll assume premium zinc carbon batteries are used.

If you replace the four Rx batteries after four flights and the eight Tx batteries after six flights, your "running costs" will be two and one-third batteries per flight, and the money used to buy these for about 60 flights (say 6 months' flying) would have bought you a set of nicads and the charger. So if you fly regularly you'll certainly save money by converting to recharge operation as soon as you can afford the outlay.

Convenience. Changing the batteries in the Tx is no problem, but changing those for the Rx is a bit of a pain. As explained in the next chapter, the battery box should be wrapped in a cushion of foam plastic and tucked away neatly at the bottom front corner of the model's radio compartment. The receiver is similarly wrapped and wedged with foam plastic above and/or behind the battery box, and all the leads have to be wedged with foam or otherwise protected from vibration. So the receiver and all the leads connecting it to the servos has to be disturbed and afterwards replaced each time the batteries are changed, and the wiring harness (as the leads are collectively described) is the weakest link in the radio chain.

The Futaba Challenger is an excellent "second generation" 35 Mhz FM outfit. This photo of the Tx shows the trim levers (black) under and alongside the sticks and the "rates" switches and associated adjusting screws above the sticks. (Photograph: Ripmax Models)

Reliability. Apart from the fact that reliability is prejudiced by having to disturb the radio equipment, there can be another snag, i.e. the electrical contacts between the batteries themselves and the compartment or box into which they fit. If you buy batteries of reputable make their reliability can be taken for granted. What cannot always be taken for granted is that, as installed, they will be able to produce the electrical current that is required. Remember, each cell produces only 1½ volts, and any competent electrician will tell you that it doesn't need much electrical resistance to stop 1½ volts from the pushing the current down the wire. If the spring contacts in the battery compartment of the Tx or in the battery box powering the Rx don't press hard on the ends of the batteries, or if there is a little dirt or corrosion on the springs or the batteries themselves, the full voltage won't get through. At the best your outfit's range will suffer, at the worst it will cease to operate altogether. Dirt isn't likely to be a problem on the ends of dry batteries (which come skin-wrapped these days) and corrosion won't occur unless the equipment is accidentally left on and they get completely flat. But a small amount of corrosion can build up over a period of time on the spring contacts and these should be periodically cleaned with a cloth or tissue moistened with methylated spirits and then given a very thin smear of Electrolube, an electrically conducting oil much favoured by model railway enthusiasts and sold by most model shops. Corrosion can also be a problem on the ends of rechargeable batteries, and it is essential that you clean and oil them as described above before they are fitted. For absolute reliability we suggest they are subsequently cleaned and re-oiled, say, once a year.

5. Conversion from dry to rechargeable batteries. We mentioned earlier how important it is that the spring contacts press hard against the ends of the batteries, and this applies, of course, whether they are dry or rechargeable. Ideally the batteries should be held firmly in a tight-fitting battery box so that they cannot move sideways, and the spring contacts at the ends should be in the form of a tapering spiral of strong spring steel wire at least ½" (12) long uncompressed and no more than ⅛" (3) long when the batteries are fitted. Some low price outfits have bent metal end connectors instead of spiral springs–these cannot be relied upon to exert sufficient pressure and while they might give acceptable reliability for model cars they are not recommended for anything that flies.

Replacing the Rx batteries with nicads won't, of course, get over the inconvenience of dry batteries unless the nicads can be recharged in situ i.e. without disturbing the battery box, receiver and wiring harness. Being aimed at the bottom end of the market some dry battery outfits economise by having the Rx battery box wired directly into the switch, and to be able to recharge the batteries in situ you'll have to buy a charging plug (or it may be a socket) and lead which has to be soldered into the back of the switch. Make sure you solder it to the input or "battery" end of the switch so that the batteries can be charged while the switch is "off". If the back of the switch isn't removable so that you can't get at the solder tags, or if you are perhaps unwilling to test your soldering skills on your newly acquired R/C equipment, then you'll have to buy a replacement battery box and switch harness which has a charging lead already wired in. These can be quite expensive, and the need or otherwise of a replacement switch harness should be borne in mind when comparing prices between one outfit and another.

Let's now compare a dry battery outfit which has been properly converted to recharge operation with an outfit that comes complete with nicads and charger as standard. The latter will still, almost certainly, use nicads of the pencell type because these are mass produced for dozens of applications and are therefore relatively inexpensive. But instead of relying on pressure contact for electrical continuity, the cells (both for the Rx and inside the Tx) will be welded together into "packs". The risk of dirt and/or corrosion affecting the output voltage is completely eliminated, the only physical contact being in the plug and socket connector between the battery pack and switch harness at the receiver end, and between the battery pack and switch inside the transmitter. Reputable R/C manufacturers use plug and socket connectors of the very highest quality, the internals almost invariably being gold plated, and the risk of failure in one of these (other than as a result of physical damage) is negligible. Other things being equal the power supply of a rechargeable outfit with welded battery packs is as reliable as man can make it. One that has been converted by replacing dry batteries with rechargeable ones, after taking the precautions we mentioned earlier, will be very nearly, but never quite, as good.

Welded battery packs are, of course, available as spares for rechargeable outfits, and instead of replacing the dry batteries in the Rx battery box you can always buy a rechargeable pack instead. Similarly some, but by no means all, manufacturers market a rechargeable pack for the Tx which replaces the Tx battery box and its individual cells. Unfortunately these rechargeable packs, particularly those for the Tx, tend to be rather expensive. Those who can solder are again at an advantage, because rechargeable pencells can be bought with solder tags welded to the ends for only a few pence more than the standard ones, and it is quite easy to make up a pack of four into a rechargeable pack for the Rx, usually at much less cost than buying the manufacturer's one. Use multistrand flexible wire for the inter-cell joints and then, to ensure the wire never has to flex anyway, bind the pack tightly, round the sides and end-over-end, with plastic insulating tape. (Belt and braces every time!) Similarly a recharge pack can be made up for the Tx, but only if there is sufficient room inside the Tx case to house the pack, which will invariably be more bulky than the set of non-tagged pencells intended to be replaced.

6. Servo reversing. All but the cheapest outfits have their transmitters fitted with servo reversing switches. These enable the direction of rotation of any servo in response to a given movement of the Tx stick to be reversed simply by moving a small switch on the Tx. So if, for example, your throttle servo closes the throttle when it should open it, you don't have to re-arrange the linkage, you simply move the appropriate switch instead–a very useful feature. The switches should obviously be positioned where they cannot be moved accidentally, preferably behind a cover to exclude dust and moisture.

7. Rates or Variable Rate Switches. Many beginners are puzzled by the purpose of these, partly because they don't vary the rate (or speed) of anything. What they do is to control the amount of movement that will result at the flying controls for a given movement of the Tx sticks, and "variable response switches" would have been a far better term. To give a good example, most aerobatic competitions require a slow roll, in which the model must be made to roll quite slowly onto one side, then upside down, then onto the other side, and then back to upright. Such a slow roll would only need a

very small movement of the aileron stick on the Tx–perhaps a fifth of its total sideways travel – and it is anything but easy to hold in this small sideways movement while moving the stick vertically to operate another control at the same time. By using the appropriate switch on the Tx the competition pilot can make his aileron stick "change gear" as it were, so that it needs to be pushed through its full sideways movement to produce the slow rotation required. He can then devote all his attention to progressively feeding in and taking out rudder and elevator to keep the model flying absolutely straight and level throughout the manoeuvre (yes - they really can do it!) Each switch is linked with a small adjusting screw so that the amount of movement of the flying control, when the switch is in use, can be adjusted, usually between about 20% and 100% of its full travel.

When first introduced you only got rate switches on the most expensive outfits designed for competition flyers, but now they appear on many outfits aimed at the normal "fly for fun" weekender.

They are useful for fun flying, but can obviously be downright dangerous if one of them gets knocked or moved into the wrong position without the pilot knowing it, or if he forgets to switch back to "full response" after using the reduced response position. While you're learning you will, of course, want the normal full response on all your controls. So make sure you set those little adjusting screws so that you get maximum response in the reduced position, then if a switch gets knocked accidentally (or moved by one of the children) there will be little or no difference. But at the same time get into the habit of checking, before *every* flight, that the rate switches are in their intended positions, otherwise one day you'll suddenly find you get a whole lot less response to a control signal than you expected.

8. TTC. As well as rates switches the more upmarket outfits have another facility, sometimes called TTC or total travel control. This enables the total movement of the servo outputs (and hence the total travel of the controls to which they are connected) to be varied by small adjusting screws inside the Tx. This is another useful but by no means essential facility. As explained in the next chapter, you have to arrange the linkages to give the correct amount of control movement to rudder and elevator and this is normally done by selecting the appropriate hole in the servo output and the correct hole in the "horn" or lever fixed to the control surface. It never comes out right first time and quite a lot of chopping and changing usually has to be done at both ends of the linkage to get it right. With TTC you simply connect your linkages to the outermost holes on both the servo outputs and on the rudder and elevator horns (by using the outermost holes you reduce free play or "backlash" to the minimum). You then merely have to turn the appropriate adjusting screw until full movement of the Tx stick gives you the correct angular movement of the control surface. TTC also makes it much easier to match the movement of the throttle control to the output of the throttle servo.

9. "Buddy Box" lead. This is the Americanism for a cable that can connect two transmitters *of the same make* in such a way that control can be passed from the Tx held by the instructor to the Tx held by the pupil, and regained instantly by the instructor whenever required. In practice the instructor actually holds the Tx belonging to the pupil, and the pupil holds the instructor's Tx which remains switched off. The instructor can, of course, take off and get the model to a safe height before instruction commences. He then presses a transfer button on top of the Tx which he is holding. This renders his Tx sticks ineffective and, by means of the buddy box lead, brings those of the Tx which the pupil is holding into use. If (or when!) the pupil gets into difficulty the instructor only has to release the transfer button to regain control. This is obviously a much quicker and safer arrangement than the pupil having to pass the Tx back to the instructor if things start to go wrong, and the writer can vouch for the fact that it makes the instructor's task *very* much easier. Because the second Tx remains "off" it needn't be on the same frequency as the pupil's, in fact it needn't have a crystal fitted at all – only the control sticks are brought into use when the transfer button is pressed. Unfortunately sockets for a buddy box lead are rarely fitted to outfits at the lower end of the price range, and it would be a waste of money getting an outfit with a buddy box socket unless your instructor's Tx also has this facility, and is of the same make that you intend to buy.

10. Coupled controls. Again at the top end of the market your outfit will give you the facility of coupling some of the controls, the usual combinations being rudder with ailerons and elevator with flaps. The former can be useful on scale thermal soarers which have very little dihedral and often need a judicious combination of rudder and aileron to turn the model with minimum loss of height. When the coupling switch is engaged movement of either rudder or aileron stick on the Tx will produce movement of both these controls and an adjusting screw will be provided on the Tx so that the amount of movement of one relative to the other can be varied. Some outfits enable you to couple elevator and flaps so that if, when the flaps are lowered, a change of trim occurs (e.g. the model may tend to go into a dive) this can be compensated for by a change in the elevator neutral which will come in automatically when the flaps are lowered. All this is, of course, a long, long way into the future for the average beginner.

The output disc of the rotary servo has holes at two different radii. The outermost holes are used whenever possible to reduce free play or "backlash".

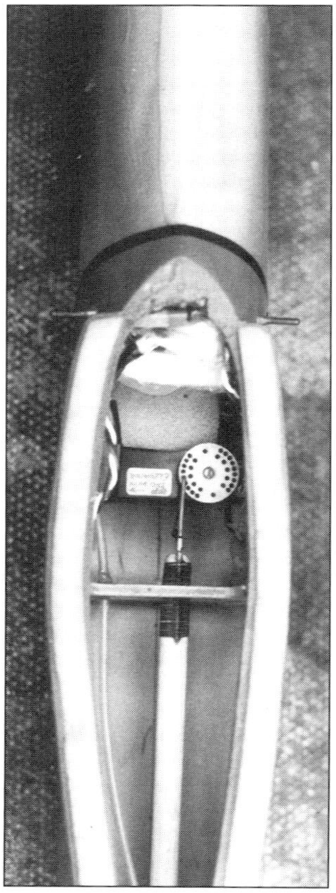

11. Computerised transmitters. The latest

computerised transmitters don't just enable you to adjust the total travel of the controls, they enable you to adjust the character of the response as well. Take for example a lightweight "fun" aerobatic model with a huge elevator moving 45° up and down to make the looping radius incredibly tight. If the elevator responded progressively to movement of the Tx stick it would be difficult to fly the model level – the slightest movement of the stick would have an exaggerated effect. So the Tx is adjusted to give very little response to movements of the stick near neutral, the response increasing progressively so that, say, the last 10° movement of the stick produces 20° movement on the elevator. The same Tx might next be used on a very stable canard that needs a lot of movement on the elevator fitted to the foreplane to have any real effect. So adjustment is made the other way to give large control surface movements intially, reducing as the stick is move further away from neutral.

Computerisation offers the ability to couple any control with any other(s). So if the side thrust is wrong and the model pulls to the left at full throttle you can correct this by coupling in a little right rudder (and a little right aileron if necessary) with movement of the throttle stick. Ugh!

Because the features – or imperfections – of models vary the computer has a number of different memories so you don't have to re-programme all the controls every time you fly a different model.

Computerisation also offes a huge advantage to those "devils for punishment" who fly helicopters as well as fixed wing aircraft. Although the control requirements are completely different that clever little electronic "chip" at the heart of the Tx enables it to cope with both.

12. Ground test facility. Some outfits have a cable which can connect the Tx to the Rx in such a way that the controls in the model can be operated without the Tx actually transmitting. This can be useful at a club flying field where you could, for example, make adjustments to the linkages to give more or less movement at the controls (or make similar adjustments to a computerised Tx), and see the result of such adjustments, while another member is actually flying on "your" frequency. Without this facility you would, of course, have to wait until your frequency is clear before switching on.

13. Receiver battery check. All transmitters have a meter which gives an indication of the voltage of the batteries, or preferably, an indication of the power of the signal actually being transmitted. This is obviously desirable but a bit illogical in that the Rx batteries are usually the ones that run down first. To enable the state of the Rx batteries to be monitored some outfits have a cable that connects the Rx batteries to the Tx so that the Rx battery voltage is indicated on the Tx meter. As explained later, this feature is only of real value when dry batteries are used.

14. Choice of Servos.

(a) Type of output. Servos can have two types of output, rotary or linear. The former have an arm or disc which is turned by the servo and this rotary movement is connected, by a push-rod or flexible linkage, to the throttle arm on the engine or to the control horn (lever) on elevator or rudder. The rotary arm or disc has a series of holes at different radii from the centre so that the amount of movement of the linkage can be adjusted by selecting the appropriate hole.

Linear servos have two lugs projecting from the top which move in opposite directions in a straight line when the servo is operated, and are accordingly sometimes called push-pull servos. The total amount of this movement (usually about ⅝" (15) from one end of travel to the other) cannot be varied. Because the linkages are connected above the tops of linear servos they can be mounted closer together if not actually touching – useful in ultra slim fuselages of advanced soarers. Linear servos have largely gone out of fashion and are now offered by only a few manufacturers.

(b) Ball-bearing Servos. The resolution of modern R/C gear, by which is meant the accuracy with which the servos respond to a given movement of the Tx stick, is of a very high order, and accuracies of around ½ per cent are claimed. But there is little point in having a servo with an output that rotates accurately to a tiny fraction of 1 degree if the shaft on which the disc is mounted can slop about 1/16 inch (1.5) or so in its bearings. The mechanical parts must wear in time and to combat this leading manufacturers produce servos with ball bearings to the output shaft. These are particularly beneficial in helicopters, where servos suffer from high, vibrating loads, and for the steering servos in cars, but the extra cost is hardly warranted for the flying controls of a normal fixed wing model. A ball bearing servo must obviously be better for a steering noseleg, but if some form of springing is incorporated in the linkage a normal servo will suffice.

(c) Cassette Type Gears. Briefly, every servo contains an electric motor to provide the power to move the model's controls. This motor rotates at very high speed and has to be geared down to provide a usable speed and more physical power, rather like bottom gear on a car. This is accomplished by a train of gears (usually plastic) on metal spindles mounted in the plastic body mouldings. Thus distortion of the servo body could affect the gear train. A cassette type gear train is nothing more than a self-contained miniature gearbox, usually with metal gears, that is entirely independent of the servo body, and cannot be affected by any distortion of the body mouldings.

(d) Remote Potentiometers. Remote potentiometers are less easy to explain without getting too technical. Suffice it to say that every servo needs to contain a variable electrical resistance that varies as the servo output disc or arm is turned. The technical term for this variable resistance is a feedback potentiometer, which comprises a rotating metal arm, called the wiper, moving over a circular electrical conductor called the track. Normally the wiper is mounted under, and moves the same amount as, the output disc or arm, and the total travel is about 90 degrees. With remote potentiometers the wiper is geared to, rather than fixed to, the shaft carrying the servo output, and can thus be made to rotate through a much wider arc, up to say 300 degrees. The servo's resolution is thus even further improved. We must stress that cassette gears and remote potentiometers are refinements at the very top end of the market. We've all managed perfectly well without them for many, many years, so don't let the adverts persuade you that they are vitally necessary!

That just about wraps up all the various features you should take into account when deciding which outfit to buy, so we'll finish this section with a check-list to help ensure nothing important gets forgotten.

- 1. Number of functions, taking into account future ambitions as well as present training needs?
- 2. Ordinary 35 Mhz FM or PCM?
- 3. For dry batteries, or rechargeable as standard?
- 4. If for dry batteries are the batteries held so they cannot move sideways, and are they compressed by strong tapered spiral springs for good end-to-end contact?
- 5. If conversion to recharge batteries is intended:
  (a) What more has to be bought so that the Rx batteries can be charged *in situ* by means of a charging lead?
  (b) Is the Tx already fitted with a charging socket?
  (c) Is a welded Tx battery pack available?
  (d) If not, is there room in the Tx for a homemade one to be fitted?
- 6. Does the Tx have servo reversing switches?
- 7. Does it have rates switches?
- 8. Does it have TTC?
- 9. Does it have a socket for a buddy box lead?
- 10. Which, if any, controls can be coupled?
- 11. If the Tx computerised?
- 12. Does the outfit have a ground test facility?
- 13. Does it have a receiver battery check cable?
- 14. Does the manufacturer offer a good range of alternative servos, e.g. (a) Ones with linear outputs? (b) Extra powerful ones for retracting undercarriages? (c) Extra small lightweight ones if, say, electric flight is envisaged?

Don't be downhearted if you can't afford most of these "extras". You can fly with the best and win places in club competitions without *any* of the features listed 6-14 above. A "no frills" four or five-function outfit with good battery compartments and good battery connections will be as reliable, if not more reliable, than one with every conceivable gimmick. After all, if you don't have rates switches or TTC adjusters on your Tx then you can be absolutely certain that they will *never* go wrong! Quite seriously, you don't have to go top price to buy reliability in the radio link, though you do sometimes have to move a little from the bottom to get good battery compartments and connections. But go for a rechargeable outfit with proper welded battery packs if you can possibly afford it.

Having discussed, at very great length, the features you should look for we now come to the most difficult bit – choosing between one manufacturer and another. Here we can only echo and amplify the advice given at the end of the chapter "About Engines". If one or two makes are most popular in your local club get one of these – as well as the benefit of the club members' experiences you have a better chance of being able to use a buddy box lead and the local model shop will probably have a reasonably good range of spares and accessories. If you have to decide on your own then you won't go far wrong if you buy an outfit made by one of the major manufacturers and stocked in depth by all the big retailers. But don't get anything too complicated. It could be 5 years or more before you actually find a need for any of the mind-boggling features available on the latest computerised outfits. And by then, what you are looking at now will almost certainly be out-of-date.

All reputable makes are guaranteed for one year but if your radio is going to misbehave it will probably do so in the first few hours of operation, possibly as a result of having been mishandled in transit. Should you be unfortunate enough to have trouble don't let *anyone* go poking about inside any part of your radio – this could well invalidate the guarantee. Take or send it back to the shop or direct to the service department instead.

Radios, like cars, sometimes develop intermittent faults. If yours does, help the manufacturer or service agent to help you by giving a clear, concise account of what happened, how many flights since the last time the batteries were changed or recharged, range at the time trouble started, how many controls failed to operate, etc. etc. Always remember that the guarantee covers repairs to the radio caused by radio failure and not by pilot error, jammed linkages or someone else switching on on your frequency! These manufacturers have a reputation to live up to and in all cases of genuine doubt you will get the benefit of that doubt. Don't push it by trying to get them to pay for your mistakes - it's not playing fair and could prejudice your treatment if you *do* get genuine radio failure in the future.

Before closing this chapter we must write a little more about rechargeable batteries. If you're fed up with reading about them already please bear with us - the best R/C outfit in the world won't be any good at all if the batteries fail.

Beginners converting their outfits to nicads are often dismayed to find that they are marked 1.2 volts whereas dry batteries are marked 1.5 volts, and wonder if their outfits will work as well on nicads as they did on dry ones. In actual use the difference isn't so great as the figures might suggest, because the voltage of a dry battery will drop to 1.4 volts or less when a reasonably heavy current is taken from it, whereas a nicad will "hold" virtually its full voltage on the same load. That's why we referred to the "nominal" voltages of dry batteries earlier. Some manufacturers use voltage compensating circuitry which will allow for the change, one manufacturer used a "dummy" dry battery in the Tx which was taken out when the conversion was made, so that 7 dry cells were replaced by 8 nicads. You can rest assured that any outfit of reputable make designed to be converted to nicads will perform "up to specification" after conversion.

Something that must be borne in mind, however, is the fact than nicads have less capacity than dry batteries, possibly not much more than half that of "premium" zinc carbon ones and not much more than a quarter of alkaline ones such as Duracell. The safe way to find out is by putting a fresh set in your Tx (make sure the aerial is fully extended) and see how long this set lasts compared with those batteries previously used. We are often asked how long (in terms of years of use) a set of nicads should last. In our experience 6–8 years appears to be about the norm, so the prudent modeller will change his after 5 – 6 years use. Experience shows that nicads used regularly will last longer than those that are left unused for long periods of time.

Nicads have other characteristics that need to be appreciated, even if not fully understood. They need two or three charge and discharge cycles before reaching their full capacity. And they will lose some of their capacity (hours of safe operation per charge) unless they are *fully* discharged and then recharged at fairly regular intervals.

The average power flyer has three or four flights on a Sunday, puts his gear on charge the following Saturday night and takes it off charge before he goes out flying the following morning. This routine is followed most weekends (weather and household commitments permitting) with the result that the nicads in the Tx at least are regularly overcharged and never have to give their full capacity. This overcharging does no harm but in human terms the nicads get "lazy" through "lack of exercise" and lose some of their capacity. So once or twice a year you should leave everything switched on until they are completely flat and then leave them on charge for 15-18 hours. The Christmas break and summer holidays are obviously good times to do this. You'll see nicad "cyclers" advertised in the magazines which do this automatically but the writer has always thought these an unnecessary luxury.

Another characteristic of nicads is that the voltage they give (and hence the reading on the Tx meter) doesn't give any real indication as to how much of their capacity has been used. Put a zinc carbon battery in a small torch and leave it switched on and it will lose its brightness slowly at first and then progressively more and more quickly as it nears the end of its life. If we assume this life to be one hour and draw a graph showing the voltage of the battery during this time the result will be approximately as shown here:

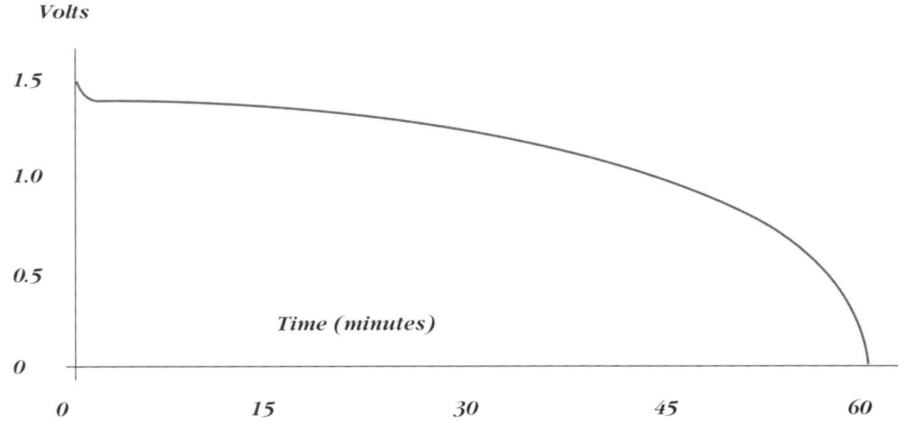

Zinc – Carbon 'Dry' Battery

If the dry battery is replaced by a nicad the bulb will be less bright initially but will lose only very little brightness over most of the hour. When it is nearly exhausted the voltage will then fall relatively quickly to zero. This is shown graphically here and will help explain why the Tx meter can be misleading when nicads are used. These meters are quite small and there will be very little difference in the reading when the batteries are fully charged than when they are at point "A", shortly before that quick fall to zero occurs.

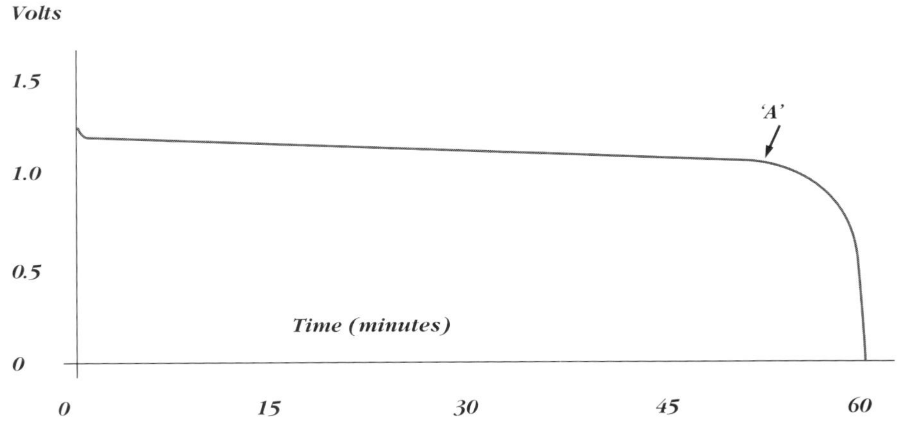

Nickel – Cadmium Rechargeable Battery

Chapter 17

Radio Installation

Whatever make of radio you finally buy, treat it with the respect it deserves. Always remember that the wiring harness and the plugs and sockets are the weak link in the chain. You should never make a habit of pulling plugs from their sockets by tugging at the wires. In our view manufacturers have carried miniaturisation too far in this respect - some connections are so small that old and less sensitive fingers can barely get a grip. The trick here is to cut a few strips of fine sandpaper and contact cement them round the offending plugs or sockets.

If, because a socket is shrouded, sandpaper cannot be used and you have to pull the wires, then you should coat the end of the plug and the first inch (24) or so of the wires with contact adhesive, applying additional layers until a solid tapering shroud of adhesive has been built up integrating the plug with the wires. It is particularly important to do this if you have to disconnect the battery from the receiver every time the battery has to be charged. This is a poor arrangement at the best of times – a separate charging socket which enables the "inflight" wiring to remain undisturbed is far better.

Later on you should take similar precautions, if necessary, with the lead to the aileron servo, which has to be disconnected each time the model is taken apart. Integrating a plug to its wires with contact adhesive in this way takes time and looks a mess, but taking precautions like this is always quicker than building a new model!

We will deal first with fitting the radio into the model, then with connecting it to the controls, though in practice these two operations go on at the same time. Because it is heaviest the battery goes at the front of the radio compartment or under the fuel tank. Pack it really well in foam plastic, the tubular "low-bounce" foam plastic sold by model shops is far better than the foam sold for making cushions, etc. Next comes the receiver, which should if possible be installed so that the printed

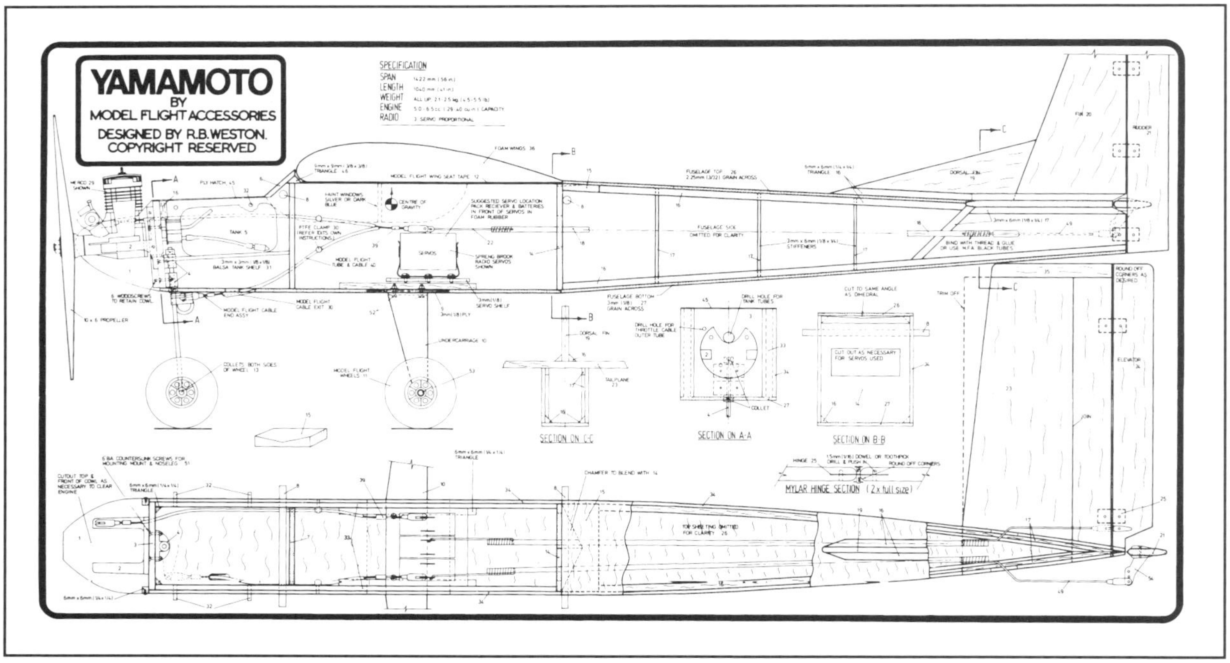

This reproduction of the Yamamoto plan warrants close study. It shows the rudder and elevator pushrods and the tube and cable linkages to throttle and steering nosewheel. Also shown are the "internals" of the clunk tank. Omitted for clarity are the receiver battery, which is wrapped in foam plastic and placed at the bottom of fuselage behind the bulkhead or "former" below the leading edge, and the receiver which is similarly wrapped and wedged between the battery and the servos. Note the thick, strong wing and the utilitarian appearance of the model generally – a thoroughly sound and practical trainer, although the undercarriage is not above criticism. (Model Flight Accessories Ltd drawing)

circuit board is vertical and the "top" of the receiver case is facing rearwards. This way the components will be pressed onto the board if you are unfortunate enough to crash head-on into something. The receiver is packed in a tube of foam like the battery and then the normal practice is to protect the throttle control and then go on wrapping foam around the receiver until all the available space is filled. The plastic is held around the receiver with rubber bands and further bands should be used across the top of the fuselage to ensure the receiver can't fly out if the wing comes off in a crash. The foam wrapping to the receiver should be bulky rather than tight to give maximum cushion effect, and you should be able to move the receiver a little in its cushion with slight finger pressure. We have known receivers survive appalling crashes completely undamaged if protected properly in this way, including one occasion when a model hit the concrete runway with such force that the battery smashed completely through an ⅛ inch (3) plywood bulkhead and concertina-ed the plastic fuel tank from about 4 inches (100) long to about 1 inch (25) long.

Surplus wiring can be wedged down the fuselage sides and will be held in place by the foam plastic to prevent vibration. Leave enough slack in the aerial so that the receiver can move fully forward in its cushion. Lead it up to near the top of the fuselage and back along one side so that it exits below and behind the trailing edge of the wing. This way the aerial will be kept the maximum distance from the servos, which are potential causes of interference. It should be secured with adhesive tape or fed through a thin plastic tube glued to the inside of the fuselage to prevent it vibrating. Where it emerges through the top of the fuselage it should be fed through a short length of flexible tube to prevent vibration weakening it. Before it exits it should be tied round a match or something similar so that if it gets knocked the strain can't be transmitted back to the soldered joint inside the receiver. The remainder of the aerial then goes up to the top of the fin where it is held in slight tension by a thin, weak rubber band. The aerial is knotted around one end of the band, the other end of the band is looped over the head of a modelling pin pushed fully into the top of the fin. Then if the aerial is knocked the band will either break or fly off the pin. There is usually 6 inches (150) or so of surplus aerial, this should not be cut but just left trailing out behind the fin.

The servos are normally fitted behind the receiver and are positioned so that the model balances correctly. Most R/C outfits include a plastic tray that holds three servos and the on/off switch and this speeds up the installation considerably. Usually one servo is held across the fuselage and the other two are held side-by-side along the fuselage. Obviously the single servo should go at the front to work the throttle and the other two at the back for rudder and elevator. The throttle servo should have its output arm or disc towards the ri ght-hand side of the fuselage (as seen from behind) because the engine's throttle arm is invariably on the right. If the switch is mounted in the servo tray it is operated by a piece of rigid wire or some other push-pull device which should project through the left-hand side of the fuselage (since the silencer exhausts on the right). The writer prefers "in" for "off" as "push off" is easy to remember!

The servo tray is mounted on two hardwood bearers about ⅜ inch (10) square which are glued across the fuselage, and is fixed to these by small screws or self-tappers. The latter are preferable because they require constant-diameter holes through the bearers, which are easily drilled, whereas a screw really needs a tapered hole to bite properly. Also, self-tappers are made from very hard steel and can be removed and replaced repeatedly without the heads becoming damaged.

If your outfit doesn't include a servo tray all three servos are normally mounted side-by-side, with the throttle servo at the right, again on hardwood bearers. The servos' mounting lugs are fitted with rubber grommets to absorb vibration and the screws or self-tappers go through these. Each has a washer which compresses the grommet - don't tighten these screws so tight that the grommets become ineffective. If the switch isn't mounted in the servo tray it is fixed to the left-hand side of the fuselage with the slide lever projecting outside. The leads from the servos should be led away underneath the servos and again wedged in place with foam plastic to eliminate vibration.

Before dealing with the linkages to the controls we must digress briefly to explain how the movement of the controls is usually arranged in relation to movement of the control sticks on the transmitter. As stated previously, if you have a tutor lined up it is essential that your installation matches his both as regards the controls operated by each stick and their direction of movement. If, despite all our warnings, you intend going it alone the following is probably the best arrangement for a right-handed person:

- (a) Have the throttle operated by the right-hand stick, arranged so that the stick is pushed forwards (towards the top of the Tx) for full throttle and pulled back for low throttle (i.e. working in the same "sense" as an accelerator).
- (b) Have the rudder controlled by the same stick as the throttle, arranged so that the rudder moves to the left (and the model turns to the left) when the stick is pushed to the left, and vice-versa.
- (c) Have the elevator control on the other stick, arranged so that the elevator moves down (and the model dives) when the stick is pushed forwards, and up when it is pulled back. (This is the same as fullsize practice.)

If you are left-handed you'll probably find it easier to fly "throttle left", i.e. to have throttle and rudder on the left stick and elevator on the right. The "sense" of each control should still be as stated above. Those with full-size flying or gliding experience may wonder why rudder and elevator are not controlled by the same stick. We can only answer by pointing out once again that flying full-size and flying a model are two entirely different things (the writer has also done a fair amount of fullsize gliding as well as a great deal of model flying and he *knows*).

Many full-size flyers have learnt to fly R/C with the two primary flying controls operated by the same stick, but many more have made absolutely no progress at all until they have been persuaded to divorce the two and have rudder and elevator controlled by separate sticks. To give just one example, assume you have rudder and elevator on the same stick. You are coming in to land

and are holding in a little down elevator to keep the airspeed high, because of a blustery wind, before flaring out. A sudden gust tips the model sideways and immediate rudder correction is needed. Working the transmitter stick with your thumb (the usual practice) you'll find it very difficult, if not impossible, to move it sideways without altering the amount of "down" you are holding in.

We mentioned before that each stick on your transmitter has small trim levers alongside and/or below it and that these alter the neutral slightly without the stick being moved. So if, for example, your model has a tendency to turn left all the time you can correct this by moving the rudder trim to the right, instead of having to hold in a bit of right rudder to fly straight.

Once the model is down on the ground again the linkage should be adjusted so that the rudder is in its "flight proved" neutral position when the trim lever is central.

Obviously both rudder and elevator trims must be central when you first fit the linkages in the model and adjust them for length. Usually the throttle trim is arranged so that when fully forward the engine idles safely with the stick at low throttle position. When the trim is moved back the engine will stop. Much more impressive than chucking a rag at the prop! But don't waste time trying to achieve this before your engine has had a good hour or so in the air as you probably won't be able to get a slow, safe idle with your new engine anyway.

The traditional way to work elevator and rudder is by pushrods, these being made up of ¼ inch (6) square hard balsa or preferably ⅜ inch (10) balsa dowel with short lengths of 16 gauge (1.6) wire at each end. The wire ends are bent, pointed and pushed through the balsa about 2 inches (50) from each end and bound tightly to the balsa with thick cotton or button thread, liberal coats of cement or glue being applied to the balsa before binding and to the thread afterwards. The front wire is bent to go through the hole in the servo output (arm or disc) and held there by some form of keeper. The rear wire is bent to go out through a slot in the top or side of the fuselage and bent again to go back to the control horn (lever) on rudder or elevator. The wire is threaded for about ¾ inch (18) at its end and a nylon connector, or clevis is screwed onto its thread. A clevis is nothing more than a small U-shaped nylon moulding, with a nylon or metal pin moulded in, that goes through one of the holes in the horn. The clevis can be sprung apart for connection and disconnection, a thin plastic sleeve around the outside preventing it springing apart, and coming off the horn, unintentionally.

Sometimes a clevis is used at the servo end as well so that the length can be adjusted at both ends.

Pushrods are light and efficient but take a lot of time to make up. You can't bend the wire at the back end while it's in the model, you have to bend it first, poke the whole thing down the fuselage, feed

End of wire is sharpened and bent, balsa rod is pierced and coated with glue, wire is forced through balsa and bound with strong thread, thread is coated with glue for additional security.

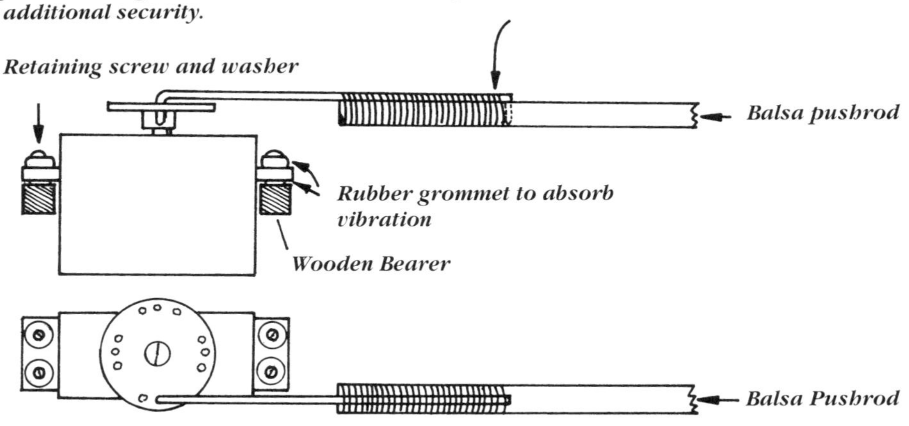

Side and top view of the wire end of a pushrod connected to the output disc of a servo. Some form of retainer or "keeper" as it is called is obviously required to prevent the wire coming out of the hole in the disc. Three of the many types of keeper are illustrated below.

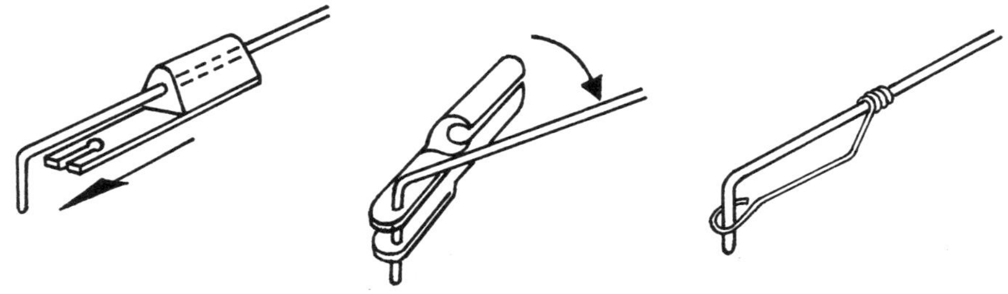

The 'push forward' keeper has to be slipped over the wire end before the final 90° bend is made

If you forget you can still use the 'swing in' type of keeper which snaps over the wire from the side

A third type is simply a coil of very thin wire of the correct internal diameter extended forward and looped around the end of the pushrod wire. This also must be fitted before the final 90° bend is made

Side view of the wire end of a pushrod emerging through the top of the fuselage, (on many models it emerges through the side rather than the top).

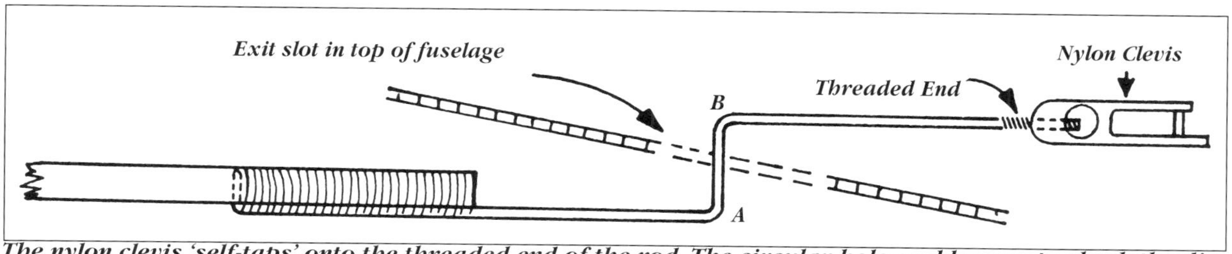

The nylon clevis 'self-taps' onto the threaded end of the rod. The circular hole enables you to check the distance the clevis is actually threaded onto the rod, and its diameter represent the amount of safe adjustment available here. Larger adjustments can be made by bending wire at angles A and B to more or less than 90° as appropriate.

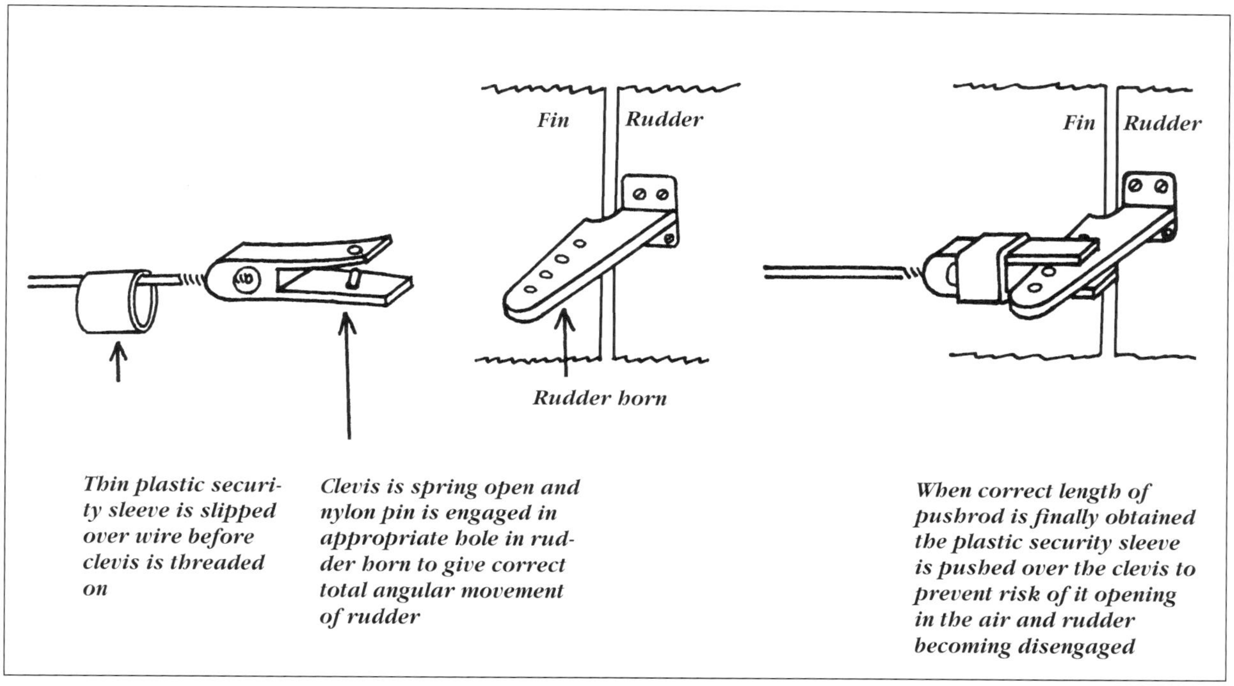

Drawings show how the clevis is secured to the rudder horn. Connection to elevator horn is, of course, similar. Ideally, the holes in the horns should be in line with the centre of the hinges holding rudder and elevator.

the end out through the slot and check that the wire is bent correctly. If your radio doesn't have servo reversing you'll be wise to check at this stage that the control will move the correct way, e.g. when the rudder stick on the Tx is pushed to the left the rudder will swing to the left. Then fit the clevis and adjust for length.

The clevis should thread at least $\frac{3}{16}$ inch (4.5) onto the wire so that it can be extended by about $\frac{1}{16}$ inch (1.5) if flight tests prove this necessary, still leaving about $\frac{1}{8}$ inch (3) of the clevis threaded onto the wire. This is the minimum for safety. At the front end you may find the clevis binds against the output disc of the servo when it is pulled forward, in which case part of the disc must be cut away to clear the clevis (arms, rather than discs, are preferable for this reason). Also, of course, you have to select the appropriate holes in the servo output and in the horn so that the total movement of the control surface is correct. (A good rule-of-thumb is 30 degrees each side of neutral for rudder and 20 degrees above and below neutral for elevator, but these angles obviously vary with the relative area of the control surfaces in question. Always use the outermost holes where possible to reduce free movement or backlash to the minimum.

Correctly installed, pushrods should move freely and easily, without causing any strain on the servo output or on the control horn and without touching anything in between (other than perhaps rubbing gently against the fuselage exit slot) whatever the position of the Tx stick and its appropriate trim. If it all works out right first time you'll either be very clever or very lucky!

Some designers prefer a tube and cable linkage rather than pushrods. These comprise a tube, usually of nylon, in which a stranded metal cable can slide. They work on the same principle as the brake cables on a bicycle – so long as the tube is firmly anchored a couple of inches from each end (and preferably anchored or wedged against vibration midway between) they will link your servos to the controls just as well as pushrods. We emphasise "firmly" because if the tube

Side view of tube and cable rudder linkage emerging through the top of a fuselage. Linkages can rarely be arranged exactly straight as shown here but should always be as nearly straight as practicable.

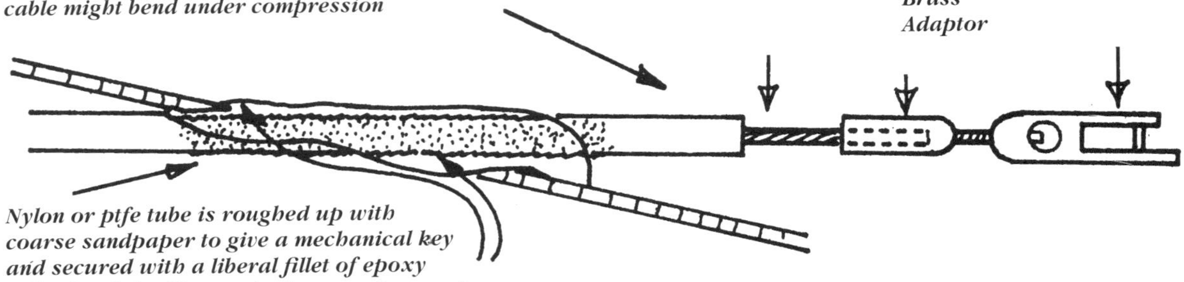

Additional adjustment can be made by re-soldering the threaded brass adaptor but at least 1/8" of cable must enter the adaptor for safety. Clevis must be removed during re-soldering. DANGER! PTFE gives off poisonous fumes when heated, so cables with PTFE rather than nylon tubes should always be soldered outside, not in the workshop.

comes loose the control won't operate and you'll probably smash your model. One way to do this is to roughen the tube with coarse sandpaper thoroughly for a length of about ¾ inch (18) before it goes into the fuselage, and epoxy it to the fuselage side while it is temporarily wedged or pinned in position. A second coat of epoxy (preferably surplus from another mix that is beginning to go stiff) should then be applied round the tube to form a collar. You can use a preformed nylon clamp round the tube but always use epoxy as well as the clamp. Instead of roughening up the tube with coarse sandpaper you can bind it tightly with paper masking tape, to which epoxy will stick admirably well.

The cable has to be cut to length which requires a sharp pair of cutting pliers or sidecutters. When it is cut the strands tend to spread out so it's a good idea to tin the cable with solder before cutting it. You're going to have to tin the end before soldering it into the brass adaptor anyway. The nylon tube should end about 1 inch (24) short of the adaptor so that the cable can flex sufficiently to accommodate the movement of the servo output or control horn. Obviously, the less unsupported cable the better so leave the nylon overlength to start with and cut it away a bit at a time when you can see how it all performs.

Another form of flexible linkage or "snake" has a nylon inner instead of the cable. Just a little more friction occurs but providing sharp bends are avoided a free linkage can be obtained. One type has brass threaded connectors that self tap on to the outside of the nylon inner, another type has a hollow nylon inner and steel threaded connectors that self tap inside. No soldering is needed with either type. These nylon in nylon linkages are clearly not as strong as cables and would be dangerous in a 10 cc aerobatic model. But they are plenty strong enough for a trainer. If your soldering is suspect you should use them anyway.

These flexible types of linkage usually come coiled up in a packet and will have developed a semi-permanent curvature. It's a good idea to unpack them and hang them up in the workshop, weighting the bottom ends, to get rid of this curvature as far as possible before they are installed.

We make no apology for defining the bits and pieces of the linkages, as in some kits the poor beginner is confronted with a bewildering collection of connectors, clevises, keepers, horns, hinges, undercarriage bolts etc. all in the same packet, with not much guidance as to which bit goes where.

Hinges are usually moulded in nylon with a thin, flat extension each side of the pivot that is let into the balsa by first cutting a slot with the modelling knife. A very simple but equally efficient substitute is a short length of flexible mylar or flat nylon strip which again is slotted into the balsa, leaving about 1/16 inch (1.5) clear between the fixed and moveable surfaces to allow the material to flex. Neither nylon nor mylar can be glued in with safety. Both must be mechanically anchored in place by very small screws or lengths of cocktail stick or matchstick going right through the balsa and the hinge material and afterwards cut off flush at the ends. Most nylon hinges already have holes in the flat part where these can go, and the positions of these can be marked on the surface before the hinges are slotted into the balsa.

With mylar strip the balsa and mylar should be pierced with a modelling pin and the hole widened out with something sharp and pointed (the end of a dart does the job splendidly). The hole is then filled with glue and the screw or cocktail stick inserted. Modelling pins alone will not hold mylar in place.

Before leaving rudder and elevator we will just state once again that the linkages and hinges must be free. Modern servos are very powerful but you will get slower and less accurate response if they have to struggle against friction and binding to move the controls. They will also take more current, and safe flying time before recharging will be appreciably reduced.

It is particularly important that the throttle control should be arranged so that the servo can move to its commanded position at full and slow throttle positions, whatever the position of the trim control on the throttle stick. Most of your flying will be done at full throttle and if the servo is prevented from reaching its full throttle position by an incorrect linkage there will be a continuous and heavy extra current drain which may

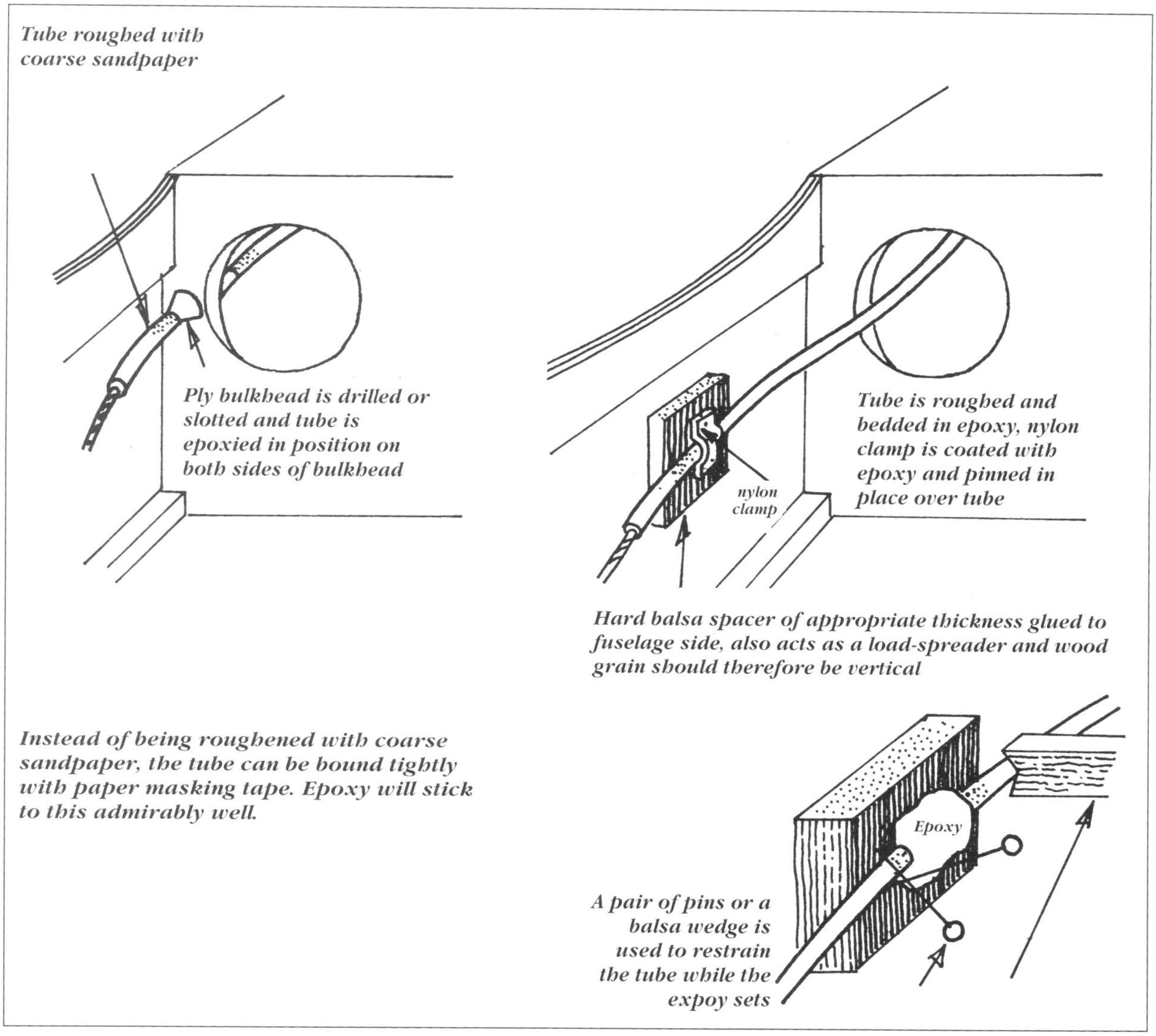

Three methods of securing the forward end of a tube and cable linkage operating rudder or elevator.

not harm the servo but which will reduce safe flying time very considerably. If your radio outfit doesn't have some form of total travel control you must be prepared to spend some time matching the throttle lever to the servo. Sometimes it is helpful if you drill your own hole in the servo output disc at exactly the correct radius.

If your model has a snake type of throttle linkage you may even find it necessary to solder a short length of spring to the end of the cable or the connector, the other end of the spring being epoxied into the end of the throttle clevis. Suitable springs can be obtained from disposable cigarette lighters. The writer prefers to connect the throttle with very thin wire (20 gauge or .85) running in a loose tube such as a plastic drinking straw to prevent it buckling up on compression. Usually a couple of 90 degree bends are required where the wire emerges through the front bulkhead to line it up with the throttle arm, and these will give the linkage adequate springing. Simple, light and inexpensive!

That just about buttons up the installation of the radio. Now perhaps you'll appreciate just why it takes so long to do it correctly! Try to position the servos so that the CG will come in the correct place, remembering to allow for the weight of the pushrods or whatever are used to operate the rudder and elevator. The correct way to check the position of the CG is explained later.

You will have unknowingly tested your radio outfit during the installation, but this doesn't prove it has adequate range. So give it a range check before the first flight. You should have full control at 400 yards (365 metres) with the model on the ground or not more than waist high, and with the nose of the model pointing at the transmitter so that the receiver aerial is end-on. If you have this range on the ground you'll have at least a mile in the air – far more than you will ever need. This check takes about ten minutes. How long will it take to repair the model if you only find out that your outfit lacks range when it's airborne?

If you ever get a malfunction in the air, cut the throttle and land the model as quickly as you can. If you cannot find anything obviously wrong, rangecheck the radio. If it fails, send it back for a checkover.

Every club has its tame electronics "expert" who is

only too willing to delve into the internals of your radio in an attempt to rectify some minor fault. If the fault is something simple like dirt on the feedback pot of a servo you may save time and money in this way. But decline all such offers of assistance while your gear is still under guarantee, and be wary of them afterwards.

In particular we don't like to see receivers and servos pulled apart on the flying field. Oily fingers, dirty tools, fuel and dust thrown up when someone starts his engine, these can do no good at all. If you must pull your radio apart a clean workbench or kitchen table is the place to do it.

But in our experience the flyers who rarely, if ever, have trouble with their radios are generally those who leave well alone, and send their gear back to the maker or service agent if service or repairs are necessary.

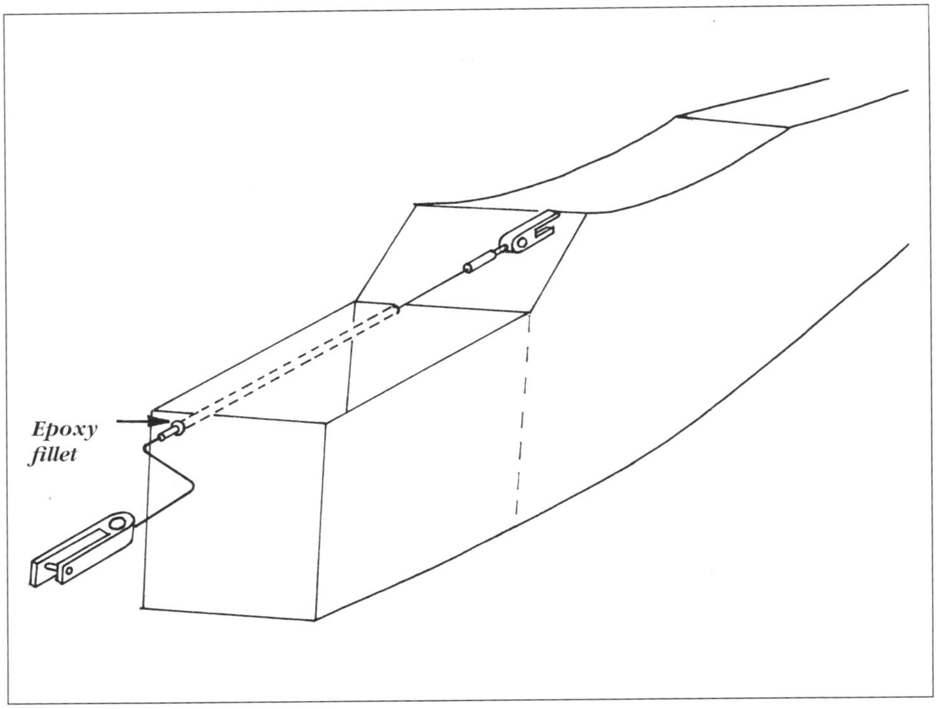

The simplest throttle linkage is a length of very thin (20swg or .85) wire running through a plastic drinking straw or similar tube of about 1/8" (3) diameter to stop it buckling when in compression. A fillet of epoxy is built up around the tube where it emerges through the front bulkhead to prevent ingress of fuel. The two bends in the wire in front of the bulkhead provide a degree of springing which will prevent the servo stalling at full throttle position if the adjustment of the linkage is not quite correct. There is usually insufficient space for adjustment at the engine end and the wire is normally bent back upon itself and epoxied into the nylon clevis. At the servo end it is similary bent back and soldered into a brass adaptor on to which the nylon clevis is fitted.

Treat your radio with respect and it will reward you with trouble-free operation.

Chapter 18

Balancing and Checking the Model

The correct position of the CG will be marked on the plan and it is imperative that your model balances at this position or a little, say ¼ inch (6), in front of it. A slightly nose heavy model responds sluggishly but safely to the controls, but a slightly tail heavy model will over-respond to the controls, and be more difficult to fly. Many beginners try to check the CG by supporting the model under the wing tips. This will not give an accurate indication – the generous dihedral on the average trainer will ensure that the fuselage hangs about level even if the CG is badly out. The easy way is to insert two modelling pins into the underside of the wing at the correct distance from the leading edge, and about ½ inch (12) outside the fuselage. The model is supported by one finger of each hand placed under the pin heads, and should take up a level or slightly nose-down attitude with the fuel tank *empty*. If positioning the pins at the CG would result in their piercing the main wing spars they should be put immediately in front of the spars.

If you find you have to add weight to get the CG correct is should obviously be added as close as possible to the nose or tail. At the nose small pieces of steel or brass can be held by the lower ends of the engine mounting bolts, larger pieces will have to be epoxied and bolted through the side cheeks of the engine cowl.

The writer's first low-wing model made its maiden flight in July 1969 and served seven years of club and display flying. During this time it wore out two engines – hence the unsightly gap behind the spinner. It proved that a reliable radio, a reasonably competent pilot and a modicum of luck, coupled with careful checking and maintenance, can result in a model having a very long life. Its luck finally ran out when it was hit, in mid-air, by a model build and flown (believe it or not) by the writer's son. The contrasting bands of white greatly reduced risk of disorientation in poor visability.

Because there is a greater leverage or moment only small weights are usually required at the tail, and a small bolt with a few washers each side through the fuselage under the rear of the tailplane will usually suffice.

Even experienced modellers tend to forget that the model must be balanced laterally (sideways) as well as longitudinally (lengthways). If the engine's cylinder head is on the centre line of the fuselage and the fin is vertical (which it should be!), the model can be balanced, inverted, on the glowplug and the top of the fin. Because of the weight of the silencer you will probably have to add a little weight to the port wing-tip. A woodscrew or self-tapper of appropriate size usually does the trick.

The secret of success in R/C modelling is always to adopt a policy of "belt, braces and string". In other words to be doubly sure that nothing has been done wrong and that nothing that is avoidable can ever go wrong. So now is the time to check your model and the installation of the controls.

First, check the strength of the structure. You should be able to push quite hard on either side of the top of the fin without undue flexing. Similarly, push quite hard, up and down, on each end of the tailplane. Repeat the above procedure with the rudder and elevator. Then pull quite hard on these control surfaces to ensure the hinges are firmly anchored. Next, support the model with the palms of your hands under, or as near as possible under, the wing tips. Then *jerk* the model upwards. There should be a feeling of rigidity as the wing takes the strain. Then invert the model and do it again. Check the engine and engine mount are firmly bolted in place and check grubscrews on wheel collets etc. Can you hear the clunk weight banging against the sides of the tank when the model is held vertically, engine uppermost, and shaken from side to side?

Finally, check the operation of the controls. Does the rudder move to the *left* when the Tx stick is pushed to the left? Does the elevator move *up* when the elevator stick is pulled back towards the bottom of the Tx? Do these controls move freely over their full range *whatever the position of the Tx trims?* Are the total movements of these controls correct? Does the throttle open fully (or very nearly fully) when the throttle stick is pushed fully forwards towards the top of the Tx, without the servo stalling? Do you get a reasonably slow tickover at closed throttle position?

If, while learning, you do a cartwheel landing or have some other minor mishap, *do not forget to go through all these checks before the next flight.* Similarly, following any major repair, go through them all and range check your radio as well. Discounting pilot error, probably half the crashes that occur on the average club flying field are *avoidable* – it's not bad luck if your elevator servo comes loose in its tray during a power dive, it is bad management. It was probably loosened in a nose-over landing and this would have been spotted in a systematic checkover. Following some mishap it doesn't take long to remove the wing and ensure that the receiver and servos are correctly in place, that all plugs are still firmly in their sockets, and that linkages are still operating freely. But it pays! The writer's low wing model illustrated earlier would never have survived its 1000 or so flights had such precautions not been taken. Each minute spent checking can save an evening repairing!

. . . belt, braces and string.

Chapter 19

The Legal Side

Model aircraft are potentially dangerous and no sensible person flies a R/C model without first arranging for third-party insurance. Many clubs have their own insurance scheme or are affiliated to the BMFA which has an "umbrella" policy but if you are a lone hander insurance can easily be arranged privately. See the magazines for details. Don't, however, think that because you are insured you need no longer be careful. A public park is *not* the place to fly your R/C model, even if such models are not specifically banned by the local byelaws.

Every radio control outfit goes wrong sooner or later, and even your simple trainer could be flying at forty miles per hour going downwind. The propeller will be turning at well over 10,000 revs per minute, and if it hits someone, a child perhaps, the resultant injuries could be appalling.

By the same token, never fly near a road. Even a model gliding down quite slowly with a "dead" engine could be hit by a motorcyclist with horrifying consequences.

Model aircraft are potentially dangerous . . .

Chapter 20

Final Preparations and Armchair Flying

Get a good pair of sunglasses . . .

So now your model is ready, with engine run-in and installed, the radio connected up correctly, and insurance and/or club membership applied for. It's uncanny but this usually signifies the start of a couple of weeks of bad weather! However, time need not be wasted. Apart from taking out your wife and family for a much-needed break and catching up on the garden, you can organise a simple flight box to hold your Tx, fuel, priming bottle, glowplug battery and ammeter, tools, rags or tissues, spare props and glowplugs, wing bands and all the rest.

You can also work out how it's all going to be fitted into the car. Obviously the flight box is heaviest so should go at the front of the boot with the fuselage behind it. Then if you have to jam on the brakes the fuselage won't be crushed. It's quicker to pack it the same way every time and once you have a mental picture of it all in place you'll see at a glance if anything is missing – it's galling to arrive at the flying field after a thirty mile drive only to realise the Tx is still on the workbench!

Get a *good* pair of sunglasses and always keep them in the car or in the flight box. If your club has a frequency control system that requires a numbered clothespeg get this ready as well. Get a 15" (375) length of ribbon about 1" (24) wide and fix one end to the top of your Tx aerial to act as a "windsock". If your outfit operates on 27 Mhz its colour should correspond to the frequency in use. If it's on 35 Mhz then, under international convention, it should be orange.

During the waiting period you can also find a deserted spot and range-check the radio. You'll need a helper to do this. Leave him with the Tx and explain he must extend the aerial fully and switch on when he sees you signal you are ready. Then he should slowly go through the sequence of left rudder, right rudder, up elevator, down elevator, holding each position for a second or so and repeating the whole sequence until you signify with a different signal that all is OK. If you have more than one set of crystals show him how to change the one in the Tx and take the Rx ones with you. Write down the order in which the crystals should be tested and take a copy to avoid confusion.

When you get to the flying field your instructor will be more than a little impressed that you have done all the groundwork and the model is actually ready to fly. Don't be upset if he wants to check the model for himself, as he probably will. He will be taking on the responsibility of getting it into the air and bringing it safely down again, so bear with him while he is checking things you know to be right, and be grateful that you have found someone prepared to be so careful.

Your instructor will trim the model for you so that it flies straight and level with both sticks at neutral. Once this is done the rudder trim will be left alone, but elevator trim has to be adjusted several times during each flight to maintain the correct height. Usually a certain amount of "up" trim is used for take off, and as the flight progresses this has to be taken out to compensate for the slight rearwards shift of the CG as the fuel is used up. So you'll need to be able to find and adjust the elevator trim with your thumb without taking your eyes off the model. This requires a little practice - now's the time to do it. Any more spare time can very usefully be employed pretending to fly the model indoors at home.

"Armchair flying" as this is called requires the assistance of a very patient helper, who must appreciate that left rudder turns the model to the left and that up elevator makes it climb, and vice versa. If you can explain to him very briefly why these things happen he is much more likely to remember them, and it is very important that he has a clear understanding of the effect of the controls because he will be tilting and tipping and rotating the model to simulate their effect, while you sit in your chair "flying" the model. You should also explain to him how the model can be made to stall.

Initially he holds the model 6 feet (2 metres) or so away with the tail pointing at you and tells you what manoeuvres to do. When he demands "turn left" you and he should expect to see the rudder move a little to the left and the elevator rise slightly to prevent the nose dropping in the turn. He then banks and rotates the model to simulate the turn.

In the early stages you will be teaching him – if you "forget" to signal a little up elevator in the turn he should allow the nose to drop progressively and lower the model as it rotates. Similarly if you "forget" to neutralise the elevator when he says "finish turning" he should slowly raise the model and point the nose upwards until it's climbing at about 30 degrees, and then suddenly push it down into a 45 degree dive to simulate a stall. You will be facing "upwind" and therefore sitting at the "downwind" end of the room and it's worth moving your chair to one end of the room and shifting the other furniture out of the way so that he can walk with the model as it "flies" the way it is pointing. You must avoid flying him into a wall!

He should walk very slowly when going upwind and rather quicker when going downwind to simulate the real thing. When you "stall" the model he should stop walking and lower it quite quickly towards the floor, keeping the nose pointing downwards until he sees up elevator applied. He can then correct the dive and raise the model slowly as you "climb" gently back to the correct height.

When you have taught your patient helper how to "fly" your model correctly round the room he can start telling you what to do. At this stage it is better to forget about left and right, he should tell you to fly "upwind" or "downwind" or "towards the window" or "towards the door" or whatever. You may find it helpful to imagine yourself actually in the model, so that if it is flying towards you and he instructs "fly towards the door", which is on your right, you will mentally look out of the cabin window towards the door, which would then be on your left, and correctly give left rudder. Sooner or later you're bound to give the wrong signal when the model is coming towards you; he'll continue turning and banking the model more and more while you signal more and more incorrect rudder, until he finally pushes the nose of the model into the carpet and tells you you've crashed.

All this can get quite hilarious and if your wife happens to come into the room she'll probably conclude you've both gone stark raving mad, but this "armchair flying" really is time very well spent. You can simulate take offs and landings and engine failures, and your helper will get a good deal of pleasure watching you trying to correct a gentle dive while he continues to lower the model towards the floor.

Now is the time also to learn that golden rule of power flying – *if you get into real trouble throttle back immediately.*

Things will then slow down and you may then be able to get the model pointing into wind. If this happens on the flying field just keep it pointing into wind and let it land itself. You'll probably do far more damage in the early stages if you try to use the elevator than if you leave it strictly alone.

Having exhausted your helper there is now nothing more you can do but wait patiently for the great day, ensuring that your gear is fully charged the night before.

This is a reproduction of the plan of "Solo", a simple and utterly practical 72 inch (1800) span trainer from the R/C Model World Plans Service.

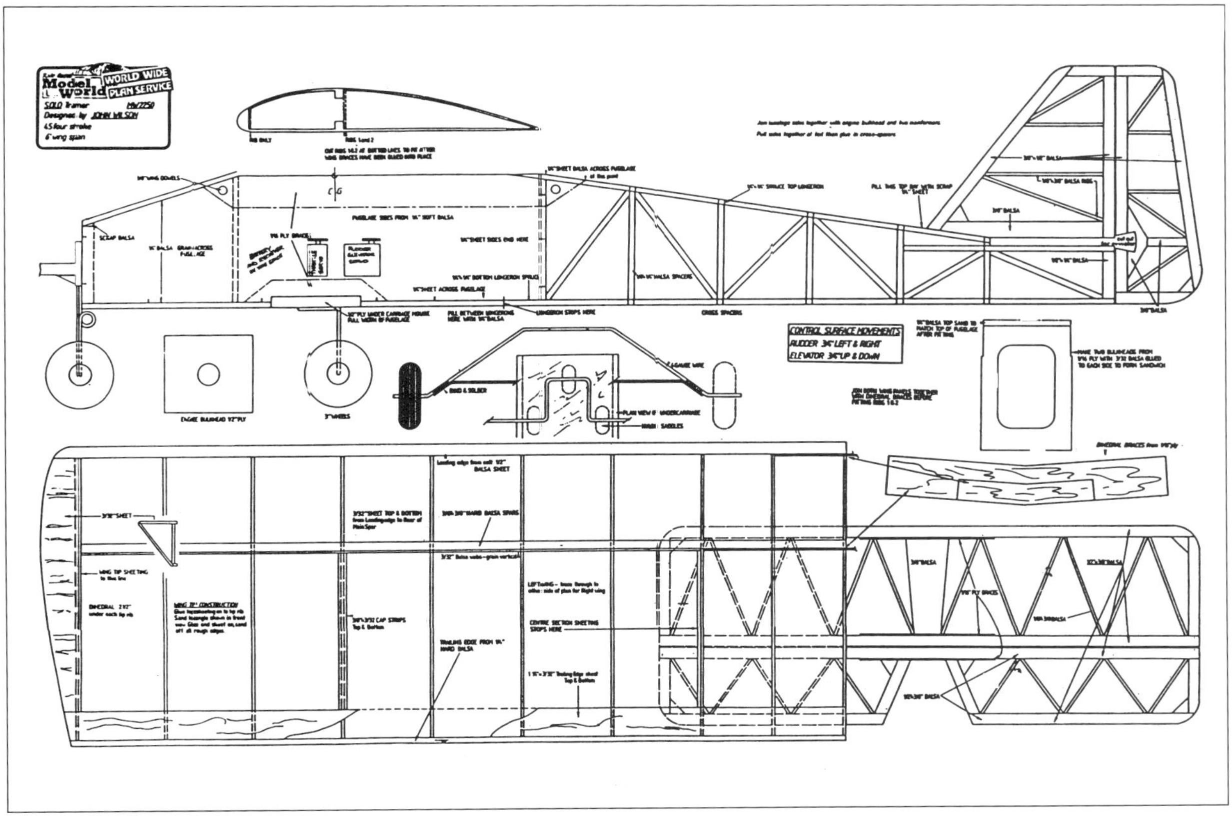

Chapter 21

Learning Solo with a Power Model

The best advice for anyone intent on learning to fly solo is, of course, "DON'T". However, there are those who, because of unusual working hours or geographical location, simply cannot get help. If you belong to this category, read on. If you don't, but want to learn on your own because of pride or prejudice or because the nearest R/C club is forty miles away, read on also. You are intent on ignoring the most important advice this book has to offer, and we may yet be able to persuade you to learn an easier way.

"Expert" is an overworked word, but having taught, or helped to teach, between 50 and 100 beginners the writer *can* claim to be a fairly expert tutor. But neither he nor anyone else can claim to be expert at learning solo, because this is something you can only do once! Nevertheless most lessons learned in teaching others apply to the solo learner, and will greatly help to reduce the risk of a bad prang in the early stages.

Despite the title of this chapter much of what follows applies to soarers, and potential soaring enthusiasts are asked to please read right through it all, though they can, of course, ignore any references to engines, sidethrust, downthrust etc. More detailed advice for "the silent brigade" follows later. First we must recap on some points made previously, emphasising those that become doubly important to the solo learner, and introduce a few new ones:

1. The first flight will be a test both for the model and for you. You will be taking the place of the test pilot yet trying to teach yourself to fly at the same time. The model can only be tested in the air, but you can be tested on the ground. If you've had two or three hours armchair flying you should be able to find and adjust the trim controls on the Tx without looking for them. If you are armchair flying the model towards you and your helper tips it off course you should be able to move the rudder in the correct direction to get it back on course ten times out of ten. If you can't, bribe your helper with beer or chocolates as appropriate and go on armchair flying until you can. It's plain stupid to risk your model in the air when so much learning can be done on the ground.

2. Checking the model is even more important, particularly the engine's needle valve setting at full throttle and at its idling speed. With the tank full you should

. . . hold the model pointing vertically upwards . . .

have the needle valve set just a little bit leaner than when you get that very occasional falter back to four-stroking mentioned earlier. With this same needle valve setting hold the model with its nose pointing vertically upwards for ten seconds. It will lean out and speed up considerably but should maintain its new speed without any signs of tightening up and slowing down. If it slows it still hasn't had enough running in. If you later find that this setting doesn't produce enough power for a safe steady climb after take-off you'll need to set the engine a little leaner. Be sure to repeat the "nose pointing vertically upwards for ten seconds" test at this new setting. With the tank a third full and the throttle trim in mid position the idle should be slow enough to prevent the model moving forward on a reasonably smooth paved surface. When you come into land the last thing you want is the engine going so fast that the model barely loses height and floats along way past you. It's better to risk the engine stopping altogether than to be faced with this situation. Oh, and make sure the prop isn't fitted back-to-front!

3. Remember your model is safe at a good height in the sky, so long as it is upwind of you. It is potentially at risk anywhere near the ground and *always at risk when downwind*. The only time it should be allowed downwind is when practicing or flying the landing approach.

4. Bear in mind that there is always a wind gradient, i.e. a wind held back to 10 mph by ground friction could be blowing at 15 mph only 20 feet (6 metres) up, and at 20 mph at, say, 200 feet (60 metres) up. If you give a wrong rudder signal or merely have a mental seizure and do nothing when the model is upwind it will almost always turn or drift back towards you. Do it downwind and you're half way to a "flyaway", even if you chop the throttle. Under power it's even worse. If the model has a full throttle speed in still air of 30 mph (this is probably typical for a trainer) and is flying downwind from you in a 20 mph wind, it will be going away at 50 mph, or very nearly 25 yards (22½ metres) every *second*. Since it takes between 5 and 10 seconds to do the sort of safe gentle turn you will be aiming at, it's going to be a long, long way away before you've turned it back, and it will take a long time to *get back* because its speed over the ground will only be 10 mph.

5. Modellers have evolved basic circuits or flight patterns to minimise the dangers of too little height or a downwind position. So, of course, did their fullsize counterparts many years before them. By following these circuits and flying the model in a disciplined rather than a haphazard manner the dangers will be greatly reduced, and the model will be better positioned to be landed safely should the engine fail. The first flight will comprise three phases and the circuits are rather different in each phase as explained below. The three phases are:

- (a) A climbing phase which will last until the model has reached a safe height, usually regarded as about 200 feet (60 metres). During this phase you will be flying oblong circuits with 180 degree turns at the upwind and downwind ends of each circuit. The model must be kept upwind of you throughout this phase, and you'll probably need two or three complete circuits before safe height is reached.
- (b) A testing phase to establish whether the engine's sidethrust and downthrust are correct, and also to establish the settings of the rudder and elevator trim controls to achieve a straight safe glide. During the tests the same oblong circuits should again be flown, with the upwind leg directly away from you, so that you can best observe the model's reaction to these tests. When tests have been completed you should change to box pattern or rectangular circuits with 90 degree turns at each corner. Throughout this phase the model is again kept upwind of you at all times.
- (c) A landing preparation phase during which the rectangular circuits are extended so that, for the first time, the model is allowed to get a little downwind from you. When you have flown two or three of these extended circuits the engine is throttled back, and this final circuit leads you into the landing approach. The landing, like the take-off, should be made directly into wind.

6. You'll need a helper, not just to release or launch the

model, but also to move the Tx trims if these prove to be badly out while the model is still too low for you to take your thumbs off the sticks with safety. Teach him or her what each trim does, and stick temporary labels on the Tx in case he or she forgets. Explain that "a little" means move the trim about 1/16 inch(1.5), and a lot means 3/16 inch (4.5). Your helper will also need pencil and notebook to record what happens when you make the tests referred to earlier. Make no mistake – after the excitement of the first flight you just won't be able to remember, and hard-earned information will have to be obtained again on another flight.

7. You'll find the model will climb away quickest if you can get the elevator trim correct. You'll almost certainly over react if you try to adjust the angle of climb with the elevator stick. Every unnecessary movement on the stick wastes energy (the model's, not yours!) and costs height.

8. Most modellers find left-hand circuits easier than right-hand ones, and, as explained previously, you'll need to hold in a little less up elevator to maintain height in the turns. You are less likely to give a wrong signal if *all* turns are to the left, since you will need to move the stick in the same direction to increase the angle of bank every time, and will need to move it in the same opposite direction to decrease it.

9. During the first flight you should only use the elevator to maintain height during turns, to take any corrective action after the glide tests, and to "flare out" for landing. For the rest of the flight you should use the elevator *trim* to gain, maintain or lose height. The engine (providing it's the right size) should be flown at full throttle throughout the flight except, of course, during the glide test, until you throttle back in preparation for the landing.

10. You must learn to recognise the correct attitude and behaviour of the model as it climbs to gain height, particularly during the climb out after launch or take-off. If there is insufficient up trim she will fly steadily and fast, getting smaller and smaller as she flies away from you, but won't be at a safe height before you are forced to make the first turn. If you have the correct climbing angle she will still be moving purposefully through the air but steadily gaining height at the same time. She will need only occasional minor corrections with the rudder to keep on course. If you have too much up trim she will no longer fly purposefully but will be waffling about in a nose-up attitude, very much at the mercy of the wind. You'll find she's being blown off course, first to one side then the other, and virtually continuous corrections with the rudder are necessary. In this attitude she will be uncomfortably close to stalling and will hardly be gaining any height at all.

You must hold in a little (say 1/8 inch (3)) down elevator on the stick until your helper has moved the trim about 1/16 inch (1.5) in the same direction.

11. Similarly you will need to establish the correct glide angle with the engine at low throttle. In this situation the model should settle into a slightly nose-down attitude, flying at about three quarters the full throttle speed, losing height steadily but not steeply and without increasing speed. If the speed seems to be getting faster or the descent quicker you obviously need a little more up trim. Too much up trim will result in that same lack of purpose as in the climb – the model being at the mercy of the wind and requiring constant work with the rudder to keep her on course. *Your first landing is doomed to failure if you have the model trimmed in this way.*

12. You will probably find that no great alteration to the trim controls is required to get a safe, straight glide. But knowing what action you'll have to take will help enormously should the engine cut prematurely during the flight. (Get your helper therefore to record the correct glide trim positions, e.g. rudder 1/8 inch (3) right of centre, elevator 3/16 inch (4.5) towards bottom of Tx.

13. You must appreciate that it is quite easy to concentrate so hard on the model in the air that you can lose your bearings on the ground, and not realise that she is getting too low or is in the wrong part of the sky. This comes as a surprise to many beginners and the writer fell into this trap hook, line and sinker. His first power model was badly out of trim, trying very hard to turn one way all the time, and what had at first been a slight tendency to stall was becoming a positive determination to do so as the fuel level dropped and the CG moved rearwards. Transmitters didn't have trim controls in those days, nor (on this particular radio) could more than one signal be given at a time. Consequently the "flight" which had lasted for perhaps five or ten minutes, was rapidly becoming nothing more than one crisis after another. With no means of throttling back the ultimate end was probably inevitable but was hastened by the writer's over-intense concentration on the model. He had forgot-

Your first landing is doomed to failure . . .

ten upwind, downwind, height and everything else, his whole attention being concentrated on trying to cure the stall and the turn. *No-one* could have been more surprised than he when an enormous area of concrete suddenly came up from below and smashed the model to pieces!

Make a habit therefore of taking your eyes off your model and glancing down at the ground to collect your bearings every thirty seconds or so, and more often during the landing approach. Make a point also of memorising the features of the upwind skyline, so you can instantly identify the "safe" part of the sky, and of the downwind skyline, so that you will at least know when you are in trouble!

14. You will have to teach yourself to time the last turn before landing so that she comes out of the turn at about 30 feet (9 metres) high. On a calm day she should then be about 75 yards (70 metres) away, in a light wind probably no more than 50 yards(45 metres). Ideally the model should touch down before she reaches you, for there is a real risk of you becoming disorientated if you have to turn quickly to follow the model as she glides past. Should you find yourself in this situation it's better to leave the sticks alone and let her glide in on her own. You should only use the elevator in an attempt to flare out if the model is close enough for you to observe its reactions instantly. If in doubt leave the elevator alone at this stage.

15. You must appreciate that during the first flight, and during the next few flights at least, it will be easier to make the landing approach with the engine throttled right back. Later on you can open the throttle a little to

Side view of the ideal climb pattern for the first flight. If it becomes apparent that model will not have climbed at least 50 feet (15 metres or 2 houses) before the first turn becomes necessary it is better to throttle back and land. The model gains more height on the upwind legs because these take longer to fly. The model is turned back into wind well before it reaches the pilot, who should not have to look upwards at more than, say, 60°.

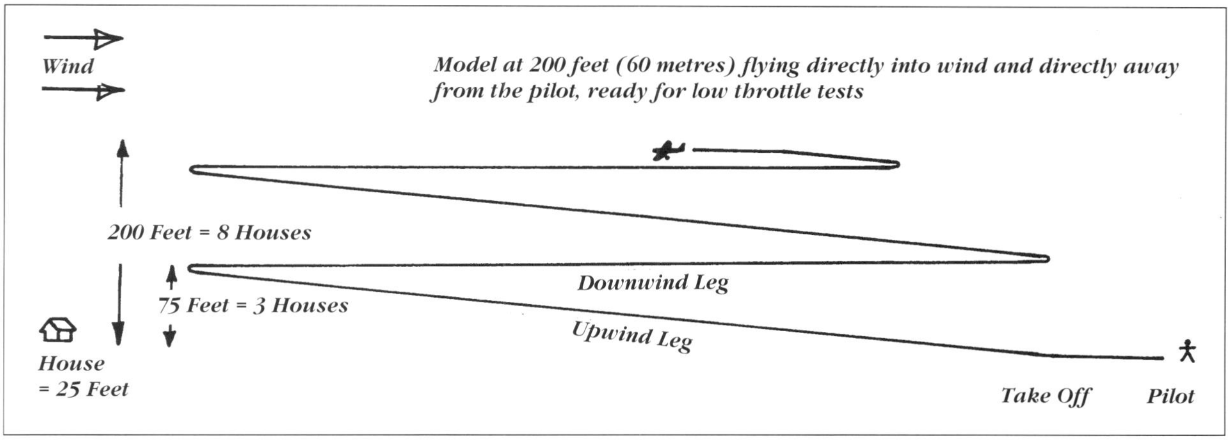

Plan view of the same pattern. The upwind legs are flown directly away from the pilot so that the effects of throttling back and adjusting trims to compensate can best be seen. The distance to the first turn is a compromise depending on the pilot's eyesight at distance and the speed at which the model is gaining height. The distance between the upwind and downwind legs is not critical though the less distance the better. It is determined by the diameter of a 180° turn flown in a gentle but purposeful manner with the wing banked over at about 20° from the horizontal.
Should the engine cut during the low throttle tests the circuit is shortened as shown dotted to turn downwind. The model is turned back into wind so that it is (ideally) heading directly away from the pilot and about 30 feet (9 metres or "a house and a bit") high as it comes out of the turn. The glide is then continued directly into wind, no attempt being made to "flare out" unless the model is still reasonably close to the pilot.

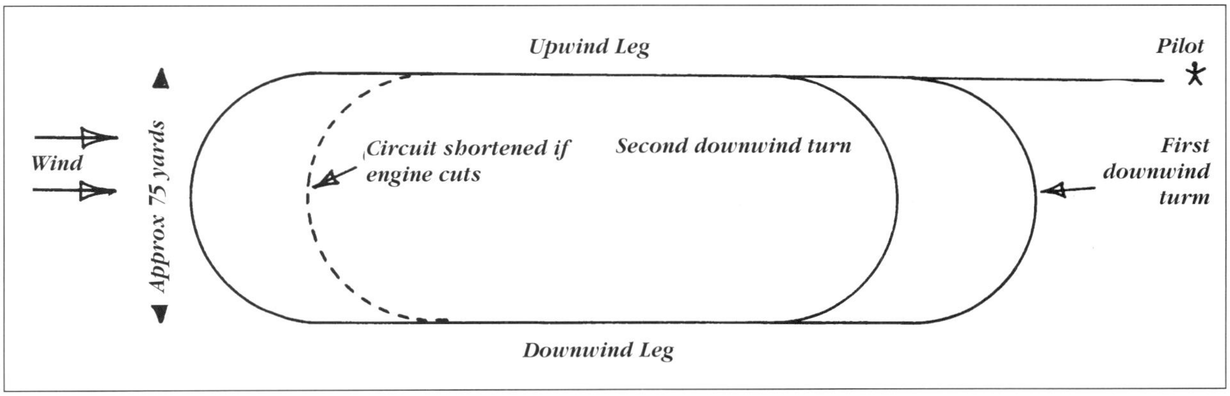

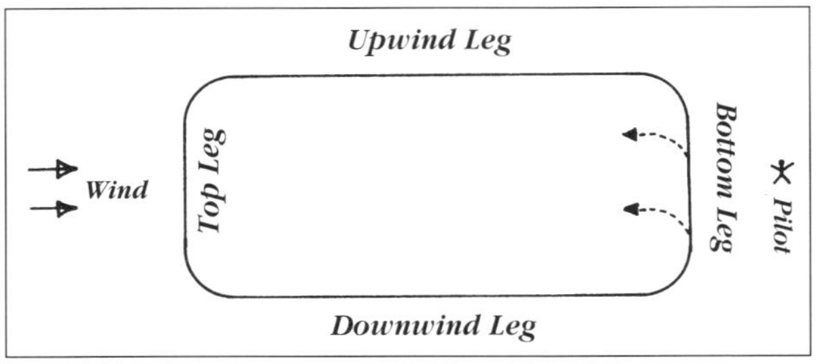

Drawn to about half the scale of the climb pattern drawing, this diagram shows the rectangular pattern than can be commenced once low throttle tests have been completed and the model trimmed for level flight. The distance to the top leg and the distance between the upwind and the downwind legs should be well within the maximum at which the pilot is still mentally "with" the model. After a few circuits, as confidence is gained, the distance to the top leg can usually be increased. If you are getting mentally tired at this stage, it is better to cut the throttle at the end of the top leg, and glide the model in to land on the same pattern, making the final 90° turn into wind wherever appropriate, as shown dotted. If, on the other hand, you are beginning to feel confident, and are able to fly the pattern reasonably accurately, you can extend the circuit so that the model flys a little downwind as shown in the next column.

maintain height if the model seems to be getting too low. But on your first and early flights it's better to leave the glide undisturbed and shorten or extend the approach circuit to get the model in the right position at the right height.

16. The site should be the biggest and most deserted open area you can find, devoid of nearby trees, overhead power lines and other hazards. The nearest house should preferably be 500 yards (450 metres) away. There should be little or no wind and plenty of daylight left (for you to search for the model if you have a flyaway). You should be armed with sunspecs for flying and gumboots and a powerful torch for searching!

17. The above may sound a bit depressing, so be encouraged by the thought that you are unlikely to damage a suitable model badly if you use the throttle to prevent a cross-wind take off or to abort the flight if the model misbehaves badly during the initial climbout. You'll also be a little unlucky to damage it badly providing you never forget the golden rule that if you get into

This is the ideal extended rectangular pattern, in which the model is allowed downwind from the pilot for the first time. The ideal landing circuit will follow this pattern, and the final turn into wind can be made anywhere along the bottom leg as shown dotted – it is more important to come out of the final turn at the correct height and directly into wind than it is to have the model heading directly towards the pilot.

bad trouble once it's up in the air – cut the throttle and leave the sticks alone.

Let's now clearly establish the objects of, and the actions to be taken, during the ideal first flight. (We'll go into the actions to be taken when it doesn't prove ideal later!)

- (a) to get it into the air to prove that, after all your efforts, it does actually fly!
- (b) to climb into wind to the safest possible height (consistent with visibility) before making the first wide, gentle 180 degree turn;
- (c) to fly the downwind leg and complete the second 180 degree turn well before the model gets downwind from you;
- (d) to continue these oval circuits until the model is about 200 feet (60 metres) high;
- (e) to chop the throttle back on an upwind leg at this height to observe and record the model's reaction, and to establish and record the position of the trim controls that will give a safe, straight, purposeful glide. As mentioned earlier this latter information will be invaluable should the engine cut unexpectedly;

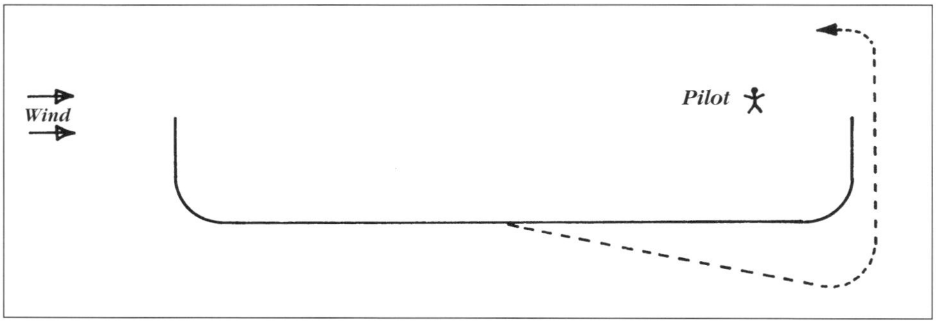

If it is obvious that the model is too high the landing circuit can be extended away from the pilot and a little downwind, as shown dotted, to lose more height.

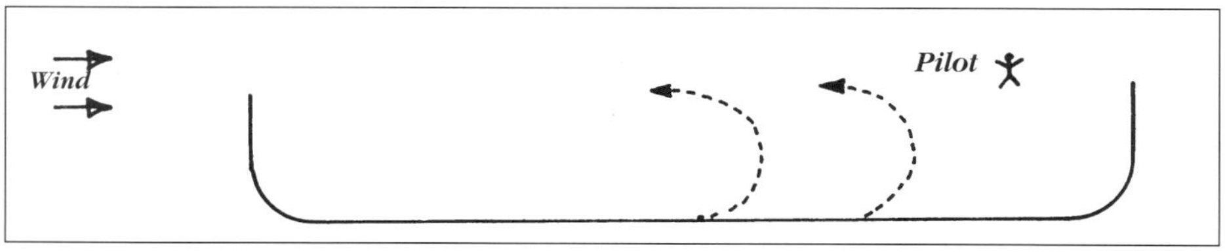

If the model is too low then makes a 180° turn into wind aiming to have about 30 feet (9 metres) of height at the end of the turn.

- (f) to get back to 200 feet (60 metres) and change to a rectangular circuit, i.e. with 90 degree turns at each corner not 180 degree turns at each end, learning to judge the start of the turn out of the downwind leg so that, as it flies crosswind, you are looking upwards at no more than about 60 degrees. It's easy to get disorientated if you have to crane your neck because the model is almost overhead;
- (g) to extend this circuit so that the model gets 50-75 yards (45-70 metres) (no more) downwind as it will do on the landing approach;
- (h) to fly this extended circuit a few times (your concentration permitting) still at full throttle, learning to judge the turn out of the downwind leg so that you get this distance as near as possible correct every time;
- (i) to fly it again at lower throttle openings so you become familiar with the model's behaviour in this state, learning to adjust the elevator trim if necessary to maintain safe purposeful flight as power is reduced;
- (j) to turn one of these circuits into the landing approach before the engine runs out of fuel and does it for you! The ideal position to start the landing approach is 200 feet (60 metres) up at the start of the downwind leg;
- (k) to reduce gradually the throttle opening during this downwind leg to give a steady even descent so that the model passes you at about 100 feet (30 metres) with the throttle fully closed;
- (l) to make the last two 90 degree turns so that the model is heading straight back towards you, and directly into wind, about 30 feet (9 metres) high and as close to the ideal position as possible (50 yards (45 metres) away in a light wind, 75 yards (70 metres) in a dead calm);
- (m) to let it glide in straight towards you, only using the elevator to flare out if the model is close enough (say within 30 yards (27 metres)) for its reaction to be clearly and readily seen.

That was the ideal first flight. Let's now go through it all again for real (bearing in mind that no solo first flight was ever ideal), and dealing with the pilot's problems as and when they occur. We'll assume your site has a take-off area. You and your helper are at the downwind end of this, all necessary tests have been made, the model is resting on its undercarriage, engine at low throttle, and your helper is stooping down restraining the model with one hand in front of each side of the tailplane.

Emphasise to your helper that he must *not* release the model until you shout "OK", and when he does so he should move his hands quickly forwards and upwards out of the way so that the model's natural attitude on its undercarriage is not disturbed. He should then move away sideways, so as not to obstruct your view, and quickly come to your side to adjust the Tx trims if necessary. Emphasise also that this will not necessarily be the first flight – if something drastic goes wrong you will cut the throttle and abort. This should impress him a little and will help give you a little much-needed confidence!

Test rudder and elevator controls, check all trims are at neutral. Open the throttle fully and test them again. This is standard practice for beginner and expert alike. Use the ribbon on your Tx aerial as a windsock to check the model is pointing exactly into wind. Memorise the upwind and downwind skylines. If all is well, shout "OK".

The model gathers speed and a little rudder correction will probably be necessary. If it turns badly off course chop the throttle. Bend or adjust the noseleg and try again. As it accelerates the engine will speed up and rudder control will become more definite. If it adopts a nose-down attitude, seeming to be in danger of nosing in, hold in a little (1/16 inch to 1/8 inch [1.5 to 3]) up elevator. Keep it on course directly into wind. After about 30 yards (27 metres) it will have reached flying speed and may have bounced into the air. If not, apply a quick touch of up elevator and return the stick to its previous position. She's airborne! Use the rudder to keep the wing level and to correct any tendency to turn away from the wind. Be ready to apply a quick touch of down elevator if the nose starts to get too high. She's climbing away into wind and you, yes you, are in control!

At this exciting stage we must unfortunately break off and assume you don't have a take-off area so that hand launching is essential. The model should be launched into wind, with the wing level and into level flight. The speed must be above its flying speed. This is no easy task and unless your helper has experience in launching R/C models he'd better read this paragraph. It is essential that the model is kept level throughout the launch – it's no earthly use swinging your arm back so that its nose is

. . . the last thing you want is the model directly overhead . . .

pointing upwards and then swinging your arm forwards, hoping the model will be about level when you let go. Your hand must be level with, or a little above, your shoulder from the time your arm is drawn right back until it is extended fully forward and the model is released. Practice with the model in slow motion, ensuring it stays level all the time. Then practice outside with a 6 foot (1800) bamboo cane – if it leaves your hand nose up your technique is wrong.

We have said before that fuselages become oily and this presents an additional hazard – the model can slip in your hand and change its attitude as you heave it forward. You daren't grip it *too* tight for fear of damaging the structure, and its best to contact cement some sandpaper to the sides of the fuselage where your hand grip will be. The sandpaper should be 3 or 4 inches (75 or 100) behind the CG because you'll be pushing below the CG and below the centre of drag, both of which will tend to make the nose rise.

As well as heaving the model forward you should also be running forward – that extra 10 mph could make all the difference. Practice again with the bamboo cane, running this time. When you have got it right, and the cane leaves your hand fast and level *every* time, you are ready to launch the model. If you are right-handed you should position your run so that you pass about 10 feet (3 metres) away from the pilot, on his left. Run forwards with your arm drawn fully back, checking the model's attitude, and when you are a few yards in front of the pilot give the model a straight, hard heave, releasing it just before your arm is fully extended forward. As far as he is concerned the more speed you can give the model the better, but a controlled launch just above flying speed is infinitely better than a wild fling in a nose up attitude twice as fast. As soon as the model is released you should move away to your left (so that you don't obstruct the pilot's view) and then quickly get alongside him to give any help that he requires. Now back to the pilot, who has the model finally climbing into wind.

If the climb seems sluggish you need to find out quickly whether you lack engine power. Ease in a little more up elevator and watch the model closely. If it adopts a more nose up attitude but still fails to climb you do. Chop the throttle, get the nose down and just let her glide in, using the rudder to keep her into wind. Set the throttle a little bit leaner, repeat the "nose vertically upwards for 10 seconds' test, and start again. If she continues to progress purposefully and gains height more quickly you have enough power.

Get your helper to put in a little up trim and take your thumb momentarily off the elevator stick. Adjust the trim further as necessary. Keep her flying away from you, directly into wind, until you have enough height to start that first 180 degree turn. 50 feet (15 metres or two houses) is minimal, 100 feet (30 metres) ideal. You know what to do – ease in a little left rudder until she's banked over to about 20 degrees. Don't move the elevator stick more than you have to – you shouldn't aim to gain much height during this first turn, be content that the nose isn't dropping. But watch the angle of the wing all the time and apply more or less rudder as required to keep it at 20 degrees from level. If things go badly wrong and the turn gets tighter and tighter she'll start to lose height. The worst thing you can do is to put in up elevator, you won't stop her losing height, you'll just make the turn worse. Back to the golden rule – chop the throttle and let go of the sticks. When she's very nearly completed the 180 degrees, and therefore very nearly heading downwind, release the rudder and she'll straighten out. Aren't you glad you built a safe, stable trainer?

Now she's coming downwind the ground speed will be higher, and it won't be long before you must start the second turn. Start it sooner rather than later, the last thing you want is the model directly overhead. You won't be able to judge the angle of bank nor see if she's gaining or losing height.

When you've got her going back once more into wind you can relax a little, and adjust the rudder trim so she flies straight with the minimum action on your part. You'll still need occasional corrections with the rudder – no trainer will keep exactly into wind indefinitely – but again, if you have to apply almost continuous corrections she has too much up trim. Ease in a little down trim and she'll speed up and gain more purpose. When the trims are finally sorted out you'll find that the upwind leg is the one that gains most height, the downwind leg seems to take so little time that you're turning out of it before any real gain can be noticed.

If you've got this far you can congratulate yourself – you may not yet know very much about flying, but as a builder and test pilot you're doing fine! All you now have to do is to repeat this oval circuit until she's about 200 feet (60 metres) high. Then you can ease in a little down trim and do one circuit at a constant height. Now she's no longer climbing the speed will increase, and both elevator and rudder will become slightly more sensitive than before.

When she's completed this circuit get her exactly into wind, warn your helper to be ready with pencil and notebook, and chop the throttle. Watch the model closely and call out what you see. "She's turning left and diving steeply" or whatever. As soon as results have been established you can go back to full throttle, take any corrective action and get back into the circuit. Don't try to analyse your findings at this stage, just make sure they are recorded. When she's once more back at about 200 feet (60 metres) and on the upwind leg you can chop the throttle a second time and move the trims to establish their safe glide positions. Yell out "rudder trim ⅛ inch (or 3) right of central, elevator 3/16 inch (or 4.5) towards bottom of case", or whatever. Technically elevator trim is 3/16 inch (4.5) "up" but this could cause confusion. At this stage it's better to be safe than pedantic.

Make sure that these, again, are recorded. Now you really *can* relax, because should the engine cut you will be able to get the trim positions approximately correct for a safe glide in the minimum possible time.

You can now change to the rectangular circuit. On a calm day the turns will be 90 degrees at each corner, but if there's a bit of wind the turn out of the upwind leg need only be about 80 degrees, because the model will drift downwind towards you on the crosswind leg. More important, the turn out of the downwind leg needs to be more like 100 degrees than 90 degrees, again to allow for drift. Don't expect to get a precise rectangular circuit at your first attempt – it's easy to draw on paper, much more difficult to fly in the air! If you find she's struggling on the upwind leg, tending to drift off course all the time, ease in a little more down trim. Remember, you are using up fuel and that invisible but very important CG is moving backwards all the time.

After two or three rectangular circuits you are now ready for the landing preparation phase in which the model is allowed for the first time to get downwind of you. Bearing in mind that on a calm day the distance it is allowed to go should never exceed 75 yards (70 metres) you can start the turn out of the downwind leg almost as soon as she passes you. If there's a bit of wind you may even have to start the turn earlier. Always remember that when she's flying crosswind at the downwind end of the circuit she will be drifting away at the speed of the wind. So make that turn out of the downwind leg more than 90 degrees.

You may not realise it but by now you will be getting mentally very tired – although your legs may feel like jelly and your pulse rate may be too high for comfort it's the poor old brain that needs a rest most of all. Make a conscious effort to relax and don't forget to glance down at the ground frequently to get your bearings.

You can now throttle back in preparation for the landing approach. Don't panic, this will be another circuit just like the ones you have already flown. The only difference is that you'll throttle back progressively to lose height during the downwind leg, and have the throttle fully closed as she passes you at about 100 feet (30 metres). Adjust the trims if necessary as soon as possible after closing the throttle. If she appears to be too high for the ideal approach you can let her go a little further downwind, do a 90 degree turn, let her lose a little more height on the crosswind leg, and then finally turn her into wind. If, as happens more often, there seems to be no height to spare, you can combine the two 90 degree turns into one of 180 degrees to get her into wind more quickly. She should now be about 30 feet (9 metres) high, and the worst thing you can do is to let the nose get too high and/or the airspeed too low so that she loses that purposeful glide. Don't worry if the engine cuts, now you're committed to landing it won't be helping anyway. Just keep her into wind, steadily losing height. Providing she's sufficiently near, you can progressively ease in a *little* up elevator to flare out, starting when she's about 10 feet (3 metres) high. Don't overdo it. She'll come to less harm gliding in without any elevator correction than if you make a perfect "landing" 6 feet (2 metres) up, followed by a stall. Suddenly you realise she's on the ground. She's down! She's down in one piece! The sense of pride and elation is absolutely unbelievable!

Have a rest, have a drink (providing someone else is driving!), have a smoke, have lunch or tea or whatever, but above all relax. You deserve to. On no account try to fly again for half an hour at least. Let your brain and your body decide when the next flight shall be. If you feel inclined to pack up and call it a day, do so. You'll be taking the model home in one piece, and that's what matters most of all. Just make sure you thank your patient helper and keep his notebook.

Before the second flight you should adjust the sidethrust and downthrust so that straight level flight at full throttle becomes a straight safe glide when the throttle is cut, and adjust rudder and elevator linkages so that the trim controls on the Tx are approximately central when this pleasant state of affairs is achieved. This is best done in the peace and quiet of the workshop, where the necessary equipment is readily to hand – another excuse for going home after the trauma of the first flight!

Let's deal with the engine's thrustline first. What happened when you cut the throttle? You've forgotten already! Happily the notebook records that the model turned to the left and started gliding too steeply. So the engine had been pulling the model to the right and pulling the nose up. Pulling the model to the right meant it had too much sidethrust, so this needs to be reduced a little. Pulling the nose up means it had too little downthrust, so this should be increased a little.

If your engine is mounted on a paxolin plate you may have to enlarge the bolt holes in the paxolin a little so that the engine can be straightened by, say, 1 degree. At the same time a couple of 6 BA washers must be introduced between the engine mounting lugs on the crankcase and the paxolin plate around the rear two bolts only. This will increase the downthrust a little. If your engine is fixed to a preformed engine mount bolted to the front bulkhead you may have to withdraw these bolts and introduce washers as appropriate. But it's better to get the thrust line correct by moving the engine in relation to its mount if you possibly can.

Next you can adjust the linkages so that the trim levers are central when the model is in its correct glide trim. Back to the notebook. It tells you that for a straight, safe glide the rudder trim lever was ⅛ inch (3) right of central and the elevator trim lever was $^3/_{16}$ inch (4.5) towards the bottom of the Tx case. So put the fuselage on the bench, switch on and put the trims in these positions. Lay a straight edge against one side of the fin and measure and record the position of the trailing edge of the rudder. It could be, say, ⅛ inch (3) right of neutral. It may not look correct but this was its position to give a straight glide. So disconnect the clevis from the rudder horn, screw it in two or three turns if the horn is on the right of the rudder (screw it out if the horn is on the rudder's left), and reconnect the clevis. Then centralise the trim lever on the Tx. Following this adjustment the rudder should again be at its correct glide position. It probably won't be and further adjustment is usually needed. Don't forget that the clevis has to be screwed onto the threaded end of the metal rod or cable adaptor for at least ⅛ inch (3) for safety. If these adjustments leave you with less than this you'll have to bend the metal rod or re-solder the cable adaptor as appropriate. Don't forget – belt, braces and string!

The linkage to the elevator is treated in a similar fashion. With a straight edge measure and record the deflection at the trailing edge of the elevator. It could be about ⅛ inch (3) above neutral. This again was the position proved in flight to give the correct gliding angle, and you can similarly adjust the linkage so that the elevator is in its flight proved position when the trim control is in the centre of its slot. This, however, is not the ideal answer – the fact that the model only glides correctly with a little up elevator indicates that either the CG is a little too far forward and/or that the wing has fractionally less incidence than it should. The opposite (CG too far back or wing with fractionally too much incidence) would apply if a little down elevator were needed for a safe glide. If the elevator needs only to be $^1/_{16}$ inch or ⅛ inch (1.5 or 3) out of neutral you can safely take the easy way out and adjust the linkage. Being a slow-flying, inherently stable trainer it

The Hawk 70 (70"-1750 span) proved to be a near-perfect first low-wing model when powered by a 40 engine, being exceptionally easy to fly with excellent low-speed handling due to the "washout" which a careful study of the picture will reveal. The same engine can be transferred to a fully aerobatic model of about 50" (1250) wingspan when the Hawk's potential for training has been fully exploited. (Photograph: Skyway Models).

will forgive you curing the symptom rather than the cause, whereas a high speed aerobatic model would show its displeasure by being distinctly unpleasant to fly. But if the elevator has to be, say, 3/16 inch or 1/4 inch (4.5 or 6) out of neutral you must cure the cause.

Assuming the CG is correct (and it jolly well ought to be after all we have written) the wing's incidence must be adjusted fractionally. This word "fractionally" has now been written three times quite deliberately, because even a very small change to the wing's incidence has a powerful effect. Wedging the leading edge of the wing upwards by 1/16 inch (1.5) will probably have the same effect as adjusting the linkage to give 3/16 inch (4.5) up elevator. So regard an adjustment of 1/16 inch (1.5) at a time (at the leading or trailing edge as appropriate) as the absolute maximum.

The traditional flying field adjustment is made by inserting a length of flat hardwood of appropriate thickness (usually the stick from an iced lolly!) between the wing and its seating, relying on the wing bands to hold it in place. The stick has, of course, to be snapped but not broken apart at its centre to accommodate the dihedral angle of the wing. Obviously this is a temporary measure and if you find that an adjustment to the wing's incidence is required it's better to glue the necessary wedges to the underside of the wing itself. Contact cement will do the job adequately (providing plenty of meths has been used to remove fuel first) but needs to be protected with fuel proofer because fuel residue will soften it. The wedges should always be hardwood, balsa will probably submit to being squeezed continually by the wing bands. You'll be lucky if all these adjustments come out exactly right when you fly the model again, but certainly they'll make it easier to fly.

After a few more successful flights you can start doing right-hand circuits. Yes – they *are* more difficult, aren't they! After perhaps twenty or more flights, as experience and confidence are acquired you can indulge in a few mild aerobatics, provided, of course, you don't get over-confident and these are *always* flown when the model is at a safe height and well upwind.

Probably the easiest to fly is the loop, but we have seen many trainers fold their wings while being looped, either because the pilot forgot to chop the throttle as the model started to descend, resulting in a high-speed pull out, or because the wing, having been weakened in a few end-over-end "landings", no longer had the strength required. So back to the "jerk upwards to feel the rigidity" test mentioned earlier. If you're happy with this, get her exactly into wind and ease in a little down elevator to build up speed. A dive of about 15 degrees held for 3 seconds or so will usually suffice. Check that the wing is exactly level and ease in up elevator, increasing the amount progressively as she climbs and slows down. You should be holding in full up as she goes over the top. As soon as she's coming down the other side chop the throttle (to ease the strain on the wing) and start progressively letting out the elevator as speed increases, so that she emerges flying level with the elevator stick at neutral. Open the throttle again and – you've done a loop! A manoeuvre that is less testing on the model, but more difficult for the pilot, is what modellers called the "Immelman turn". It comprises a little more than half a loop followed by half a roll, so that the model, in theory at least, comes out of the manoeuvre in more or less the same position as it entered it, but travelling in the opposite direction. This is, once you have mastered it, a very easy and quick way to change direction, as well as looking quite impressive. Get her exactly into wind and ease her into a gentle dive to build up speed, ensure the wing is level again, then haul in up elevator, increasing the amount progressively as before. When she's passed the top of the loop, and beginning to descend, and therefore building up speed, let go of the elevator stick completely and push in full rudder (it doesn't matter which way). As the speed increases the rudder will roll her back the right way up and you've done a very quick 180 degree turn. The ability to do this manoeuvre liberates you from the restrictions of the circuit and, once enough experience is acquired, it is a quick and safe way to change direction.

Rather less spectacular but more difficult to get exactly right is the stall turn. The model isn't actually stalled, it is pulled up slowly into a vertical climb at full throttle and held there until it's nearly stopped and almost "hanging on its prop". Then full rudder is applied to push the tail out of the way sideways. This rotation continues until the nose is pointing vertically downwards. The rudder is released and (for safety) the throttle is cut. Obviously she speeds up very quickly and a bit of up elevator gets her back into level flight again, heading in the opposite direction to before. The throttle is opened and you're back in business.

It was never the intention that this book should be a manual on aerobatic flying, and we are already a little outside our brief. Nevertheless it is pointless to abandon your basic trainer before its full capabilities have been exploited, and in doing this you will be gaining experience and confidence which will be invaluable in the future. During the learning stage you should have been reading at least one of the R/C magazines, and your future ambitions should now have crystallised.

Let's just recap by stating that an aileron wing is the obvious next step, and you will certainly frighten yourself a few times while learning to fly inverted. By now it should be obvious that when the model is upside down and losing height one needs to push in down elevator to make her climb, and vice-versa. Sooner or later *every* aspiring aerobatic pilot gets into trouble when the model is inverted, and suddenly develops an overwhelming desire to see her the right way up again, and quickly! Experience has shown again and again that the *only* safe way to do this is to use the ailerons to "roll her out" as this is called, though in practice you only do half a roll. Don't *ever* try to get a trainer the right way up again by pushing in full down elevator in an attempt to do half a loop. The inverted wing will produce less lift than anticipated and she'll probably run out of speed about half way up the climb, resulting in the father and mother of all stalls. Also, of course, if you are disorientated or confused there's a fair chance you will give up elevator instead of down, and she'll hurtle downwards into an inverted loop. Probably the ground will get in the way or the wing will fold, but even if neither of these disasters occur she'll come out of the bottom flying so fast, and you'll be so confused, that something else will almost inevitably go wrong.

Chapter 22

Learning Solo with a Powered Soarer

Let's turn from the hair-raising stuff at the end of the last chapter to the first flights of the lonehander learning with an engine-powered thermal soarer. If you are in this category please re-read the chapter entitled "The Ideal Trainer" where a fair amount of background advice was given.

Again you should find a large site free from nearby hazards, but you won't need a take-off area as you'll hand launch anyway, and noise will hardly be a problem. Don't attempt your first flight if the wind is much more than about 5 mph. You can judge this by puffing out or otherwise creating a cloud of smoke. If it drifts away at more than a really brisk walk it's getting marginal.

Re-read the advice on hand launching if you're going to do it yourself, though you probably won't have to run as the flying speed of a powered thermal soarer will be well below that of a power trainer. Don't have too much fuel in the tank because you want to be able to climb into wind, and keep into wind, until the engine cuts. During the climb, which will be quite leisurely, you'll have time to adjust the rudder trim so that she keeps more or less straight, and to adjust the elevator trim so that no movement of the elevator stick is necessary. Again if she's drifting off course all the while, first to one side and then the other, it's a sure sign you have a little too much up trim.

When the trims are sorted out just let her get on with it, keeping her into wind and glancing down at the ground occasionally to keep your bearings. The engine will probably splutter a few times before it finally cuts and this will alert you to be ready to record, either mentally or via a helper, the changes of trim that then occur. Subsequent action to cure these is, of course, the same as for a power model. You must now keep her exactly into wind (don't forget your Tx ribbon is a good airsock) while you get the trims correct for a straight and reasonably purposeful glide. Note the word "reasonably". If you get the glide so fast that hardly any rudder corrections are necessary the wing will be operating at an incidence far below its ideal, and the model will lose height much more quickly than necessary. So you'll only have a relatively short flight. You'll have to compromise a little and accept fairly frequent, but not continuous, rudder corrections to obtain a reasonably long flight. But again you must avoid so much up trim that she's wallowing around without any sense of purpose.

If you're lucky enough to have found a day when there is hardly any wind you can now go into the rectangular circuit (always upwind) described for power models. Make no attempt to use the elevator during turns, you are flying a completely stable model using just the rudder to steer her in the sky. The only time you may need to use the elevator stick is if she puts her nose up as she turns into wind. Give just a brief touch of down to get the speed up again, then leave well alone. Again it's better to fly left-hand circuits exclusively for the first few flights, and after the first two or three circuits you can extend these so that she goes 25-30 yards (23-27 metres) downwind.

When it's obvious she's running out of height adjust the circuit to try to position her so that she comes out of the final turn about 15 feet (4.5 metres) high and 20-30 yards (18-27 metres) downwind from you. Check the wind with your Tx ribbon and just let her glide in. If she's sufficiently near you can attempt a gentle flare-out starting about 5 feet (1.5 metres) high. But don't overdo it.

All this sounds very easy and could well be so, providing you've built up to the "full power full tank" situation in easy stages as described earlier. If something goes wrong during a turn, and the turn develops into a spiral dive, don't attempt to fight it. Just let go of both sticks and let the model's inherent stability sort it out. If you're flying the sort of model we recommend it will do a better job than you can! If the wind proves stronger than you thought, or increases during the flight, it's better to abandon the idea of a circuit and fly her across the wind, first one way then the other, with a 180 degrees turn, always into wind at each end. As height is lost you can let the model gradually drift downwind towards you and finally a little way past you, starting the final 90 degrees turn into wind when she's about 25 feet (7.5 metres) high.

Chapter 23

Learning Solo with a Slope Soarer

We must now advise, as best we can, the intrepid modeller who has built a slope soarer, who has found what appears to be a suitable slope, and is intent on learning solo. Again, the best advice we can give is DON'T! But if you must then you should re-read the chapter on learning solo with a power model, because a lot of what is written there will equally apply to you – you'll be the test pilot yet trying to teach yourself to fly at the same time, and you must have done your armchair flying. It will help if you can get a good mental grasp of the fundamentals before taking the model out on to the slope, so we'll list these out as before:

1. The model you have built should belong to the "slope or thermal" category, and should be capable of flying in a 10 mph wind on the slope you have selected. It's no use hoping you'll be able to cope in a wind of 20 mph or more – you won't stand a chance. Be patient and wait until the wind is blowing directly against the slope, a 10 mph wind that is exactly right will give more lift and less turbulence than a 15 mph wind that is 20 degrees off course.

2. Many beginners fail to realise that the choice of the landing area is every bit as important as the choice of the actual slope. If the ground at the top of and behind the slope is reasonably level the wind over it will be reasonably smooth, though there will always be a little turbulence just above at the top of the slope. You should therefore plan to land about 50 yards (45 metres) behind the edge of the slope. If the ground is all nicely covered with grass

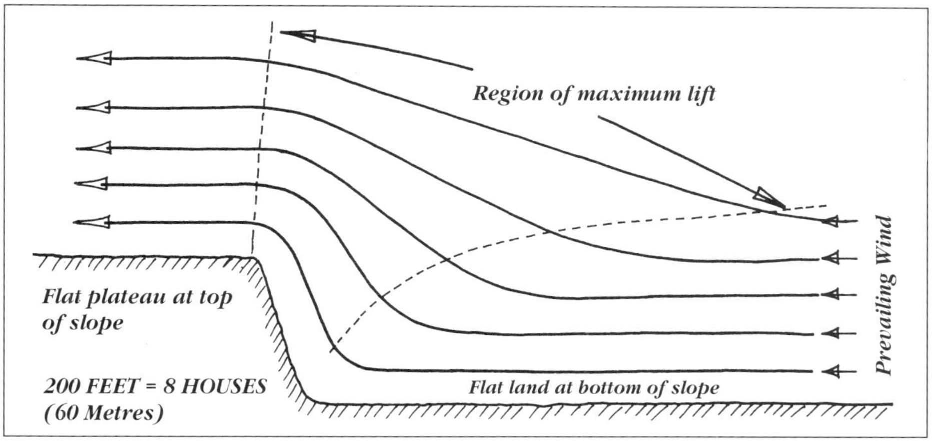

The ideal soaring slope rises steeply from a wide expanse of flat land below, faces the prevailing wind, is long enough for the wind to be forced up the slope rather than go round the ends, and has a flat plateau liberally endowed with unobstructed landing areas at its top! The arrows indicate the way in which a light wind is diverted upwards, but please bear in mind that this is a theoretical drawing. The sort of wind pattern shown will, at best, only be true for a limited range of wind speeds. Really expert full-size gliding enthusiasts, with 30 or 40 years experience behind them, will tell you that no slope ever gives the same lift in the same position two days runnng. Air is very volatile and unpredictable, and shafts of sunlight, patches of ground warmer or cooler than their surrouding, the brief passage of a heavy cloud under the sun, or any one of countless other factors can trigger off a local upcurrent or downcurrent of air that will disturb the pattern. These factors are vitally important for the thermal soarer, be he flying a model or a full-size glider. The only thing that can be stated with any degree of certainty is that you'll never finish learning!

For the model slope soarer the following generalisations can be made:

- ***(a) The higher the slope the less wind speed will be required to give you sufficient lift to fly your model.***
- ***(b) The more the wind speed the more lift you will find but the more will be likelihood of you damaging your model.***
- ***(c) Only an experienced model slope soarer can tell you if your model will be flyable on any slope at any particular time. Without help you can only hold the model slightly nose-down at the edge of the slope and perhaps sense if it is trying to lift out of your hand. If no clear indication is obtained you can only launch it and find out the hard way!***

you can pick the smoothest area, avoiding the lee (downwind) side of small hillocks or depressions which will cause local turbulence. If the ground is littered with stones or outcrops of rock it's worth spending some considerable time searching for, or creating, a relatively rock-free area. If you find a fair-sized patch of ferns or bracken you'll do better to land by flying your soarer into these than risk a true landing amongst the rocks. In stronger winds the turbulence just over the top of the slope will extend further downwind, and your landing area will have to be further back.

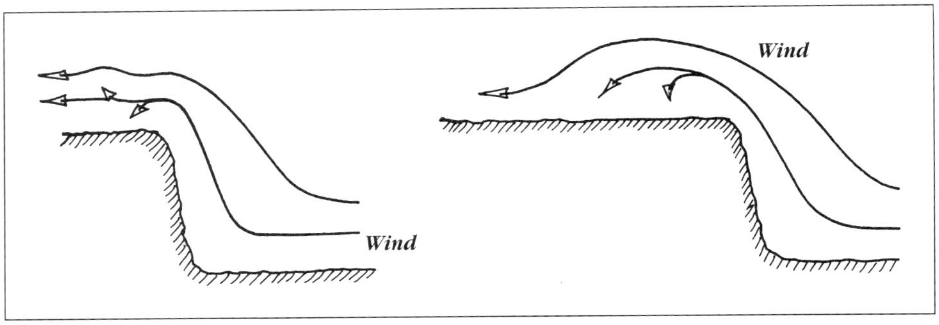

There will always be a certain amount of turbulence above the top or "lip" of the slope. In stronger winds turbulence will be noticeable and will extend down-wind.

3. If the ground slopes away on the leeward as well as the windward side of the slope, so that you are flying from a ridge rather than from the edge of a plateau, considerable turbulence will be caused over the ridge, even in light wind conditions, and this turbulence will extend a long way back from the ridge. Flying through this turbulence could result in your model, literally, losing 20 feet (6 metres) of height in less than half a second. If there is a level and reasonably smooth patch of ground say 100-150 yards (90-135 metres) further back you may be able to make a long-distance landing into this ground. (Actually it will be a controlled descent into wind until the ground stops it – you'll not be able to make any intentional landing at this sort of distance.)

4. If there is no potential landing area at all behind the top of the slope you'll either have to land the model along the slope (difficult even for the expert) or have a helper catch it (not quite so difficult but by no means easy) or simply fly it away from the slope until it runs out of lift and glides down somewhere into the fields below. Your only other hope is to find a patch of ferns or bracken somewhere along the slope itself and fly her into these. This won't be anything like as easy as it is on the flat plateau behind.

So if you have found a slope that gives adequate lift in a light wind, faces the prevailing wind and is convenient as regards distance and access *it might* be worth risking a "catch" landing or flying her into the ferns. Please take us literally here, it might be worth risking. You'll only avoid these risks by finding a different slope that has a suitable landing area.

5. The lift generated by the slope will extend a considerable distance to the windward, usually at least three times the height of the top of the slope above the ground at its foot. So if your slope rises 200 feet (60 metres) above the flat land below you should be able to fly 200 yards (180 meres) out from the slope without significantly losing lift.

6. You must bear in mind that, if the model is flying along or parallel to the slope and you turn her downwind the airspeed will decrease and she'll lose height while airspeed is being regained. At the same time she will be heading towards the slope at a speed equivalent to the speed of the wind plus her airspeed. It follows that you should never turn a model towards the slope unless you are sure that you have enough height for her to clear the top of the slope after losing height in that downwind turn, or that you have her so far out from the slope that the turn will be completed well before the slope is reached. The safe height or distance for a downwind turn will depend on the strength of the wind, the angle and height of the slope, the speed of the model and half a dozen other factors – there can be no hard and fast rule. Just be doubly sure you have enough height and/or distance before starting a downwind turn. The writer's Slingsby Skylark illustrated later was badly damaged because he hadn't!

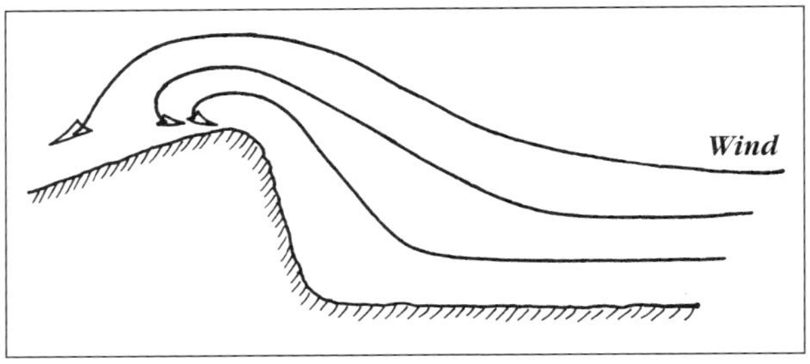

In really strong winds turbulence can extend downwind for a considerable distance.
And this is made worse if the slope falls away to the leeward, i.e. if you are flying from a ridge rather than a flat plateau.

7. Certain safe flight patterns have evolved for slope soaring just as they have for full-size soaring, and the safest one (and therefore most suited for the beginner) merely comprises a series of passes or legs parallel to the slope with 180 degree turns away from the slope at each end. Again, of course, the turns are actually less than 180 degrees because the model will be drifting towards the slope at the speed of the wind and the nose must always be pointing upwind a little to compensate.

8. Assuming you can land on the plateau the landing circuit is similar to that described for power models i.e. rectangular with 90 degree turns, but the amount of height that will be lost in each circuit cannot be predicted with any degree of accuracy. For this reason the first "landing" circuit is made at a considerable height, and, instead of landing, the model should pass over the pilot's head with at least 30 feet (9 metres) to spare. Subsequent circuits are made, each following the same flight path but each starting with a little less altitude. As the circuits get lower the model will be more prone to local turbulence caused by minor hillocks or valleys in the plateau, and the circuit may have to be modified to avoid these areas. This process of steadily losing height and "sniffing out the wind" should continue until the model barely clears

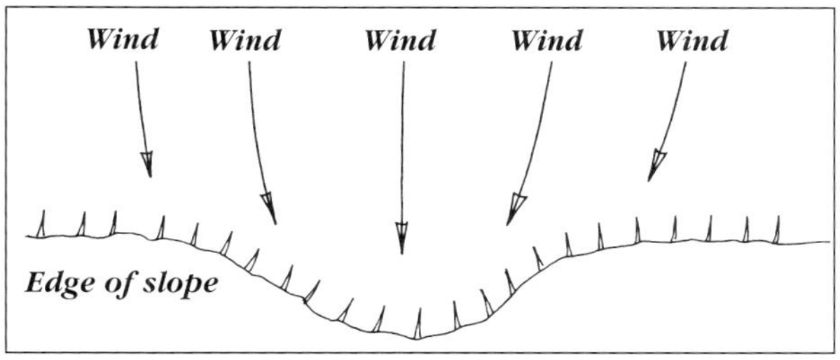

The wind will always be funneled into any bowl in the slope and this is where maximum lift will be found.

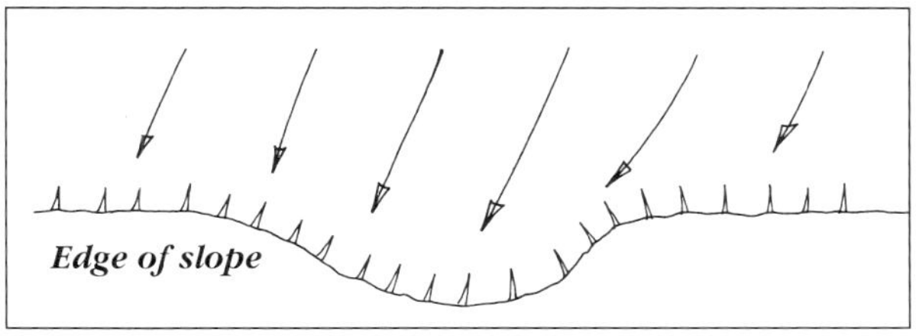

Similary adequate lift can sometimes be found over one face of a bowl, even though the wind is not blowing directly onto the slope as a whole

the edge of the slope; on the next circuit, all other things being equal, it can be landed.

Anyone who soars regularly in the Swansea area will have met the arch exponent of this technique, a short cheerful character whose weather-beaten face reflects what by now must be thousands of hours of soaring in all kinds of wind and weather conditions. His first landing circuit usually ends 10-15 feet high and he invariably does three or four subsequent circuits before finally landing. By the same token he *never* has to take more than two or three paces to pick up his model when it finally come to rest! This, however, is an illustration of what can be achieved by experience, and the beginner should aim for safety rather than perfection. It is better to run out of height and land behind the intended area, despite minor hazards, than to risk the model touching down just short of the top of the slope, bouncing into the air and starting what will be a very short circuit indeed as it goes out again with little speed and in a stalled condition.

9. You'll need to recognise the correct attitude of the model and its correct reaction to the controls, both while climbing and during level flight, and these are even more important on a soarer than on a power model. You'll remember the point was made earlier that, without an excess of speed, a soarer must always be moving downwards through the air that surrounds it. This means that it must be launched with the nose pointing about 5 degrees *downwards* and must be climbed with the nose pointing about 5 degrees *downwards*. If it loses purpose and starts waffling about the nose still isn't pointing sufficiently *downwards*.

You think we're overstressing this? We're not! If the nose gets too high after the launch the wind coming up the slope will get under the wing and push it up even higher. She'll stall, of course, but the wind will hold the wing up and she'll lose all forward speed before the nose finally drops. With no airspeed not even the weather-beaten gentleman referred to earlier could now save your model – it is, quite simply, incapable of being controlled. It will either turn to one side and smash into the slope near the top or drop into a vertical dive and smash into the slope further down. The end result will be no different. The golden rule for power flying "when in trouble chop the throttle" is replaced by the platinum rule for slope soaring – "when in trouble get the nose down".

10. As well as testing your soarer you'll be testing your slope as well – you don't yet know what wind speed is necessary to provide sufficient lift. Experienced soarers puff out a mouthful of smoke or nonchalantly toss a bit of dry grass into the air and base their decision on this. You won't have the necessary experience and any beginner will find it's well worth trying to buy a wind meter. They are not expensive but not always readily available – if your model shop can't get one for you it may be worth trying the big mail-order model shops or even the ships chandlers that advertise in yachting magazines.

If you record the wind speed before and after the first flight you will at least have some guidance as to the wind speed required for future occasions. It's also well worth arming yourself with a compass so that you can record the wind direction as well. Bear in mind that the lift will be greatest only when the wind is blowing at 90 degrees against the face of the slope. A deviation of only 15 degrees could cause the lift to be reduced by a third.

11. You'll need a helper to launch the model, to adjust the trims when it is dangerous for you to take your thumbs off the sticks, to record any trim changes that may prove necessary, and to help pinpoint the model's position should you find that there is insufficient lift, and you have to fly her away to an uncontrolled "landing" somewhere past the bottom of the slope. A pair of binoculars, a large scale ordinance survey map and your compass can be of immeasurable help in plotting the position of the model and subsequently locating it if you are faced with this situation.

Now lets do it for real. We'll assume you have the model on the slope, have located a suitable landing area, are wearing sunglasses, have "educated" your helper, have the Tx trims duly labelled, and have drummed into your helper that he must launch the model downwards. The model has been assembled, rudder and elevator response has been checked, and the trims are at neutral. You should be standing a little below the top of the slope, so that there is no risk of the model being caught in the turbulence at the edge of the plateau. Your helper,

Side view of the ideal climb away from the slope.

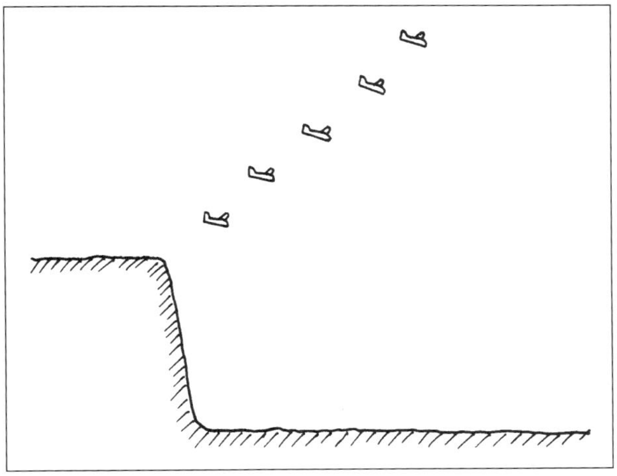

if he is right handed, should be standing a few feet away to your left, holding the model in the nose-down attitude in which it will be launched. Move behind him and check that the wing is level and that the model is pointing exactly into wind. Move back to your former position and shout "OK".

A reasonably hard heave should have her going out from the slope, nose down, yet actually rising. It's true – they really can climb in an apparent dive!

Since each yard flown away from the slope increases the amount of air under the model no panic reaction should be necessary. Your first concern will probably be to apply a little rudder to correct any slight turning tendency. Your next will be to establish the correct position of the elevator trim control to achieve the best climb. If she's not gaining much height you need to determine whether this is due to under-elevation or to insufficient lift. Move the trim back fractionally and watch the model closely. If she gains height more quickly yet still continues to move forward purposefully you've found a slope that is flyable in these wind conditions. Congratulations! If she starts waffling about put the trim forward until speed is regained and then ease it back a tiny bit at a time, watching the results very carefully. Be patient – getting the best trim takes time but can make an enormous difference. If, despite your best efforts, you simply cannot get her to a safe height let her drift very slowly along the slope, pointing nearly into wind all the time. There may be a bit more lift within a flyable distance on one side of you or the other. If this fails also then put in a bit more down trim and tell your helper to dig out the binoculars, for you're going to have to fly her away from the slope and ditch her somewhere in those fields below.

If you find lack of lift is no problem you can begin to enjoy yourself. With the model 50-75 yards (45-70 metres) out from the slope and 50-75 feet (15-22 metres) above it you can drift rather than turn her away from you and you'll probably find one or two places within flying distance where the lift is better than average. Make a mental note of these and head for them should the wind drop and you find lift is needed. Similarly you'll probably find places where she loses height, and make a mental note that these are to be avoided. When you do your first downwind turn resist the temptation to pull in a little up elevator to keep the nose up. This is fine with a power model but not with a soarer. Let her "feel her own way round' – if properly trimmed she'll do a better job without interference from you. You may need a quick touch of down elevator as she comes back into wind – she may put her nose up too high for comfort. And again, when you do your first high landing circuit, she may put her nose up as she flies out over the top of the slope. These two examples apart you should, on your first flight, leave the elevator alone and fly her as a "rudder only" glider.

The landing circuits have already been described and we can now deal with the landing itself. The technique here is rather different than with a power model or thermal soarer. If you are going to land her on the ground (rather than into ferns) a little behind the top of the slope you must resist the temptation to flare her out so that she's flying level a couple of feet above the ground, hoping she'll settle in to a featherlight touchdown. She won't.

In the turbulent air just above the ground she'll probably drop a wing and do a cartwheel, or she may suddenly drop vertically, bounce back up with her nose too high, and possibly be turned over onto her back. The safest landing for the beginner is to ease in just a little up elevator to reduce the speed of descent and then fly her gently but deliberately into the ground, pushing in down elevator as she touches to stop the nose rising again.

After the first flight you should thank your helper and relax with a capital R! You've done something that only a small fraction of slope soarers have done, you've got her down in one piece without tuition. Follow the advice given for power models: if you feel reluctant to fly again, don't fight this feeling. Record the trim positions, wind speed and direction, pack up and go home. You deserve a rest!

After the initial climb the model is "crabbed" along the slope, first to one side and then to the other.

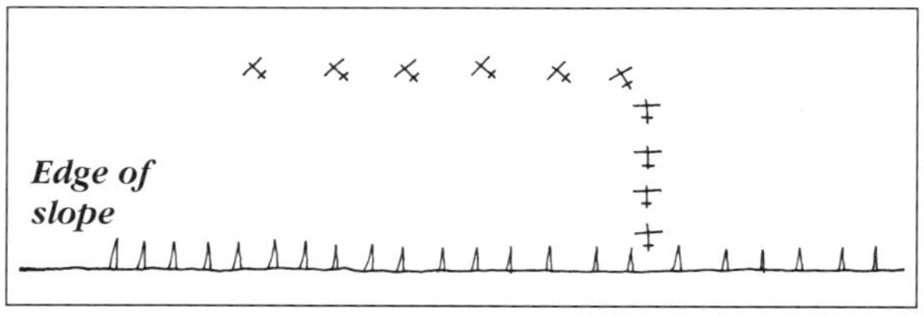

This drawing, about 1/3 scale of the drawing above, shows the ideal flight pattern for the first flight. When you are sure that you have enough height and distance you can turn towards the slope and fly high over what will be the landing circuit.

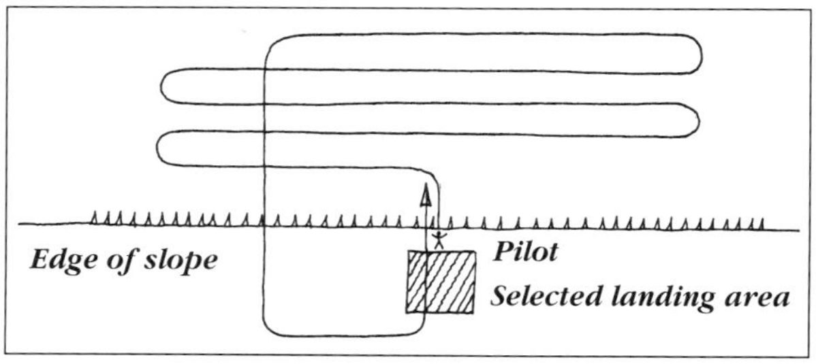

A scale soarer, the writer's Slingsby Skylark was badly damaged when he made the fatal mistake of turning towards the slope with not quite enough distance to spare.

Chapter 24

Power Trainers Compared

Author's Note

When this book was first written we had doubts as to whether or not chapters dealing with individual trainer kits should be included. It was obvious that some kits would subsequently be discontinued, the contents of other kits could change, and that new and better kits would be introduced in the future. Yet any book claiming to be a complete guide for beginners must include some detailed comparisons as well as general advice. We therefore apologise in advance if this and the next chapter has become a little "dated".

A good all balsa trainer from the early days of R/C is the DB Models TYRO MAJOR (54" – 1350 span). It has a two-wheel undercarriage (more suitable for rough fields) and the engine is mounted on a paxolin plate. This is easily cut to accommodate engines of different crankcase widths, and can break away in a crash and perhaps save both engine and front fuselage from serious damage. The kit contains ready-cut wing ribs, wheels, fuel tank and many, but not all, accessories and is good value for money. But the instructions are very brief and there is no real indication as to how the radio is connected to the controls. If you lack previous aeromodelling experience you should buy a more modern kit. Suitable engines 19 – 25.

One of the earliest "second generation" trainer kits was the MFA YAMAMOTO TL (British despite the funny name). This is the Mark II edition of a 56" (1400) span trainer that dates back to the early days of R/C in Britain. It has a thick flat-bottom foam wing, balsa fuselage and solid sheet tail surfaces. The tricycle undercarriage has a ready-bent wire noseleg and a preformed aluminium main leg assembly. The foam wing core is exposed at the trailing edge and we prefer to see it finished off with a strip of ⅛" (3) square hard balsa glued on and rounded off with sandpaper. Balsa for this is not included in the kit. The TL part of the title stands for "Top of the Line", which is another way of saying that the kit contains very nearly everything needed to finish the model except covering and finishing materials, engine and radio. You get an engine mount, fuel tank, wheels, pins, PVA glue, a single sided razor blade (always a good modelling knife), glassfibre tape for joining the wing halves, wing seating tape and all linkages for connecting the radio to the controls. Apart from the balsa previously mentioned you will only need epoxy glue and fibreglass resin, for joining the wing halves, and covering material to complete the model.

The plan is first class (it is reproduced in chapter 17) but the instructions are far too brief. The plan shows the main undercarriage bolted to the plywood underside of the fuselage. The instructions suggest that, as an alternative, the undercarriage is held on with rubber bands looped over ¼" (6) dowels just like the wing. We strongly suggest the builder uses this alternative. If ¼" (6) dowel is not readily available pencils will do.

Flat bottom wings have the reputation of stalling rather more sharply than semi-symmetrical ones but this certainly does not apply to the Yamamoto, which for many years was one of our favourite trainers. Not even the makers claim it to be good looking, it looks what it is – rugged, purposeful and thoroughly sound. An aileron wing kit is available for follow-on training. Use a 25 Schnuerle-ported engine if you must learn to fly on your own, but if tuition is available a 30-35 will be suitable and will give more scope for aerobatics when the aileron wing is fitted.

We have repeatedly said that a trainer is a means to an end not an end in itself. Good looks should therefore not be classed as particularly important. Nevertheless if a trainer can be given a certain amount of style without detriment this can only be good, and David Boddington certainly achieved this when he designed the DB MASCOT (59" (1475) span). Originally it was kitted in both built-up and foam wing versions but now only the latter is available. The wing has a semi-symmetrical section and each half is grooved for two plywood "dihedral braces" (full depth spars which join the wing halves, give added strength to the centre part of the wing and make the joining very easy). These should be glued in with slow-setting epoxy. The fuselage is of balsa and the tail surfaces are solid sheet. The tricycle undercarriage has ready-bent wire legs. The kit is very nearly complete – as well as the engine mount, tank, wheels, PVA glue and all linkages you also get a spinner and the all-important fuel filter. But you do not get a modelling knife or pins.

All the accessories included in the kit are of good quality, the plan is first class and the instructions are among the best we have seen. The Mascot flies every bit as nicely as the Yamamoto and an aileron wing kit is available. Use a 30 or 35 engine for learning solo, a 40 if you can get tuition.

Those with limited skills or building time should seriously consider the PRECEDENT HIBOY (62" (1550) span). It has a semi-symmetrical foam wing with plywood dihedral braces (very similar to the Mascot) and a sheet balsa tail and again an aileron wing is available. Where it differs from the others is in the construction of the fuselage, which is made entirely from pre-cut plywood. The ply is light "aircraft" grade and there are large cut-outs between the wing and tail positions to help keep the weight down.

The DB Mascot – a thoroughly sound trainer from the drawing board of David Boddington. (Micro-Mold Drawing)

The formers or bulkheads have projections on their side edges and these fit into slots cut into the fuselage sides, so that it is impossible to assemble the fuselage incorrectly. The makers claim, with justification, that the whole fuselage can be assembled "dry" in two minutes. It can then be held together at nose and tail with rubber bands while PVA glue is squirted into all the joints and smoothed off with a fingertip. Fully integrated into the fuselage construction are a plywood tray for the servos and hardwood engine bearers. Obviously it will be easier if these are cut, if necessary, to the exact size of the servos and engine before the fuselage is built. The kit contains the tank, fuel tube, hinges, linkages, preformed wire undercarriage legs, but no wheels or spinner. There is an excellent "exploded diagram" of the fuselage construction which is just as well because the written instructions are rather poor.

Note that the "windscreen" is removable to give access to the tank. Being slightly larger and heavier than its rivals it requires a 40, either for learing solo or with tuition.

The Precedent HiBoy, a quick build model with an ingenious pre-cut ply fuselage. (Photograph: Balsacraft [International] Ltd)

Chapter 25

Soaring Trainers Compared

Those looking for an introduction to electric flight, or for a thermal soarer that is large enough (88 inch (2200) span) and light enough to fly off a gentle slope, should seriously consider the Precedent Electra Fly. It is designed round an electric motor fitted in the nose and driving a folding propeller and comes complete with an ingenious switch coupled to the elevator servo so that the motor can be switched on and off during flight. Thus a simple 2 channel R/C system can be used, though it must be stated that a beginner learning alone will find it much easier if his R/C has another channel so that the motor can be switched without moving the elevator. It is also available as a "pure" soarer with a dummy spinner to replace the propeller and without motor, switch, etc. Construction of both versions is virtually identical. To keep it light the construction is intricate. The wing has spruce spars, vertical grain balsa webbing between the spars and additional diagonal ribs between the spars and the trailing edge to resist warping. It is jointed at the centre with tubes and a metal dowel for easy transport. The fuselage is of balsa strip and sheet construction and the tailplane and fin are both built up (saving weight where it matters). So this really is a "builder's model". But we have rarely seen a kit that makes building so pleasureable or so easy. All the wing ribs, webbing strips, etc. are beautifully cut out, so are the fuselage bulkheads, hatch cover, noseblock etc. The leading and trailing edges are shaped and slotted for the ends of the ribs and you even get a little plastic jig to ensure the centre of the ribs stay vertical! Everything is included to connect the radio to the controls (though we would *never* rely on glue alone to hold the hinges in position) and you get fourteen pages of A4 size instructions that many manufacturers would envy. They should

There's a lot of building in the Precedent Electra Fly but design, kit quality and instructions are simply superb.

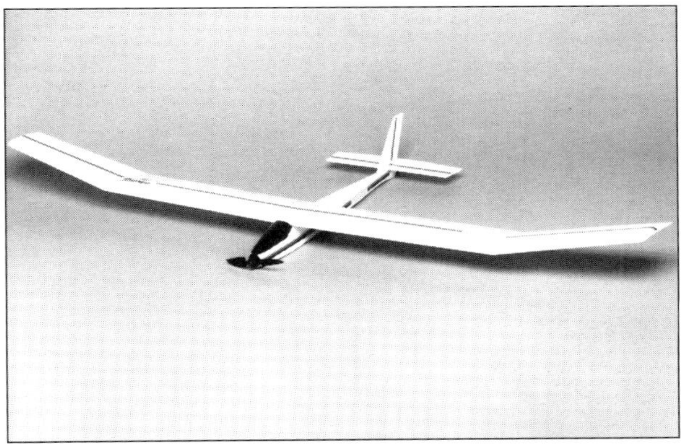

also envy the separate set of ten A4 size assembly drawings and a wiring diagram. Because the drawings are separate you can have the right one open in front of you while you read the instructions, instead of having to break off and turn backwards or forwards to find the right drawing as is so often the case. To gild the lily the instructions end with a whole page of thoroughly sound flying instructions. To sum up, there is a lot of building but the quality of the contents of the kit and the excellence of the instructions remove the need for aeromodelling experience or skill. You just need a fair bit of patience. With this, a superb model should result. Unhesitatingly recommended.

Let's next look at a few, smaller, training kits designed for slope soaring alone with no real capability for thermal hunting.

The PRECEDENT HIFLY (63" (1575) span) has a very carefully designed built-up wing with spruce spars and pre-cut webbing strips of a vertical-grain balsa which go between the ribs and are glued to the back of the spars to integrate them into a true beam, just as is done in full-size design (and in their much larger Electra-Fly). So the wing will take some time to build. In contrast the fuselage is of the same quick-build pre-cut plywood construction as the Precedent HiBoy described in the last chapter. The tailplane is shown held in place with rubber bands and dowels. As stated in "The Ideal Trainer" we don't like this arrangement-glue it in place and fit a small tail skid of, say, ⅛" (3) light ply or 3/16" (4.5) hard balsa (grain running vertically) about 1½" (36) high to keep the tailplane further off the ground. The kit includes excellent linkages and comes complete with materials for constructing a power pod (for the Cox 049 engine). The wing is in two halves and the base of the power pod slots between them, being held in place by the thick wire rod which slides into tubes to form the dihedral brace. The power pod is thus instantly detachable. If you have no intention of using the power pod then glue the wing halves together and reinforce the joint with a strip of tape or ribbon ½"-1" (12-24) wide glued round the joint. A thoroughly sound "builders " kit with good instructions.

One of the most respected designers in R/C soaring is Chris Foss, who has developed, honed and perfected a whole range of soarers over many, many years. His current trainer is called MIDDLE-PHASE 2 (61" (1525) span) and is available in Primary and Advanced versions. They come in identical boxes rubber stamped according to version – don't buy the advanced one by mistake! The Primary version has, as can be seen from the photo, plenty of dihedral and is, of course, designed for two function control. The wing halves are foam with balsa leading and trailing edges to be glued on. The fuselage is remarkably slim and this is achieved by using $\frac{1}{16}$" (1.5) hard plywood for the sides. For economy each side is in two pieces which have to be joined together – join up the second side on top of the first one to ensure perfect alignment.

The rest of the fuselage construction is fairly intricate, resulting in a structure that is not only slim but exceptionally light for its strength. All this is reflected in the flying performance, this model was rated "the best trainer I have ever flown" by a friend of ours who has taught dozens of beginners. All the linkages are included and the designer has selected these with a view to saving weight wherever possible.

You can buy the Advanced wing kit by post direct from the manufacturer when initial training is complete, and turn your trainer into the very sleek aerobatic job in the foreground of the photo. A power pod can be obtained in the same way. Our only niggle is that the instructions cover both versions. Cross out the Advanced parts in pencil to make reading easier, don't rush the building and you'll have a model that should stay up better in light winds, penetrate better into strong ones and respond to the controls more crisply than almost any of its rivals. This kit is sometimes in short supply and may not be readily available at some model shops.

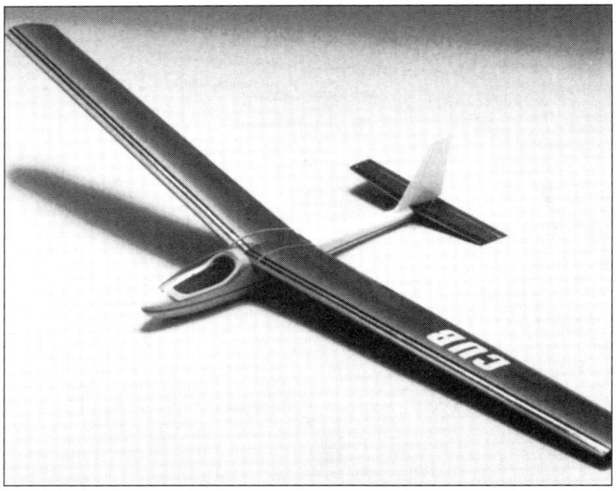

The Avoncraft Cub, one of the smaller soarer kits, is highly prefabricated. (Photograph: Micro-Mold)

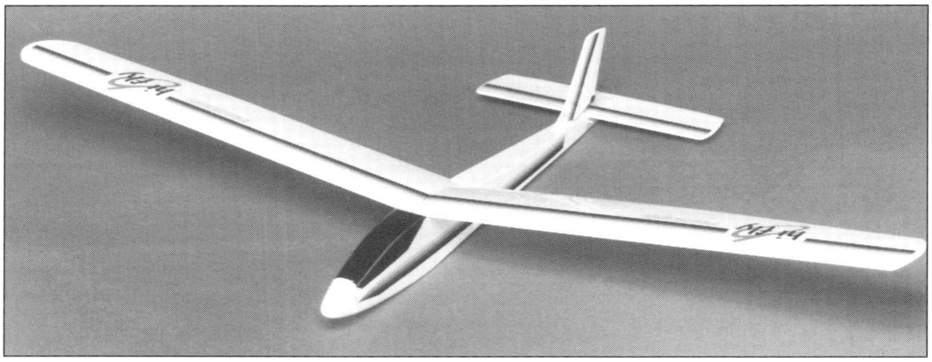

The Precedent HiFly, an excellent slope soaring trainer for those who want to build up the wing. (Photograph: Balsacraft [International] Ltd)

The middle-phase 2 in Primary and Advanced versions (Photograph: Chris Foss Designs)

For those who want to "get airborne" as quickly as possible Chart Hobby Distributors produce the AVONCRAFT CUB (60" (1500) span). It features an ABS fuselage (which has to be reinforced at the nose with pre-cut pieces of thin plywood provided in the kit) and foam wing halves.

The wing splits into two for transport, being joined by wire rods which slide into metal tubes already fitted in the wing halves. A 60" (1500) wing can easily be transported in virtually any car and we would prefer to join the wing halves permanently. The instructions are better than average and the linkages are above reproach. A preformed plastic power pod (again for the Cox 049 engine) is available as an extra. This is held in place by the wing bands so the wing halves can be permanently joined whether you intend using a power pod or not. Despite its small size it flies very nicely, the streamlined plastic fuselage aiding penetration.

Chapter 26

Further Reading

This book has been written solely for the outright beginner and deliberately ignores the more advanced aspects of our hobby, which are more likely to confuse the beginner then to assist him. When you have finished learning you'll find the transition to more advanced models greatly helped by further reading.

Look out for the following Traplet books:-

- **"Model Jet Aircraft"** by Mike Cherry, which covers spectacular models powered by true miniature jet engines as well as ducted fans where a piston engine drives a turbine to produce the jet.

- **"Scale Gliders"** by Cliff Charlesworth, which specialises in true scale models of classic, vintage and modern sailplanes.

- **"Basic Aeronautics for Modellers"** by Alastair Sutherland which explores the science of aerodynamics in real depth.

- **"Designing your own Models"** By Peter Miller

Also in the pipeline is a book specialising in Electric Flight by Stephen Mettam.

As well as books, there are, of course, the monthly magazines and most enthusiasts take at least one regularly and two or more when they begin to specialise. "Radio Control Model World" keeps you abreast of all the latest developments in kits, engines, and radios, publishes plans, kit reviews and engine tests and reports on the major shows and competitions.

"Radio Control Jet International" covers the huge range of jet and ducted fans models and "Electric Flight incorporating R/C Gliders" covers true soarers and anything powered electrically from simple power assisted soarers and single engined "fun" models to multi-engine scale models ideally suited for electric power such as the great pre-war Handley Page HP42 biplanes which flew so sedately and safely between Croydon and Paris in what was, if you could afford it, the golden age of flying.

Chapter 27

Conclusion

R/C flying is, like many other hobbies, expensive. The beginner will almost certainly suffer some disappointments and frustrations, and one must accept that the older one is the more difficult it is to learn to fly a radio-controlled model aircraft. But it can be done (we taught a gentleman of nearly sixty who came along very nicely) and the fact that it is not easy makes each success that much more rewarding. When you see your first model high in the sky you will inevitably say to yourself, albeit subconsciously, "this is something I have built, I created it, and it works!" In fact almost every beginner, when asked if he is ready to take over his model on its maiden flight, answers by saying something like "you just fly it around, I'm perfectly happy seeing it up there and knowing it actually flies!" And, later, when you make your first really smooth landing, and the model rolls to a stop near your feet, you will go home with a sense of indescribable pride and a deep satisfaction that no other hobby can provide. We hope this book will help you achieve that goal. Fly safely, fly quietly, and happy landings!

Appendix

Tutor's Checklist for a typical unflown high-wing trainer

1. GENERAL SAFETY

1.1 Does pupil realise the danger of switching on the Tx without first ensuring that his/her frequency is "free" and/or without first complying with club frequency control procedures?

1.2 Does the frequency of the crystals in use accord with the channel number displayed on the Tx aerial?

1.3 Does pupil realise the danger of a spinning propeller?

1.4 Is pupil suitable dressed, e.g. no loose tie, scarf or anorak strings dangling loose?

It is important that both Tx and Rx remain switched on while *all* the following checks are made, even though many do not require use of radio.

2. BEFORE MODEL IS ASSEMBLED

2.1 Are all controls operated by the correct Tx sticks and are they working in the correct directions?

2.2 Is the total movement of all controls approximately correct? (Typically rudder 30° each side, elevator 20° up and down, ailerons (if fitted) 10° average but more up than down).

2.3 Are horns fixed securely and are linkages free of apparent friction or jamming when controls are moved to extreme positions, *whatever the position of the Tx trims?*

2.4 Are keepers fitted to all linkages wherever required?

2.5 Are all servos mounted securely and is fuel tank securely fixed?

2.6 Are all plugs tight in their sockets and are all wires secured against vibration?

2.7 Are battery pack and Rx properly packed in low-bounce foam, and can Rx be moved fully forward in its "cushion" without strain on the aerial?

2.8 Is aerial protected against vibration inside the fuselage, is it knotted around a match or whatever before it is led out under or behind the wing, and can it be knocked free of its rear fixing without strain?

2.9 Can clunk weight be heard banging against sides of tank when fuselage is held with nose vertically upwards and moved smartly from side to side?

3. VISUAL CHECKS AFTER MODEL IS ASSEMBLED

but first, have all Tx trims been returned to their neutral positions?

From front:

3.1 Does incidence of each wing half appear equal?

3.2 (3-function models only). Does dihedral appear adequate?

3.3 Is fin vertical and in line with fuselage and is rudder in line with fin?

3.4 Is tailplane horizontal and is elevator in line with tailplane?

From side:

3.5 Does wing appear to have slight positive incidence in relation to tailplane?

3.6 Does engine appear to have approximately 3° downthrust?

From above:

3.7 Does engine appear to have 2° or 3° sidethrust towards starboard side?

4. MANUAL CHECKS

4.1 Is wing seating correctly so that incidence cannot vary during flight?

4.2 Are wing bands adequate in number and strength and is wing sufficiently strong to feel rigid when model is supported by the palm of a hand under each tip and jerked smartly upwards?

4.3 Does wing feel equally strong and does nothing come loose when this test is repeated with the model inverted?

4.4 Is C.G. in correct position both longitudinally (25%-30% back from leading edge unless otherwise recommended) and laterally (balance model upside down resting on top of glowplug and fin)?

4.5 Are fin and tailplane soundly secured to fuselage, are rudder and elevator soundly hinged (pull them reasonably hard) and are the linkages sufficiently strong to resist reasonable pressure on rudder and elevator both ways? (and on ailerons if fitted?)

4.6 Does the u/c track straight?

4.7 Are the carburettor and silencer securely fixed and is engine itself securely mounted?

4.8 Is propeller fitted the right way round and approximately level (a quarter to three) as engine comes onto compression?

4.9 Is prop: washer in correct position, is prop: nut really tight and is spinner correctly secured?

5.CHECKS ON RADIO

(assumed to be brand new or second-hand untried).

5.1 Has radio been fully charged (and if new or with new nicads, preferably cycled)?

5.2 Has it been range checked? (400 yards/360 metres on the ground with the model pointing at the Tx. Without a car this can take 10 minutes, but how long will it take to rebuild?

5.3 Have there been any twitches or glitches while this testing has taken place, indicating over-sensitive Rx or interference?

6. CHECKS WITH ENGINE RUNNING

(The tutor should hold the model and the pupil should operate the Tx, both for safety reasons and for the pupil to learn or demonstrate familiarity with the controls.)

6.1 Does throttle control give full throttle and a reasonably slow idle and does mixture sound right at full throttle?

6.2 Will engine run for 10 seconds at full throttle with the nose pointing vertically upwards, without distress?

6.3 Is the tank now full or nearly full?

6.4 Do all controls operate correctly at full throttle and at idling speed?

7. FINALLY

7.1 Is insurance O.K?

7.2 Are sunspecs being worn if needed?

7.3 Has pupil been reminded to hand back Tx *before* a minor crisis becomes a potential disaster?

7.4 Prayers?

Notes

Notes